THE ART OF THINKING:

A GUIDE TO CRITICAL AND CREATIVE THOUGHT

VINCENT RYAN RUGGIERO
State University of New York, Delhi College

HARPER & ROW, PUBLISHERS, New York
Cambridge, Philadelphia, San Francisco,
London, Mexico City, São Paulo, Sydney
1817

7-11   # 9853798

To Betty,
for caring

Sponsoring Editor: Phillip Leininger
Project Editor: Rita Williams
Designer: Michel Craig
Production: Delia Tedoff
Compositor: ComCom Division of Haddon Craftsmen, Inc.
Printer and Binder: R. R. Donnelley & Sons Company
Art Studio: Fineline Inc.

The Art of Thinking: A Guide to Critical and Creative Thought

Library of Congress Cataloging in Publication Data

Ruggiero, Vincent Ryan.
  The art of thinking.

  Includes bibliographical references and index.
  1. Thought and thinking. 2. Thought and thinking
Problems, exercises, etc. I. Title.
BF455.R828 1984   153.4′2   83-12992
ISBN 0-06-045665-5

Contents

Thinking is an art, with its own purposes, standards, principles, rules, strategies, and precautions. And it is an art well worth learning, for every important thing we do is affected by our habits of mind.

To the Instructor

Throughout this century, many educators felt that thinking was learned automatically when certain subjects (notably science and math) were studied, and that therefore it need not be formally taught. Others believed that thinking could not be learned, at least not by the average student. As a result, high schools did not generally offer formal instruction in thinking, and colleges confined their offerings to formal logic courses inaccessible to students outside the discipline of philosophy.

This situation has never gone unchallenged. There have always been dissenters, here and abroad, who urged that systematic training in thinking be offered to all students. But when they were heard at all, such people were either misunderstood, like John Dewey, or dutifully applauded and then ignored, like Alfred North Whitehead and Jean Piaget.

Now, thanks to the persistence of those prophets and that of the small but determined number of educators who continued to press for the reforms those prophets championed, a new era seems to be dawning. Prestigious studies, such as the one released by the U. S. Department of Education in November 1981, call attention to the lack of critical thinking and problem-solving skills in today's students. A respected group of educators, headed by Mortimer Adler, published *The Paideia Proposal,* a comprehensive plan for the reform of public education giving prominence to intellectual skills. And colleges all over the country are responding to the needs of their students. At least one state university system, California's, has instituted a critical thinking *requirement* for all students in its two-year transfer and four-year baccalaureate programs.

THIS BOOK'S PREMISES

This book has been designed for both existing courses in thinking and those that are being instituted in various departments—philosophy, humanities, social science, and English. As the title *The Art of Thinking* suggests, this book is more comprehensive than most texts on thinking. The following four premises underlie its content and organization:

1. *The emphasis in a textbook on thinking should be more on what to* do *than on what to* avoid *doing.* Thinking is not an ivory tower enterprise. It is a practical matter. Moreover, it is active and dynamic, not reactive and static. Effective thinkers do not merely sit back and criticize others' efforts—they solve problems, make decisions, and take stands on issues. For this reason, textbooks focusing on fallacies are little more successful than music books that focus on avoiding the wrong notes, or typing manuals that focus on avoiding all possible misstrokes.

2. *A textbook on thinking should introduce students to the principles and techniques of* creative *thinking.* The considerable literature that has been published on thinking in the last two decades demonstrates that the creative process and the critical process are intertwined—first we produce ideas (more or less creatively), then we judge them. It makes little sense to teach one-half of a complex process. Yet that is what has usually been done. Logic has focused on the validity of *already formed* arguments. And rhetoric (although it has recently rediscovered the classical concept of invention, whereby appropriate arguments are discovered) has emphasized organization and style to the neglect of substance.

3. *A text on thinking should teach students how to critique their own ideas, as well as the ideas of others.* Human beings have a great capacity for self-deception. Accordingly, it is much more difficult for students to see their own blind spots, their own prejudices, and their own errors than it is for them to see other people's. Yet it is their own weaknesses and mistakes that pose the greatest obstacle to their effective thinking.

4. *A text on thinking should teach students how to persuade others.* Many brilliant ideas have never been put into practice simply because the originator assumed that others would recognize excellence without assistance. Students need to learn how to anticipate objections to their ideas before they occur and how to overcome them.

SPECIAL FEATURES OF THIS BOOK

Because it is based on the above premises, this book has a number of features not commonly found in textbooks on thinking. These are the most evident:

- Wherever possible, the chapters are presented in the sequence that occurs in actual problem solving. For example, identifying the problem (Chapter 7) is followed by investigating the problem (Chapter 8), by producing possible solutions (Chapter 9), and by refining the best solution (Chapter 11).

- Part Two, "Be Creative," offers direct answers to the questions that most baffle students and prevent their progress in thinking. These are questions such as: "How can I be more imaginative, more original in my solutions to problems?" "What should I do when I experience 'thinker's block,' when I get confused, or when I get in the rut of producing the same kinds of solutions?" and "How does insight occur, and what can I do to stimulate it?"
- A separate chapter (Chapter 8) explains in detail how to investigate issues quickly, efficiently, and with ingenuity, both in the library and out.
- Chapters 14 and 15 offer specific techniques for anticipating negative reactions to ideas and a helpful approach to use in persuading others.
- Appendixes B and C provide brief explanations of the fundamentals of logic and the principles and approaches of good writing.
- Three Warm-up Exercises are provided at the end of each chapter, in addition to a generous supply of problems and issues. These are problems of a general nature with no special association to chapter material. They are designed to develop students' interest and build students' self-confidence, thereby making the formal applications less intimidating.
- Applications are provided following the Warm-up Exercises in each chapter.

Since some instructors will prefer not to assign formal compositions in response to the end-of-chapter applications, and those who do so may differ in their requirements, no specific composition instructions are given in the applications. All applications, however, lend themselves to formal composition response as well as to class discussion. If the composition emphasis is especially strong in your course, you may wish to consider altering the chapter order, assigning Chapter 15 ("Build a Persuasive Case") between Chapters 1 and 2. The only application in Chapter 15 not suitable for the early weeks of the course is Application 15.11.

ACKNOWLEDGMENTS

I wish, first, to express my appreciation to all the men and women—the prophets, the researchers, the risk takers—who labored over the years to advance the cause of knowledge in a subject that was unfashionable. Without their contributions, this book would never have been written. I wish also to express special thanks to John P. Broderick of Old Dominion University, Daniel McDonald of the University of South Alabama, Brooke N. Moore of the University of California, Chico, Richard Paul of Sonoma State University, and Robert E. Yarber of San Diego Mesa College. for their constructive criticisms and helpful suggestions for improving the manuscript, and to Phillip Leininger and Rita Williams for their editorial direction.

Vincent Ryan Ruggiero

chapter *1*

Developing Your Thinking: An Overview

Claude is a high school student. His English teacher has just asked the class to identify the theme of the short story they read for homework. When no one answers, she admonishes them, "Class, you're just not thinking. Get busy and *think.*"

Claude wrinkles up his nose, furrows his brow, scratches his chin, and stares up at the ceiling. "Think, think, I've got to think. What's the theme of that story? The theme, the theme, what could be the theme?" He shifts his gaze to the right and to the left, purses his lips, then reaches down purposefully, opens his book, and begins flipping pages as if looking for something. All the while his mind is repeating "Think . . . think . . . theme. . . ."

Is Claude thinking? No. He's trying to, hoping to, but not really doing so. His mental motor is racing, but his transmission is in neutral. He's ready to go, but not going.

Let's consider another case. Agatha, a college student, is sitting in the campus cafeteria, drinking her morning coffee. To all outward appearances she is not only thinking, but totally lost in thought. Here is what is taking place in her mind:

> So much work to do today . . . must remember to meet Jim at 6 P.M. . . . I'll have to begin my term paper soon . . . that Bertha is such a slob—I wish she'd clean her part of the room sometime this semester . . . my hair looks so awful—if only I could fix it like Martha's, it would look neat, yet demand little attention . . . if winter would only end, I wouldn't be so depressed—why is my mood so dominated by weather? . . . this coffee is bitter—you'd think the staff here could at least make a decent cup of coffee . . . I can't wait to get home to have a real

meal again . . . wonder how much weight I've gained; perhaps jogging is the
solution. . . .

Agatha's mental behavior is much closer to thinking than Claude's. Ideas,
images, and notions are drifting through her mind, and she is dutifully watching
them float by. But her role is passive—she is a spectator to the activity of her
mind. Thinking, as we will view it in this book (and as most authorities view it),
is something more than aimless daydreaming.

WHAT IS THINKING?

What, then, is thinking? To begin with, it is purposeful mental activity over which
we exercise some control. *Control* is the key word. Just as sitting in the driver's
seat of a car becomes driving only when we take the steering wheel in hand and
control the car's movement, so our mind's movements become thinking only
when we direct them.

There are, of course, as many different purposes in thinking as there are in
travelling. We may be on a business trip or a pleasant drive through the country-
side with no particular destination. Similarly, we may drive in varying conditions,
and with varying degrees of success or efficiency. We may travel in darkness or
in light, proceed slowly or quickly, take the correct turn or the wrong one, arrive
at our intended destination or a different one, or find that we are hopelessly lost
en route. Nevertheless, as long as we have our hands on the steering wheel of our
mind, we are thinking.

This does not mean that thinking must always be conscious. The evidence
that the unconscious mind can join in purposeful mental activity is overwhelming.
The most dramatic example of this is the fact that insights often come to us when
we are no longer working on a problem, but have turned away from it to other
activities. (We will see a number of examples of this phenomenon in Chapters 6
and 9.)

With these important considerations in mind, we can attempt a more formal
definition of thinking. *Thinking is any mental activity that helps formulate or solve
a problem, make a decision, or fulfill a desire to understand. It is a searching for
answers, a reaching for meaning.* Numerous mental activities are included in the
thinking process. Careful observation, memorizing, remembering, wondering,
imagining, inquiring, interpreting, evaluating, and judging are among the most
important ones.

Often several of these activities work in combination, as when we solve a
problem or make a decision. We may, for example, identify an idea or dilemma,
then deal with it—say, by questioning, interpreting, and analyzing—and finally
reach a conclusion or decision.

There have been many attempts to explain the nature of thinking. One of
the most popular notions, now largely discredited, is that thinking is entirely
verbal. According to this theory, we arrange words in our minds or silently
whisper to ourselves when we think. Yet if this were the case, Albert Einstein
would not be considered a thinker. His thinking consisted more of images than

of words.[1] Contemporary authorities agree that the form a thought takes in our minds is usually verbal, but not necessarily so. Just as we may *express* an idea in mathematical symbols or pictures, in addition to words, we may also *conceive* of it that way.

NOT ONE BRAIN, BUT TWO

Throughout this century researchers have deepened our understanding of the operations of the human mind. The past three decades in particular have been rich in insights. We now know that thinking is not a mystical activity, unknowable and unlearnable. There are patterns of thought that can be studied and compared to determine their relative objectivity, validity, and effectiveness. This knowledge can be used to reinforce good thinking habits and to overcome bad ones. As James Mursell has observed, "Any notion that better thinking is intrinsically unlearnable and unteachable is nothing but a lazy fallacy, entertained only by those who have never taken the trouble to consider just how a practical job of thinking is really done."[2]

One of the most significant insights is that the brain is not a single organ, but two organs in one. The breakthrough came when a neurosurgeon began treating patients with severe epilepsy in a new way. He severed the nerve fibers connecting the two hemispheres of the cerebral cortex to relieve the symptoms of the disease. The severing made it possible to study the way each hemisphere of the brain functioned. The right hemisphere, studies revealed, governs nonverbal, symbolic, and intuitive responses. The left hemisphere governs the use of language, logical reasoning, analysis, and the performing of sequential tasks.[3]

This research gave new importance to old understanding. For decades psychologists of thinking stressed that the mind has two distinct phases—the production phase and the judgment phase—that complement each other during thinking. They stressed further that proficiency in thinking required the mastery of all approaches appropriate to each phase, and skill in moving back and forth between them.

Let's examine each phase a little more closely, noting the difference between effective and ineffective use.

The Production Phase

In this phase, which is most closely associated with creative thinking, the mind produces various conceptions of the problem or issue, various ways of dealing with it, and possible solutions or responses to it. Good thinkers produce both more ideas and better ideas than poor thinkers. More specifically, good thinkers tend to see the problem from many perspectives before choosing any one, to consider many different investigative approaches, and to make every effort to produce possible solutions before turning to judgment. In addition, good thinkers are more willing to take intellectual risks, to be adventurous and consider outrageous or zany ideas, and to use their imaginations and aim for originality.

In contrast, poor thinkers tend to see the problem from a limited number of perspectives (often just one narrow view), to take the first approach that occurs to them and to judge each idea immediately, or to settle for only a few ideas. Moreover, they are overly cautious in their thinking, unconsciously making their ideas conform to the common, the familiar, and the expected.

The Judgment Phase

In this phase, which is most closely associated with critical thinking, the mind examines and evaluates what it has produced, makes its judgments and, where appropriate, adds refinements. Good thinkers handle this phase with care. They test their first impressions, make important distinctions, and base their conclusions on evidence rather than their own feelings. Sensitive to their own limitations and predispositions, they double-check the logic of their thinking and the workability of their solutions, identifying imperfections and complications, anticipating negative responses, and generally refining their ideas.

In contrast, poor thinkers judge too quickly and uncritically, ignoring the need for evidence and letting their feelings shape their conclusions. Blind to their limitations and predispositions, poor thinkers trust their judgment implicitly, ignoring the possibility of imperfections, complications, or negative responses.

GOOD THINKING IS A HABIT

It is frequently said that good thinkers are born, not made. That idea is essentially false. There is, of course, an element of truth in it. Some people have more talent for thinking than others, and some learn more quickly. As a result, over the years one person may develop his thinking ability to a greater extent than another. Nevertheless, effective thinking is mostly a matter of habit. Research proves that the qualities of mind it takes to think well, the qualities we noted in our discussion of the production and judgment phases, above, can be mastered by anyone. Research even proves that originality can be learned. Most important, it has proved that you don't need a high IQ to be a good thinker.[4] (E. Paul Torrance has shown that fully *70 percent* of all creative people score below 135 on IQ tests.)[5]

The difficulty of improving your thinking depends on the habits and attitudes you have. Chances are you've had no direct training in the art of thinking before this, so you're bound to have acquired some bad habits and attitudes. This book will supply principles and techniques for you to master, and your instructor will supply the guidance. You must supply the most important ingredients—the desire to improve and the willingness to apply what you learn.

If at first the task seems impossible, remember that a lot of other tasks seemed just as impossible, yet you mastered them. Walking. for example, and eating without drooling food out of your mouth onto your high chair. Swimming, hitting a baseball, and driving a car were all impossible at first. The unfamiliar always seems immensely difficult.

STRUCTURE OF THIS BOOK

Becoming familiar with the contents of this book will help you meet its challenge more confidently. The purpose of the book is to *teach you how to think*. That may seem obvious enough, but it's easily confused with *telling you what to think*. The difference is this: Telling you what to think brainwashes you, enslaves you to others' ideas; teaching you how to think liberates you from others' ideas and helps you form sound and sensible ideas of your own. You will find this book introducing you to (or deepening your acquaintance with) a host of problems and controversial issues. It will guide the way you consider them—that is, the strategies you apply and the manner in which you apply them. But you will not find this book making up your mind for you. That task is yours alone.

The Art of Thinking is divided into four parts, each with several chapters. The first part is titled "Be Aware." Its importance is suggested by these words from philosopher Arthur Schopenhauer: "Every man takes the limits of his own field of vision for the limits of the world." One aim of this section is to broaden your outlook. Another is to clarify such important concepts as *truth, knowledge,* and *opinion,* each of them clouded today by confusion and misconceptions. Other objectives are to help you arrive at a better understanding of your own strengths and weaknesses, and to develop your curiosity and analytical skills.

The second section of the book, "Be Creative," focuses on producing ideas and offers practice in identifying, investigating, and solving a variety of challenging problems and issues. The third section, "Be Critical," focuses on judgment. It shows you how to apply your curiosity and analytical skill in evaluating your ideas, choosing the best ones, refining them, and overcoming their flaws.

Finally, Part Four, "Communicate Your Ideas," helps you prepare the ideas for presentation to other people.

The book also includes four appendixes. You will probably refer to them from time to time during the course. They contain considerations that will make your assignments easier to do and more effective. If, for example, you find the warm-up exercises at the end of any chapter confusing or difficult to do, you can turn to the appropriate part of Appendix A and consult the model responses presented there.

In addition, Appendix B explains fundamental writing principles, and shows you how to master the three stages of the composition process—planning, writing, and editing. Whenever you aren't sure how to begin an assignment, or when you encounter an obstacle as you proceed, there's no need to give up or wait for your instructor to clarify the matter in class. You can take the initiative yourself and turn to Appendix B. In most cases you'll find your answer there. Moreover, you'll build the kind of self-reliance and resourcefulness all good thinkers possess.

GETTING THE MOST FROM YOUR EFFORTS

There was a time when it was thought there were certain right occasions, places, and conditions for study. Today we know better. No two people are exactly alike in their needs. What works for one will not necessarily work for another. Mozart and Beethoven, for example, were both great composers. Yet they worked very differently. Mozart thought out entire symphonies and scenes from operas in his head, without benefit of notes. Later he transcribed them onto paper. Beethoven, on the other hand, wrote fragments of notes in notebooks, often reworking and polishing them for years. His first ideas were so clumsy that scholars marvel at how he could have developed such great music from them.[6]

Imagine what would have happened if Mozart had followed Beethoven's approach and vice versa. Surely Mozart's output would have been diminished. Given the unsuitability of another approach to his temperament, it might even have been choked off altogether. And Beethoven would have given the world trash.

It is not unreasonable to believe that there are thousands, perhaps millions, of people in the world today who have not begun to glimpse, let alone develop, their potential for achievement *simply because they are using work habits borrowed from someone else—or work habits they have fallen into by chance or force of circumstance.*

Your best approach is not to assume your work habits fit your needs, but to experiment a little and find out what really works best for you. What you find may not make a dramatic difference, but even modest improvements in proficiency will continue to pay dividends over the years.

Consider Time

An hour of prime time will often get better results than two or three hours of the wrong time. When are you in the habit of working? Early in the morning? Late at night? At midday? For the next week or two try different times and note the effect on your work.

Consider Place

You can observe students studying in strange places—dormitory lounges, crowded cafeterias filled with people clanging and chattering, and snack bars (often next to a blaring jukebox). You've probably studied in some of these places, too, at one time or another, and for no other reason than that you happened to be there at the time an assignment had to be done. But that is hardly a good reason for being there. If you need quiet to work efficiently, then you should seek a quiet place—if not a dormitory room, then an empty classroom, a park bench, or a parked car. (Of course, if you find that a busy place actually stimulates your thinking, by all means work there.)

Consider Conditions

Thinkers throughout history have occasionally needed some strange stimuli. Poet Johann Schiller needed a desk filled with rotten apples. Novelist Marcel Proust needed a cork-lined workroom. Dr. Samuel Johnson demanded a purring cat, an orange peel, and a cup of tea. But you'd do well not to become dependent on gimmicks or bizarre conditions, if for no other reason than the fact that they're hard to maintain. You're better off trying such approaches as taking a walk or a brisk jog across campus before beginning work, or taking a warm bath, or playing music while you work.

A word of caution is in order here. Don't confuse what you like with what works best for you. You may, for example, enjoy being in the dormitory lounge in the early evening watching TV or listening to the stereo blare new wave rock. But these might hinder more than help your efforts to write or think. Alcohol and drugs, similarly, may be pleasant but are definitely harmful. Although the notion persists that they enhance creativity, researchers are virtually unanimous in concluding that such substances have the *reverse effect*—they cloud and numb the mind.

USING FEELINGS TO ADVANTAGE

Feelings were greatly emphasized in the 1960s and early 1970s. "Do your own thing," "If it feels good, do it," and "Get in touch with your feelings" were the catch phrases of the time. Today many psychologists, educators, and social critics believe that emphasis went too far. They urge a better balance between feeling and thought. That position is a reasonable one.

We usually feel before we think, and what we feel is often intensely subjective, impulsive, and uncritical, an extension of our ego. The force of feelings is the force of emotion, passion, and so it often directs us in ways good sense would not have us go. If everyone acted as he felt like acting, there would not be enough police officers to guarantee our safety. If someone decided he liked our car, he'd drag us out of it and drive off. If someone objected to the expression on our face, he'd punch it into a shape more to his liking. If someone suddenly found us sexually desirable, he'd tear off our clothes and attack us. Thinking is necessary to sort out positive, constructive feelings from negative, destructive ones.

Yet if feeling is not a good substitute for thinking, it is nevertheless a good companion. No explanation of the human mind that excludes feeling can be completely accurate. For it provides us with hunches, impressions, intuitions, and —most importantly—with the enthusiasm to undertake difficult challenges and persevere in them. Albert Einstein spent 7 years working out his theory of relativity; Thomas Edison spent 13 years perfecting the phonograph; Copernicus devoted more than 30 years to proving that the sun was the center of the solar system. Without enthusiasm for what they were doing, these creative people could never have sustained their efforts.

The popular notion that only artists feel, that scientists and other practical people approach problems in computerlike fashion, has long been discredited by scholars.[7] Albert Einstein himself affirmed the role of intuition in science. "There is no logical way to the discovery of [complex scientific] laws," he wrote. "There is only the way of intuition, which is helped by a feeling for the order lying behind the appearance."[8] And Arthur Koestler, who studied the lives of innumerable great scientists, writes: "In the popular imagination [they] appear as sober ice-cold logicians, electronic brains mounted on dry sticks. But if one were shown an anthology of typical extracts from their letters and autobiographies with no names mentioned, and then asked to guess their profession, the likeliest answer would be: a bunch of poets or musicians of a rather romantically naive kind."[9]

As you proceed through this course, try to become more aware of your feelings. They will never be the end of your reflections. But they will be an excellent starting point.

LEARNING TO CONCENTRATE

Many people have the notion that concentration means a constant, unbroken line of thought. They imagine that scientists, writers, inventors, and philosophers start from point A and move smoothly to point B without distraction. That notion is incorrect. Concentration is not so much something done to *prevent* distraction and interruption as it is something done to *overcome* distraction and interruption when they occur. To concentrate means to return our attention to our purpose or problem whenever it wanders.[10]

Concentrating is much like steering a car. When experienced drivers steer, they don't lock their hands on the wheel in one fixed position. They turn it slightly to the right and to the left to keep the car on course. Even on a straight road, the car stays on course only a small percentage of the time. They must make constant adjustments, many of them almost imperceptible. Experienced drivers are not more talented than inexperienced ones. They have simply learned to make subtle corrections at the right time.

Similarly, the secret of efficient thinkers is not that they experience fewer distractions, but that they have learned to deal with them more quickly and more effectively than inefficient ones do. There is no magic in what effective thinkers do. It is a skill. And you can learn it as they did, by practicing.

COPING WITH FRUSTRATION

All thinkers have their share of frustration: confusion, mental blocks, false starts, and failures happen to everyone. Good thinkers, however, have learned strategies for dealing with their frustration, while poor thinkers merely lament it—thus allowing themselves to be defeated by it.

One important study of students' problem-solving processes revealed some interesting differences between good and poor problem solvers. Among them were the following:[11]

GOOD PROBLEM SOLVERS	POOR PROBLEM SOLVERS
Read a problem and decide how to begin attacking it	Cannot settle on a way to begin

Bring their knowledge to bear on a problem	Convince themselves they lack sufficient knowledge (even when that is not the case)
Go about solving a problem systematically—for example, trying to simplify it, puzzling out key terms, or breaking the problem into subproblems	Plunge in, jumping haphazardly from one part of the problem to another, trying to justify first impressions instead of testing them
Tend to trust their reasoning and to have confidence in themselves	Tend to distrust their reasoning, and to lack confidence in themselves
Maintain a critical attitude throughout the problem-solving process	Lack a critical attitude, and take too much for granted

All of these differences are matters of skill. If you have not yet learned to use the strategies of the good thinker, begin practicing. In time you will master them.

You have no need to fear difficulty in this course. As we noted, Appendix A offers guidance to help get you started doing the exercises and applications at the ends of the chapters. Now, here are two additional tips to help you begin with an extra measure of confidence. Use them whenever you begin working on a problem and encounter a mental block:

1. Reread the directions, this time *aloud.* Let your ear join your eye in determining what you are being asked to do. (Two senses are better than one.)
2. Refuse to sit passively, staring at the problem. Do something to attack it. (If you took a dead-end street by accident, you wouldn't sit in your car staring at the dead-end sign—you'd turn the car around and try moving in another direction.)

Let's take an actual problem and see how tip 2 would work. You have three unmarked glasses of different sizes—3 ounces, 5 ounces, and 8 ounces. The largest glass is full. Your job is is to end up with 4 ounces of liquid in each of the larger two glasses.

Let's say you look at the problem and draw a blank. Following step 1, you reread the problem aloud. Now you understand it. But you still don't know how to begin. What can you do to attack it, to get your mind in motion? One approach is to get three appropriately sized glasses and fill the largest with water, then go through the motions of transferring liquid to see where the difficulty lies. But an easier way is to draw the glasses, however roughly, on a piece of paper. Like this:

3 ounce   5 ounce   8 ounce

What next? Pour some liquid into one of the empty glasses (actually or in your imagination). Which one? It makes no difference. Just get busy *doing*. If you make a mistake, and encounter a dead end, so what? You can always turn around and try another approach. The point is that you will be exerting some initiative on the problem. You'll no longer be at its mercy. If you'd like to pause now and try to solve the problem, do so. (You'll find the answer on p. 213.)

Not every problem, of course, can be so easily visualized (or visualized at all). We'll see other approaches in subsequent chapters.

THE BENEFITS OF FREEWRITING

We have seen that it is possible to think without expressing the thought. Nevertheless, expressing our thoughts is a valuable way of clarifying them. And the benefit is reciprocal. In other words, expressing helps thinking, which in turn helps expressing, and so on.

You've surely had the experience of believing you have an idea clearly in mind and then trying to express it and finding out it isn't so clear after all. It's a common experience. And it hints at a deeper condition than most of us realize. Ernest Dimnet explains,

> Most men and women die vague about life and death, religion or morals, politics or art. Even about practical issues we are far from being clear. We imagine that other people know definitely their own minds about their children's education, about their own careers, or about the use they should make of their money. The notion helps us to imagine that we ourselves are only separated from decision on these important issues by the lightest curtain of uncertainty. But it is not so. Other people, like ourselves, live in perpetual vagueness. Like us they foolishly imagine they are thinking of some important subject when they are merely *thinking of thinking about it*.[12] (emphasis added)

As a cure for this problem, Dimnet suggests taking a sheet of paper and doing your thinking on it rather than just inside your mind. Then you'll be able to see if you're really thinking, and how well you're thinking. It's a simple enough approach. And it works. You'll find, too, that the very act of recording your thoughts helps to focus them better and improves your concentration.

The activity Dimnet is referring to, and which is recommended by many authorities on thinking and writing, is called *freewriting*. It consists of focusing on a problem or issue and letting your mind produce whatever associations it will, then writing down whatever ideas result, without stopping to evaluate any idea or shutting off the flow of ideas prematurely. This kind of writing is private expression, for your eyes only. Its aim is very different from that of formal writing —it is to stimulate thought rather than to communicate it. Therefore it can be —indeed, *should* be—informal, casual, and highly tentative. There's no need, either, for correct spelling or accurate typing. Freewriting can be filled with grammatical blunders. No one else will see it, so you needn't worry whether any of your ideas seem foolish. If you decide an idea is unworthy, you can cross it out later without embarrassment or loss of face.

WRITING FOR OTHERS

Now let's turn to the other kind of writing, the kind you are probably more familiar with: Writing to be shared with others. This writing is done when you have finished the thinking process, including the second, critical phase, and are ready to present your ideas for others' consideration.

The structure your formal writing takes will vary with the specific nature of the problem, the audience, and the purpose you hope to achieve by writing. All these matters will be discussed in depth in later chapters and in the appendix. For now we'll discuss only the basics.

Use the following approach for all your formal responses to the exercises and applications at the ends of the chapters, unless otherwise directed:

- State what you think in response to the problem
- Explain the reasoning by which you arrived at your view
- Add whatever supporting information or reasoning is appropriate and would be helpful to your reader in understanding your view

There is no specific length required for the responses to most exercises and applications. As a guide for determining whether your responses are satisfactory, use the test of *adequacy.* That is, ask yourself "Is my response adequate to convey my thoughts clearly and effectively to my readers?"

WARM-UP EXERCISES

1.1. Decide whether the reasoning that underlies the following statement is sound or unsound. Write a paragraph or two stating and explaining your judgment. (If you have difficulty doing this assignment, consult p. 199 of Appendix A.)

There's a possibility the price of postage stamps will be raised again soon. I think I'll stock up on them now to avoid paying the higher price.

1.2. Follow the directions for Exercise 1.1 above.

Physical fitness is very fashionable today. Yet the great philosophers agreed that the mind was more important than the body. So the physical fitness movement must be harmful.

1.3. Follow the directions for Exercise 1.1 above.

The sun has always risen in the past; therefore, it will rise tomorrow.

APPLICATIONS

1.1. For each of the following statements, write a brief response (one or two sentences) stating your position and explaining why you hold it.

    a. We know ourselves better than others know us.
    b. An unborn fetus is a human being.
    c. If guns are outlawed, only outlaws will have guns.
    d. Truth is an intensely personal matter—what is true for me is not necessarily true for you.
    e. Winning isn't everything—it's the only thing.
    f. Challenging another's opinion is a sign of intolerance.
    g. Atheists are generally moral people.
    h. Censorship is evil.
    i. Black people are better athletes than white people.
    j. The oil companies are manipulating gasoline prices.
    k. Getting your feet wet can cause a cold.
    l. Homosexuals are as likely to control their sex urges as heterosexuals.

1.2. The following passage is an excerpt from a student's letter home. Read it carefully. Then decide whether its reasoning is sound or unsound. State and explain your judgment in a paragraph or two, including whatever supporting material you believe will help persuade your reader.

The one thing that really bugs me about my schedule this term is that required course in "Introduction to Literature." Some students may not know what their future career is. I do. It's to help you, Dad, with the business, and someday to take it over. If we sold books I could see the value of such a course. But literature surely isn't going to make me a better furniture store manager.

1.3. Read the following dialogue carefully, looking for flaws in thinking. If you find a flaw, identify it and explain what is wrong with it in sufficient detail to persuade someone who read the passage without seeing the flaw. If you find two or more flaws, decide which is most serious and limit your discussion to that one. If you find nothing wrong with the thinking in the dialogue, explain why you agree with what is said. (If you have difficulty doing this assignment, consult p. 201 of Appendix A.)

    SALLY: Norma, have you begun your composition yet, the one that's due tomorrow?
    NORMA: No, I haven't. But I have done quite a bit of research on the topic. I've got a few very interesting facts I plan to refer to. Have you done any reading?
    SALLY: Not me. I want to do my own thing in my compositions; you know, be original.

NORMA: Really? Maybe I'd better not use those facts. They could work against me, I guess.

1.4. Follow the directions for Application 1.3, above.

HOMER: Excuse me, Professor Collins, may I speak to you for a minute?

PROF. C: Sure, Homer. What can I do for you?

HOMER: It's about the test we had last week. You gave me a 40 on it.

PROF. C.: That's not a very good grade. Had you read all three chapters carefully?

HOMER: *Care*fully? I read each one four times, underlined every important detail, and then studied them for about ten hours for three nights before the test. I took No-Doze and stayed up until 4:30 A.M. the night before the test.

PROF. C.: I see. That would surely seem to be more than adequate preparation. What do you think went wrong?

HOMER: I think the test was unfair . . . I mean, it's not . . . I know you wouldn't make a test unfair on purpose. I think you're a good teacher and all. Sociology is your field and I'm just an amateur, but after all that trying, I wouldn't have gotten a 40 if the test were fair.

1.5. Some years ago anthropologists discovered a primitive tribe dwelling on an island southwest of Manila. The tribe, called the Taotbato, live in limestone caves high in the walls of the crater of an extinct volcano. They hunt game with blow-guns and trap wild boar. During the rainy months they grow casava and sweet potatoes. The Taotbato are a nonviolent tribe, gentle and friendly. They run away from enemies rather than confront them. Their clothing consists of loin cloths or brief skirts made of bark, and they decorate themselves with bead necklaces.[13] Would it be correct to classify this tribe as human? On what basis? (If not enough information is given for you to decide, explain what information would be required for you to make a decision.)

one

BE AWARE

chapter 2

Establish a Foundation

If thinking took place in a mind completely insulated from the outside, an intellectually germ-free environment, there would be no need for the preliminary work in this chapter. We could just turn to techniques and strategies for thinking and begin practicing them. But that is not the case. We humans are social creatures. We live in an imperfect world, a world of conflicting ideas and values. And these affect us, for good or for ill.

Thus the ideas you have about free will, truth, knowledge, and opinion, and the debating of moral issues, will make a difference in your progress and in your development as a thinker. Some ideas will enhance your thinking; others will hinder it. Still others may paralyze it altogether. It is therefore important to examine these matters closely before proceeding, sorting out the helpful from the harmful notions, and establishing a firm conceptual foundation. First we'll consider the question of free will.

FREE WILL VERSUS DETERMINISM

Are you reading this chapter because you chose to do so or through compulsion? By *compulsion* I don't mean your instructor's direction "Read Chapter 2 for tomorrow." That is a kind of gentle (and benevolent) pressure, but it is not compulsion. Compulsion is a force you are virtually powerless to resist. Some psychologists would argue that you have no free will and so you are not reading through choice but through compulsion.

"Wait a minute," you say, "I know I have free will because right at this minute there's a party in my friend's room and I had to struggle with my conscience to read this chapter instead of going there." The psychologists smile patiently and say "Sorry, that struggle was an illusion. There's no choice—just a stimulus-response bond. You've been conditioned to behave in a certain way, and so you behave that way."

"Oh, yeah," you respond, "then watch this." You slam shut the book and head for the door. They yawn and say, "Quite unconvincing. All that your dramatic action shows is that you've been conditioned to be stubborn in the face of a disagreeable idea."

At this point your fists are clenched and you're beginning to grind your teeth. That's a normal reaction. And a lot of scholars and intellectuals—yes, and a lot of other *psychologists*— react similarly. Many of them have wisely given up arguing with the strict determinists. They realize that it's as impossible to win with someone whose rule is "Anything you say will prove my point" as it is to play cards with someone who stacks the deck.

This is not to say that reasonable people reject the idea of conditioning. On the contrary, they reject only the extreme notion that *all* human action is governed by conditioning. They take the moderate view that though we are all influenced by our surroundings and background, sometimes very strongly, we usually retain a significant measure of free will. Reasonable people would say that it is possible you are reading this chapter because of some compulsion, but more likely that you are doing so because you chose to read rather than to attend the party. What role has conditioning in your choice? They would say it increases or decreases the probability of one choice over another. A student who has acquired the habit of putting responsible action before self-indulgence would be more apt to do so in any particular situation.

It is important for you to accept this more moderate view for a number of reasons. First, you can discuss moral issues meaningfully only if you affirm that people have some control over their behavior and to that extent are responsible for it. (There is little point in discussing which of two actions is preferable if no one has the ability to choose between them.) In addition, you can profitably discuss social issues like nuclear disarmament, prison reform, or the treatment of the elderly only if you affirm that individuals (or a whole society) can change their policies and priorities. Most important, you can become motivated to approach problems creatively and critically only if you affirm that you have control over what you say and do, only if you affirm that careful thinking can make a difference.

WHAT IS TRUTH?

We live in an age that has made the true-false test not only the basis of educational achievement, but also the staple of one of our most durable (if lamentable) forms of entertainment, the game show. For this reason, it is ironic that so much confusion exists about the truth. Even otherwise intelligent people can be heard saying things like "Everyone makes his own truth," "One person's truth is another person's error," "Truth is relative," and "Truth is constantly changing." All of these ideas undermine thinking.

If everyone makes his own truth, then no person's idea can be better than another's. All must be equal. And if all ideas are equal, what is the point in researching any subject? Why dig in the ground for answers to archeological questions? Why probe the causes of tension in the Middle East? Why search for a cancer cure? Why explore the galaxy? These activities make sense only if some answers are better than others, if truth is something separate from, and unaffected by, individual perspectives.

Consider, for instance, this interesting (though hardly momentous) question—What are the most popular street names in the United States? If the truth here is relative, then any answer is as good as any other. One person says "Maple," another "Roosevelt," still another "Grove," and so on. Many people would say "Broadway" or "Main." (After deciding on your answer, check page 215.)[1] If every answer were equally correct, then few people would be interested in the question. Yet progress depends on the curiosity and interest of people, the drive to find the *right* answer, the desire to know the truth.

Truth is *what is so* about something, the reality of the matter, as distinguished from what people wish were so, believe to be so, or assert to be so. Being human and therefore imperfect, we can all too easily embrace erroneous views. And whenever we make such a mistake, for whatever reason, no matter how long we may shout "This is the truth," and no matter how deeply we may believe what we say, the truth of the matter is not changed one bit.

At various times and places, some very strange ideas were widely accepted as true. For example, the idea that a horsehair turns into a snake when placed in water. (Even Shakespeare believed this one.)[2] The reason people were deceived is obvious to anyone who has observed how refraction of light in water makes any object appear to be moving.

Similarly, many people believed erroneously that small flies, moths, and bees are babies of larger ones.[3] And the history of medicine includes an interesting and often bizarre collection of folk cures—for example, curing a headache by putting a bowl on the head, cutting the hair around the bowl, and then burning the hair; curing an earache by having someone spit tobacco juice in the affected ear; curing pneumonia by cutting a live chicken in two and placing it over the person's lungs; and curing weak vision by piercing the ears.[4]

We laugh at these ideas today, and rightly so. But it's important to realize that our very laughter underlines the fact that people do not *create* truth—they reach out to apprehend it, and construct expressions that they hope represent it faithfully. Sometimes they succeed, and sometimes they fail. Novelist H. G. Wells summed up the challenge and the difficulty of the task in a simple metaphor: "The forceps of our minds are clumsy forceps and crush the truth a little in taking hold of it."[5]

Does the truth ever change? No. It may sometimes seem to, but on closer inspection it will be found not to. Take the following case. In November 1981, a previously unknown species of fish was accidentally found deep in the Pacific Ocean.[6] We might think that the truth was that no such fish existed at first, and that the truth changed when the fish was discovered. But think of just how foolish that idea is. It asks us to believe that there was no such fish swimming in the water and that someone in a deep diving machine "looked" it into existence. How much more reasonable it is to believe that the fish existed but we didn't know that it did. In other words, that the truth of the matter was the same before and after the discovery, and only our knowledge of it changed.

Consider another very different example, the case of the authorship of the first book of the Bible, the book of Genesis. For centuries Christians and Jews alike believed that the book had a single author. In time this view was challenged, and eventually replaced by the belief that as many as five authors contributed to Genesis. Then, in 1981, the results of a 5-year linguistic analysis of Genesis were published, stating that there is an 82 percent probability of single authorship, as originally thought.[7]

Has the truth about the authorship of Genesis changed? No. Only our belief has changed. Perhaps one day we will have final and conclusive proof. On the other hand, perhaps, like an unsolved crime, the matter will never be resolved. The truth will not be changed by our knowledge or by our ignorance.

One easy way to spare yourself any further confusion about truth is to reserve the word *truth* for the final answer to an issue. Get in the habit of using the words *belief, theory,* and *present understanding* more often. This will have the added benefit of making you more willing to revise your views when new evidence appears and casts them in doubt.

WHAT IS KNOWING?

Here's a brief quiz. Don't read ahead until you have completed it:

1. Who said "I only regret that I have but one life to give for my country"?
2. What was the agreed-upon signal that was to be given Paul Revere from the tower if the British were coming?
3. What was Cinderella's slipper made of in the original story?
4. What is a camel's hair brush made of?

Most people could answer these questions quite readily. But the answers that come quite readily to those sure they "know" are wrong answers![8] (See page 216 for the correct answers.) The point is that *thinking we know* is not the same as *knowing.* We can think we know, be certain we know, proclaim loudly that we know, and yet not know at all. Our ideas do not constitute knowledge unless they correspond to reality.

Reality, unfortunately, can be deceptive. In 1972, 17-year-old college student Lawrence Berson was held for more than a week on multiple rape charges . . . until the real rapist, Richard Carbone, 20, confessed to the crime. A glance at photographs of the two will explain why the victims who identified Berson "knew" he was the rapist.[9]

It is obvious that situations where we believe we know, but really *don't* know, pose an obstacle to effective thinking. Why should anyone go to the trouble to investigate a matter or listen to opposing testimony when he believes he knows

Figure 2.1 Lawrence Berson (inset) and his look-alike, Richard Carbone. Copyright © 1974 by the New York Times Company. Reprinted by permission.

already? It is important, therefore, to understand the dynamics of knowing—how we come to know, and what kinds of knowledge are most trustworthy.

WAYS OF KNOWING

We know in one of three ways—*by experiencing situations, by witnessing others' experiences,* or *by report.* Each way can be subject to error.

Direct Experience

Of the three ways of knowing, direct experience is usually the most trustworthy. But even this way is less than perfect. We do not just receive experiences and store them, hermetically sealed, in our minds. We compare them with previous experiences, classify, interpret, and evaluate them, and make assumptions about them. All these processes may occur quite unconsciously, without our being aware of them. And any flaw in them makes our experiences seem different from the reality we encountered.

Consider this situation. Agnes has grown up in a religious family. She went to a parochial school and celebrated all the feasts of her church, including Christmas. She knows that Christmas is a Christian feast and throughout her lifetime it has always been a sacred time. From her knowledge she unconsciously creates the idea that it has always been so, throughout the history of Christianity. In time, this vague idea becomes a certainty in her mind. She can even imagine herself hearing it expressed in a classroom. Yes, she *knows* that Christmas has always been a major Christian feast.

Alas, she is wrong. In fact, in seventeenth-century England the Puritans forbade the celebration of Christmas. They felt it was a pagan custom. Similarly, it was banned in colonial New England. Christmas was not made a legal holiday in Massachusetts until 1856.

Here is another, even more common, example. All of us have experienced childhood as a stage in our development. Most of us have never conceived of anyone *not* experiencing childhood, so it is easy for us to believe with certainty that childhood always existed. Yet research shows this idea to be false. Historian J. H. Plumb writes

> The world that we think proper to children—fairy stories, games, toys, special books for learning, even the idea of childhood itself, is a European invention of the past four hundred years. The very words we use for young males—boy, *garcon, Knabe*—were until the seventeenth century used indiscriminately to mean a male in a dependent position and could refer to men of thirty, forty, or fifty. There was no special word for a young male between the ages of seven and sixteen; the word "child" expressed kinship, not an age state.[10]

Our perceptions are subjected to various mental processes and are not passively received: They are not mirror images of reality. Experience always distorts reality to some extent.

Witnessing Others' Experiences

It is certainly possible to observe accurately, but we often fall short of doing so. We usually see the world through glasses colored by our experiences and beliefs. If we believe that blacks are more athletic than whites, we are likely to "see" a particular black athlete outperforming a white athlete in a basketball game—even if that is not occurring. If we believe that Italians are violent by nature, we are likely to "see" an Italian making threatening gestures and preparing to strike another person when we observe him in a spirited discussion—even when those gestures are not unfriendly. Exactly how such distortions of observation occur may be explained as follows:

> We are told about the world before we see it. We imagine most things before we experience them. And those preconceptions, unless education has made us acutely aware, govern deeply the whole process of perception. They mark out certain objects as familiar or strange, emphasizing the difference, so that the slightly familiar is seen as very familiar, and the somewhat strange as sharply alien. They are aroused by small signs, which may vary from a true index to a vague analogy. Aroused, they flood fresh vision with older images, and project into the world what has been resurrected in memory.[11]

Report

This source of knowledge covers most of what we are taught by parents and teachers, what we hear reported in the news, and what we read in books and magazines. Most people who present ideas to us are undoubtedly trying to teach accurately and not deliberately misinform us—they themselves believe what they share with us. Yet they are human, and therefore capable of error. It is likely that a fair percentage of what we have been taught is at least partly incorrect.

An interesting example of the extent to which error can creep into news reports was revealed by George Seldes. Here is an original news story, together with the actual facts, as later determined by Seldes:[12]

THE STORY	THE FACTS
Belgrade, Oct. 27—A few moments before she should have appeared on the stage at the Lioubliana Theater last night, Mme. Alla Behr, a Slovene actress, was found hanging dead in her dressing-room. The reason for the suicide is unknown.	After the first act. Not at the Lioubliana, but the Klägenfurt. Her name, Ella Beer. Not Slovene, but Viennese. Not in her dressing-room, but in her hotel. The reason was known.

How could the reporter make such a total botch of the story? It's really not too difficult to imagine. He probably arrived at the scene late, found the area cordoned off, and got his details from bystanders or police keeping the crowd back —in other words, from people whose only knowledge was the fragments of fact and hearsay that circulated among them.

Errors are sometimes made from simple carelessness. For example, it was reported in an upstate New York daily newspaper that Thomas Simmons was arrested for striking Carl Peterson on the head. A day or two later, a corrected version was published. It seems Peterson had struck Simmons.[13] All those who read the first version but missed the second "knew" what happened, but they were wrong.

But what of magazine articles and books? These are researched more carefully than newspaper articles, and therefore ought to be more accurate. Edwin
Clarke writes:

> It is well known that secondary sources are likely to be written to harmonize with
> generally accepted beliefs and prejudices. Most popular histories, for instance
> . . . make heroes more heroic, villains more wicked, battles bloodier, and peaces
> more glorious than the best primary sources warrant. In short, they tend to
> present historical events, not as they were, but as the author likes to think of
> them, or as he believes his public likes or ought to think of them.[14]

THE PROBLEM OF REMEMBERING

Finally, all three ways of knowing—experience, observation, and report—are
subject to another problem, one that occurs days, months, or years later. This
problem is the tendency to remember inaccurately. Memory, of course, is a great
blessing. (The agony of amnesia is evidence enough of this fact.) But memory can
work tricks on knowledge. When we remember, according to authorities, the first
thing that occurs is something like an attitude. Then we reconstruct what we are
remembering, largely in conformity with our attitude. It is common to add new
details, to condense what happened, and to elaborate and invent things that
weren't part of the original experience.[15]

Even eyewitness testimony is subject to this distortion. "It has been found,"
one report states, "that witnesses have a tendency both to perceive and to remember things, first according to their expectations, second, according to their emotional bias, and third, according to their private notions as to what would be the
natural or reasonable way for things to happen.[16]

One simple example, of a kind that everyone has experienced at one time
or another, will illustrate the problem. Professor Sage is sitting captive at a faculty
meeting as a long-winded administrator drones on and on. Seeking escape, he
opens a book and begins to read. Suddenly he hears his name spoken, "Mr. Sage,
may I have your attention, please." Caught off guard, he looks up awkwardly,
accidentally drops his book, and stammers "Uh . . . I was listening . . . sort of
. . . sorry."

As he is driving home after the meeting, his mind ranges over the responses
he could have made to the speaker. Finally, he settles on the best one. He would
rise to his feet dramatically, and reply in his most withering tone, "Sir, my
attendance at this meeting you may require—my attention you must *earn.*"
Several months later, Professor Sage tells a friend the experience as it exists in
his memory. Which version is that? The one he truly believes is the correct one:
the one he imagined in his car.

This seems a rather pessimistic view of knowing, but you shouldn't be
discouraged by it. It is not the whole story about knowing—only the neglected
side. It is possible for you to know accurately and to remember with little
distortion. The point is that this seldom happens automatically for anyone. The
key to having it happen for you is to be cautious in claiming to know, be ready

to update your views, and make an effort to avoid distortion wherever possible.

WHAT ARE OPINIONS?

Opinions are intensely personal, so it is understandable that people have strong feelings about theirs. But many people carry those feelings beyond the boundaries of good sense. They take the valid idea "Everyone has a right to his opinion" to the ridiculous extreme of "Everyone's opinion is right." No one can hope to be a good thinker without acquiring a mature understanding of the nature of opinion.

The basic problem with the word *opinion* is that it is too general. It is made to carry a heavier load than it can bear, covering both expressions of taste and expressions of judgment.

Expressions of Taste

Expressions of taste describe internal states and preferences. They say essentially "I like this" and "I dislike that." For example, one may say "I find bald men attractive," or "I wouldn't buy any car but a Buick," or "When I look at a painting of a cow, I want to see something resembling a cow, not a swirl of color," or "Yellow and purple go well together." All these statements are expressions of taste. We may share the preferences or find them deplorably vulgar. But we have no business asking someone to defend these statements. No defense is necessary.

Expressions of Judgment

Expressions of judgment are assertions about the truth of things or about the wisdom of a course of action. Thus if people say "Bald men get more colds than hirsute men," or "Buicks are more economical cars than Fords," or "Paintings of cows that are unrecognizable as cows are inferior paintings," or "Yellow and purple combinations have never been in style in America," they are not expressing taste (though their taste may be lurking in the background). They are expressing judgment every bit as much as if they had commented on the question of whether the death penalty deters crime or whether the voting age should be raised.

It is not impolite or undemocratic to challenge an expression of judgment. Judgments are only as good as the evidence that supports them. History is filled with examples of judgments based either on insufficient evidence or narrow interpretation of evidence. In many cases they did untold harm because people were timid about challenging them.

For centuries people accepted the idea that the heart rather than the brain was the center of human consciousness. People believed that the planets were guided in their orbits by angels as late as the early seventeenth century. (Even the renowned astronomer Johannes Kepler did not question this belief.)[17] Fossils were known to exist long before Charles Darwin's day. In the Middle Ages they were interpreted as relics of plants and animals destroyed by Noah's flood, or as creations of Satan to deceive religious people, or as tests of religious faith put in the ground by God.[18]

At various times our ancestors commonly accepted the judgment that disordered behavior was caused by demons, and that the most effective cure was either magic, an enema, imprisonment in an asylum, beating, spinning in a rotating machine, or stoning to death.[19]

Many books were written in the past purporting to show that blacks are inferior to whites. As late as 1902, authors argued that black people were created along with animals to serve Adam, that they possessed minds but not souls, that the Adam's temptress was a black servant, and that Cain married a black and so mixed the blood of man and beast.[20]

How can you be sure your judgments are sound? There is no certain way. The best you can do is be aware of the possibility of error, and try to base your judgments on sufficient evidence, carefully interpreted, rather than prejudice, whim, or blind faith.

DEBATING MORAL QUESTIONS

Nowhere is modern thinking more muddled than over the question of whether it is proper to debate moral issues. Many argue it is not, saying it is wrong to make "value judgments." This view is shallow. If such judgments were wrong, then ethics, philosophy, and theology would be unacceptable in a college curriculum —an idea that is obviously silly. As the following cases illustrate, it is impossible to avoid making value judgments.

Raoul Wallenberg was a young Swedish aristocrat. In 1944 he left the safety of his country and entered Budapest. Over the next year he outwitted the Nazis and saved as many as 100,000 Jews (he was not himself Jewish) from the death-camps. In 1945 he was arrested by the Russians, charged with spying, and imprisoned in a Russian labor camp. He may still be alive there.[21] Now, if we regard him as a hero—as there is excellent reason to do—we are making a value judgment. Yet if we regard him neutrally, as no different from anyone else, we are also making a value judgment. We are judging him to be neither hero nor villain, but average.

Consider another case. In late 1981 a 20-year-old mother left her three infant sons unattended in a garbage-strewn tenement in New York City.[22] Police found them there, starving, the youngest child lodged between a mattress and a wall, covered with flies and cockroaches, the eldest playing on the second-floor window ledge. The police judged the mother negligent, and the court agreed. Was it wrong for them to judge? And if we refuse to judge, won't that refusal itself be a judgment in the mother's favor?

No matter how difficult it may be to judge such moral issues, we *must* judge them. Value judgment is the basis not only of our social code, but of our legal system. The quality of our laws is directly affected by the quality of our moral judgments. A society that judges blacks inferior is not likely to accord blacks equal treatment. A society that believes a woman's place is in the home is not likely to guarantee women equal employment opportunity.

Other people accept value judgments as long as they are made *within* a culture, and not about other cultures. Right and wrong, they believe, vary from one culture to another. It is true that an act frowned upon in one culture may be tolerated in another, but the degree of difference has often been grossly exaggerated. When we first encounter an unfamiliar moral view, we are inclined to focus on the difference so much that we miss the similarity.

For example, in medieval Europe animals were tried for crimes and often formally executed. In fact, cockroaches and other bugs were sometimes excommunicated from the church.[23] Sounds absurd, doesn't it? But when we penetrate beneath the absurdity, we realize that the basic view—that some actions are reprehensible and ought to be punished—is not so strange. The core idea that a person bitten by, say, a dog, has been wronged and requires justice is very much the same. The only difference is our rejection of the idea that animals are responsible for their behavior.

Is it legitimate, then, for us to pass judgment on the moral standards of another culture? Yes, if we do so thoughtfully, and not just conclude that whatever differs from our view is necessarily wrong. We can judge, for example, a culture that treats women as property, or places less value on their lives than on the lives of men. Moreover, we can say a society is acting immorally by denying women their human rights. Consider the following cases.

In nineteenth-century Rio de Janeiro, Brazil, a theatrical producer shot and killed his wife because she insisted on taking a walk in the botanical gardens against his wishes. He was formally charged with her murder, but the judge dismissed the charge. The producer was carried through the streets in triumph. The moral perspective of his culture condoned the taking of a woman's life if she disobeyed her husband, even in a relatively small matter. A century later that perspective had changed little. In the same city, in 1976, a wealthy playboy, angry at his lover for flirting with others, fired four shots into her face at point-blank range, killing her. He was given a two-year suspended sentence in light of the fact that he had been "defending his honor."[24]

Surely it is irresponsible for us to withhold judgment on the morality of these cases merely because they occurred in a different culture. It is obvious that in both cases the men's response, murder, was out of all proportion to the women's "offenses," and therefore demonstrated a wanton disregard for the women's human rights. Their response is thus properly judged immoral. And this judgment implies another—that the culture condoning such behavior is guilty of moral insensitivity.

THE BASIS OF MORAL JUDGMENT

On what basis should moral judgment be made? Certainly not the majority view —that is too unreliable. In the 1976 murder in Rio, for example, a radio poll revealed that 90 percent of the people surveyed agreed with the verdict. Hitler enjoyed the support of a majority of the German people. The American people at one time supported slavery. And more recently, the majority first opposed abortion, then approved it. Nor should the basis of moral judgments be feelings, desires, or preferences. If it were, then we would be forced to conclude that every rapist, every murderer, every robber is acting morally. Conscience provides a better basis for judgment, but it too can be uninformed or insensitive. (After all, the most heinous criminals apparently feel no remorse.)

The most reliable basis for moral judgment, the basis that underlies most ethical systems, is the principle that people have rights existing independently of any government or culture. The most fundamental is the right to be treated with respect and left undisturbed as long as one does not infringe on others' rights. Other rights—such as "life, liberty, and the pursuit of happiness"—extend from that right.

The basic principle, of course, is not itself adequate to judge complex moral questions. Additional working principles are needed. The following four are found in most ethical systems and provide common ground for the discussion of issues, even among people of very different ethical perspectives.

1. Relationships with other people create *obligations* of various kinds, and these should be honored unless there is compelling reason not to do so. There are, for example, formal agreements or contracts, obligations of family membership (parent to child, child to parent, husband to wife and vice versa), obligations of friendship, employer-employee obligations, and business and professional obligations.
2. Certain *ideals* enhance human life and assist people in fulfilling their obligations to one another. These should be served whenever possible. Among the most important ideals are: tolerance, compassion, loyalty, forgiveness, peace, brotherhood, justice (giving people their due), and fairness (being impartial, as opposed to favoring selected people).
3. The *consequences* of some actions benefit people, while those of other actions harm people. The former actions should be preferred over the latter. Consequences, of course, can be emotional as well as physical, momentary as well as lasting, and subtle as well as obvious.
4. Circumstances alter cases. Generalizations have their place, but too often they are used as a substitute for careful judgment. "Taking a human life is wrong" is useful as a general moral outlook, but it provides little help in deciding real cases. It blurs important distinctions. A hit-man for the mob takes a life when he completes a contract. So does a police officer when he kills a robber in self-defense. And so does a small child when he mistakes a real pistol for a toy and accidentally shoots his sister. But all three acts are very different from one another. Good thinking about issues means getting beyond generalizations and examining the particulars of the case.

To achieve depth in your examination of moral issues and wisdom in your judgment, you must deal effectively with complexities. The presence of two or more conflicting obligations or ideals creates complexity. So does the likelihood of multiple consequences, some beneficial and some harmful. Here is an easy-to-follow guide for dealing with such complexities.

1. Where two or more obligations are in conflict, decide which is the most serious obligation or which existed first.

2. Where two or more ideals are in conflict, ask which is the highest or most important ideal.
3. Where multiple consequences exist, some good and some bad, ask which are most significant—and whether the good effects outweigh the bad, or the reverse.

Let's look at an actual moral issue and see how these considerations apply. Ralph is a middle-aged man. In his youth he was a good athlete, and his son Mark grew up sharing his father's enthusiasm for sports. In seventh grade Mark went out for three sports, but was rather poor in two of them. Basketball was his best sport—in that he was fair, but not outstanding. Ralph decided that Mark could only be a first-string player if he received some assistance. So Ralph struck up a friendship with the junior varsity and varsity basketball coaches. He invited them and their wives to his house for dinner, opened his personal sports library to them, and got them tickets to professional games through his business contacts.

Through his friendship with the coaches, Ralph was able to help his son. He spoke to them often about Mark's intense desire to excel in basketball, and asked if they would mind giving Mark some tips to improve his game. The coaches were happy to help Mark; their help was an expression of their friendship with Ralph. They opened the gym to him on weekends and took personal responsibility for developing his skills.

Soon Mark was playing junior varsity basketball. Ralph took every opportunity not only to remind the coach of Mark's dedication, but also to point out other players' weaknesses and apparent lack of dedication. Mark received more playing time in each game than his skills alone justified, and in time became the team's scoring leader. When he moved up to varsity, Mark received further special treatment. He was almost never benched, even when his team was far ahead—instead, he was kept in to raise his point total. During his senior year, most of the team's plays were designed for him. And Ralph persuaded the coaches to write letters praising Mark's playing to a number of college coaches.

Did Ralph behave morally? Let's apply the principles we discussed earlier and see.

There are three important obligations involved in this case: Ralph's obligation to guide his son responsibly to manhood, through teaching and example; obligations of friendship between Ralph and the coaches; and the coaches' obligation to help all their players develop their potential and learn the values associated with sports.

The ideals that should be considered are sensitivity to others' needs, justice, and fairness. The first applies to Ralph—he should have appreciated the other players' needs for encouragement, support, and equal opportunity. The other two ideals, justice and fairness, apply to the coaches. They should have considered giving each player on the team the attention and help he deserved rather than concentrating their attention on one player. (This, of course, does not mean that it would be an injustice to give special attention to an outstanding player—Mark, remember, was only a fair player at the outset.) And the coaches should have considered treating players impartially (fairness). One way they could have done this was by opening the gym on weekends to all players who wished to practice, instead of to one.

The clearest and most certain consequence was that Mark's skills were developed and the other players were shortchanged because they did not have the same opportunities. Other probable consequences were that Mark's teammates developed a feeling of bitterness and cynicism over the coaches' favoritism, and that Mark acquired the attitude that it is permissible, even desirable, for him to disregard other people's rights and needs in order to achieve his own goals.

It is clear that though Ralph's actions achieved some good—the development of his son's skills—they also caused a great deal of harm to a number of people. The obvious harm was to the players. But they also caused the coaches to put friendship over responsibility to their players, and to violate the ideals of justice and fairness. (The main responsibility for the coaches' actions is, of course, their own. They could have resisted Ralph's influence.) Moreover, Ralph's actions probably even harmed his son. The self-serving attitude created in him far outweighs the development of his modest athletic skill.

In light of these considerations, we would find Ralph's actions morally wrong. Further, the fact that he knew what he was doing and actually *planned* it makes him even more blameworthy.

DEALING WITH DILEMMAS

Moral issues frequently pose dilemmas, situations in which a number of choices are available, but no choice is completely satisfactory. Such situations are frustrating. No matter what choice we consider, it seems the wrong one. "It's impossible to decide," we tell ourselves. Such situations are best approached with a clear strategy in mind. The following strategy will help you get beyond confusion and indecision:

1. Remember that you needn't classify your choices into simple good versus bad terms. It is possible to view them in a more sophisticated way. To do so, ask where each choice fits on the following scale.

Best	Better	Good	Bad	Worse	Worst

This approach will help you to distinguish between choices that at first glance seem equally moral.

2. In situations where the choices are all good, decide which is the *greater good*. In situations where none of the choices are really good, decide which is the *lesser evil*.

WARM-UP EXERCISES

2.1. Decide whether the reasoning behind the following statement is sound or unsound. Write a paragraph or two stating and explaining your judgment. (If you have difficulty doing this assignment, consult p. 199 of Appendix A.)

If Sarah were a real friend, she'd agree with me whether I was right or wrong in my idea. Even a stranger would agree when I was right. Friendship demands doing more than strangers do.

2.2. Follow the directions for Exercise 2.1 above.

The United States has been in existence for a little over 200 years, and in that time the world has enjoyed unprecedented technological progress. Therefore, it is obvious that without the United States there would have been little or no progress.

2.3. A young child is convinced that the time between 2 o'clock and 3 o'clock is longer than the time between 1 o'clock and 2 o'clock. Compose a brief explanation, with or without a diagram, that helps the child understand that the time isn't longer.

APPLICATIONS

2.1. Read the following dialogue carefully, looking for flaws in thinking. If you find a flaw, identify it and explain why in sufficient detail to persuade someone who has read the passage without seeing it. (If you find two or more flaws, identify and explain your thinking about each.)

CLEM: Can you believe that stuff Chapter 2 says about truth and opinion. I mean, it's a lot of garbage.

CLYDE: I don't know . . . it sort of made sense to me.

CLEM: Come on, man, you've got to be kidding. How can some egghead textbook writer tell *me* what truth is for me? He's himself, not me. How can he see through my eyes or make up my mind? Only I can do that.

CLYDE: But wait a minute. . . .

CLEM: Wait, nothing. You're taken in by all the words, man. Like that stuff about opinion. This is a democracy, isn't it? Maybe in Russia the Politburo can say which opinion is right, but not here. My opinion is as good as anyone else's. It says so right in the Constitution.

2.2. Read the following dialogue carefully. Then state whether Sabrina is right in what she claims. Explain your position.

SABRINA: There is such a thing as error. I can prove it.

LUCINDA: Oh yeah, then prove it.

SABRINA: I just did, with my very first sentence—"There is such a thing as error."

LUCINDA: What are you talking about?

SABRINA: I'm saying that if you examine that sentence carefully, you'll have to agree with it.

2.3. In November 1914, the German army invaded and captured the city of Antwerp, Belgium. The German press reported that the occasion was celebrated in Germany.

Other European newspapers noted the German report and wrote their own news releases. Here are the texts of the original German statement and four subsequent accounts.[25]

> When the fall of Antwerp became known, the church bells were rung [meaning in Germany]. *(Kölnische Zeitung)*
>
> According to the *Kölnische Zeitung,* the clergy of Antwerp were compelled to ring the church bells when the fortress was taken. *(Le Matin)*
>
> According to what *Le Matin* has heard from Cologne, the Belgian priests who refused to ring the church bells when Antwerp was taken have been driven away from their positions. *(The Times)*
>
> According to what the *Times* [London] has heard from Cologne via Paris, the unfortunate priests who refused to ring the church bells when Antwerp was taken have been sentenced to hard labor. *(Corriere della Sera)*
>
> According to information to the *Corriere della Sera* from Cologne via London, it is confirmed that the barbaric conquerors of Antwerp punished the unfortunate Belgian priests for their heroic refusal to ring the church bells by hanging them as living clappers to the bells with their heads down. *(Le Matin)*

     In a paragraph or two explain how such distortion could have occurred. Draw on what you learned in this chapter or in Chapter 1 to write your response.

2.4. Turn back to Application 1.1. Select one of the statements there (a–l) and recall your response to it. Examine that response in light of what you learned in this chapter about knowledge and opinion. That is, determine the source(s) of your view and their soundness.

2.5. In a small Central American village a few years ago, a visiting American student witnessed the following incident. A homosexual was dragged through the street by the police after being found in a compromising situation with his lover. When they got him in front of the police station, they made him take off his pants and bend over. The police chief proceeded to beat him on the buttocks with a riding crop until blood flowed from his wounds. Then he made the man repeat "I am a man and will behave like a man." Finally, he was taken inside the jail and forced to have intercourse with a prostitute. Discuss the moral considerations in this case and judge the moral quality of the police's treatment of the man.

2.6. The quotation that follows is by a famous American statesman. Does it challenge anything you read in this chapter? If so, identify the idea it challenges and decide which view is more reasonable. If it does not challenge anything, identify the part of the chapter it is most in agreement with.

> It is a great and dangerous error to suppose that all people are entitled to liberty. It is a reward to be earned, not a blessing to be gratuitously lavished on all alike; —a reward reserved for the intelligent, the patriotic, the virtuous and deserving; —and not a boon to be bestowed on a people too ignorant, degraded and vicious, to be capable either of appreciating or of enjoying it. (John C. Calhoun)[26]

2.7. Each of the following cases involves a moral question. (Some also involve legal questions that do not concern us here.) Identify the important moral considerations in each and then judge the morality of the action that was taken (or is proposed). Be sure to explain your reasoning carefully.

a. A doctor in Waltham, Massachusetts was convicted of raping a nurse at the hospital where he was employed. While free pending appeal of his conviction, he applied for a position at a Buffalo, New York hospital. The Waltham hospital administration reportedly wrote him a strong letter of recommendation, and did not mention the rape case. (Buffalo hospital officials learned of his conviction only when a new rape charge, involving patients, was filed against him in Waltham.)[27] Did the Waltham officials behave morally in withholding information concerning his rape conviction?

b. Dahlia Reyna, 17, was a victim of a rare disease that attacks the central nervous system and destroys brain cells. The doctors in Edinburgh, Texas gave her no chance for survival—she had no brain waves and only her respirator kept her heart pumping. Her parents requested that the respirator be unplugged so that she could die. The hospital complied and Dahlia expired.[28] Was it morally right to unplug the respirator?

c. A young U. S. navy officer sold secret electronics documents to the South African embassy. He was subsequently court-martialed.[29] There is no question that his action was illegal. Was it also immoral?

d. In Montpelier, Vermont, 11-year-old Ana Sola was struck by a car and rushed to the hospital. When her father, a Jehovah's Witness, denied permission for the blood transfusion the doctors felt was imperative, a judge revoked the parents' custody of the girl and gave it to the state so the transfusion could be administered.[30] The judge behaved within legal limits, but did he behave morally?

e. In November 1981, a statement was filed with the International Red Cross charging Iran's Khomeini regime with extracting blood from condemned prisoners before executing them.[31] Taking blood for use in blood banks under such circumstances is regarded by many people as immoral. Do you agree?

f. In Bartow, Florida a defense attorney doubted that prosecution witnesses could identify his client in an assault case. So he asked a young man he saw in the courthouse corridor to sit in place of his client at the defense table. The young man did so, the witnesses identified him as the man who had committed the assault and thereby lost their credibility with the jury. As a result of the defense attorney's trick, the defendant eventually went free.[32] Did the attorney behave morally?

g. The killer of a 14-year-old girl received a sentence of 25 to 40 years for the crime. After serving 17 years and 10 months as a model prisoner, he was eligible for parole. Yet the girl's father collected more than 21,000 signatures from people opposed to the killer's parole. The father promises, if the murderer is paroled, to make life difficult for him. "Wherever [he] goes," the father is quoted as saying, "I'll find him. Then I'll saturate that community so they know what kind of guy he is. They say time heals all wounds. That's baloney."[33] If the father does as he promises, will he be acting morally?

h. In recent years the law has tended to oppose sterilization of retarded people unless they understand the nature of the operation and freely consent to it. But in 1977 the parents of three severely retarded girls brought court action to gain the legal right to make the decision for their daughters.[34] Is their position morally acceptable?

i. Brian and Louise have been dating steadily for three years. Although they do not live together, they often stay at each other's apartment for several days at a time. Now Brian has met an attractive woman at work and isn't sure about his feelings for Louise. He would like to tell Louise that he believes he no longer loves her and wants to date someone else, but he is afraid of losing her and then having the other relationship fail to develop. So he begins seeing the other woman without telling Louise. Is Brian behaving morally?

chapter 3

Broaden Your Perspective

Do you know the story of the six blind men and the elephant? Able to rely only on their sense of touch, they reached out and touched an elephant to learn about it. One touched its side and decided that an elephant was like a wall. The second touched its trunk and decided—a snake. The third, its tail—a rope; the fourth, its ear—a fan; the fifth, its leg—a tree; the last, its tusk—a spear. Now each had a clear picture of the elephant in mind. But because all the pictures were based on a limited perspective, they were all wrong.[1]

All too often we are like the six blind men in our perspective on the world. We see narrowly, and our thinking suffers as a result. The first and perhaps saddest way we are victimized by narrow perspectives is in our view of our own potential. Most of us never come to know ourselves fully. We see only what we are and never realize the larger part of us—*what we have the capacity to be*. We never appreciate just how much of what we are is the result of accident.

Our development, for example, and our degree of success, is strongly influenced by the way others regard us. In one experiment, researchers administered an intelligence test to an entire elementary school. The researchers told the faculty that the test would identify students who were ready to undergo a "learning spurt." Actually the test did no such thing—the testers merely selected some students at random and identified them as the ones whose learning would enjoy a spurt. Teachers were subsequently observed using the same materials and methods for these students as for others. Nevertheless, at the end of the year, when the researchers again tested the student body, they found that the students that had been singled out had gained *twice as many IQ points* as the other students.

What was responsible for this gain? Obviously the teachers had formed favorable attitudes toward these students, and unconsciously transmitted their attitudes to the students. The students' self-images, in turn, ultimately changed.[2]

If that experiment seems surprising, the following one, similar in its design, will seem astounding. Laboratory assistants were assigned the task of teaching rats to run a maze. They were told the rats were in two groups, fast learners and slow learners. Actually, all the rats were identical. After the test period, the rats that had been designated fast learners were found to have learned the maze better than the other rats. Like the school teachers, the lab assistants had formed preconceived notions about the rats, and those notions had not only affected the degree of patience and the amount of attention and encouragement the assistants displayed with the rats—they had actually influenced the rats' *performance*.[3]

Studies show that confused, defeatist, helpless reactions are not inborn in us. They are *learned*. In one study people were given problems they were told could be solved, but which in fact could not be. As their efforts to solve the problems failed, the subjects experienced increasing frustration, until they finally accepted their helplessness and gave up. The real point of the study, though, came later. When the same people were given *solvable* problems, they continued to act helpless and to give up without really trying.[4]

What do these studies suggest about everyday life? That parents who are inconsistent in their demands and unpredictable in their reactions, teachers who focus on the negative rather than the positive, and coaches and activity leaders who ignore actual performance or contribution can rob us of our confidence, lead us into the habit of failure, and blind us to our real potential.

One of the distinguishing marks of many successful people is their refusal to define themselves by other people's assessments. Winston Churchill was branded a slow learner. Thomas Edison was urged to quit school because he was considered hopelessly stupid. Later, on his first job, working for the railroad, he set a train on fire with one of his experiments and was dismissed. And Albert Einstein's early record was even worse. Here are some of the details:

- He was not only an unimpressive student; he was told flatly by one teacher, "You will never amount to anything."
- At age 15 he was asked to leave school.
- When he took his first entrance exam to Zurich Polytechnic School, he failed it and was required to spend a year in a Swiss high school before he could be admitted.
- At Zurich he did mediocre work and was so unimpressive to his professors that he was rejected as a postgraduate assistant and denied a recommendation for employment.
- He eventually obtained a job as tutor at a boarding school, but was soon fired.
- He submitted a thesis on thermodynamics for a doctoral degree at Zurich. The thesis was rejected.
- Four years later, he submitted his special theory of relativity for a doctoral dissertation at the University at Bern. It was rejected.

"Wait," you may be saying, "Churchill, Edison, and Einstein were very special people. The question is whether the average person can overcome negative assessments." The answer is yes. To cite just one example, a teacher noticed that when students saw themselves as stupid in a particular subject, they unconsciously conformed to that image. They believed they were stupid, so they behaved stupidly. He set about to change their self-image. And when that change occurred, they no longer behaved stupidly![5]

The lesson here is not that legitimate criticism or advice should be ignored, nor that one can achieve competency in any field merely by belief. It is that you should not sell yourself short—your potential is undoubtedly much greater than you have ever realized. So when you catch yourself saying "I'll never be able to do this" or "I don't have the talent to do that" remember that the past does not dictate the future. What people call talent is often nothing more than knowing the knack. And *that* can be learned.

BECOMING AN INDIVIDUAL

All the philosophers and wise men of the ages tell us that individuals are rare. Yet the curious thing is that virtually all people consider themselves individuals. (Think about it—have you ever met anyone who admitted "I am *not* an individual"?) If the philosophers are right, then most people are wrong in their self-assessment. The source of the error may lie in our assumption that the very fact of our *being* (existing) is proof of individuality. That assumption is unwarranted. We are not individuals automatically. Rather, we *become* individuals by our willingness to realize our potential and our effort to be "self-aware, self-critical, self-enhancing."[6]

Acknowledging our lack of individuality is the key to becoming an individual. We must make an investment before claiming a profit, an investment of courage—the courage to take a long look at ourselves and to separate fact from fancy. That, of course, can be painful. It means giving up some cherished illusions.

How serious is *your* lack of individuality? Let's see. Ever since you lay helpless and gurgling in your crib, you have been learning. The moment you were able to use your senses, impressions rushed in on you. You received literally millions of impressions before you could interpret them with any sophistication. By the time you were able to interpret effectively, you had long since acquired a large repertoire of actions and reactions—by imitation. You endlessly practiced speaking and walking and, yes, *thinking* as your parents and siblings did.

Later, you attended school, and accepted your teachers' information and beliefs, often imitating their habits and attitudes. You learned, too, from your friends and classmates, and in time (when peer acceptance became more important) you said and did many things not because they seemed appropriate or mature, nor because you especially wanted to, but because those things promised the crowd's acceptance. If you are like most people, you are still selecting your words and actions at least in part by what others want or expect from you.

But the greatest shaper of your attitudes, habits, and values has probably not been your parents, siblings, teachers, or friends. It has very likely been the media—radio, magazines, newspapers, and especially television. By the time the average American graduates from high school, it is estimated that he has spent 11,000 hours in school and more than 22,000 hours watching television.[7]

This whole process of being exposed to society—home, neighborhood, church, school, and so on—sociologists call acculturation. Essentially it involves getting comfortable with, settling into, our culture. An unavoidable process, it has its blessings as well as its curses. Acculturation can occur subtly, creating the illusion that our values, attitudes, and ideas were formed independently of other people and circumstances. Erich Fromm was referring to this kind of illusion when he noted that, much of the time when we say we think something, we really ought to say "It thinks in me."[8] It is much like putting a record on the stereo and believing the record is itself making the music, when in fact it is just playing what was etched into it.

It's not hard to understand how we are deceived about our independence. We are much more acutely aware of having ideas than of the circumstances where we received them. What we feel and believe are present experiences for us, and so we tend to forget their origins. What we think, moreover, seems as much a part of us as the beating of our heart. The idea that our thoughts are borrowed is foreign and offensive.

To be an individual means more than claiming independence. It means achieving it. Here are three steps that will help you begin to achieve your individuality:

1. Acknowledge the influences that have shaped your thinking. Say to yourself, "My mind is full of other people's ideas and attitudes, which I received uncritically and accepted because I was young and trusting. Many of those ideas and attitudes are now hardened into principles and convictions. Yet some of them are surely erroneous or unworthy." Identify the people you have especially admired or been close to—your mother and father, an aunt or uncle, a coach or teacher, a celebrity. Consider each person's convictions and actions. Decide exactly how those convictions and actions contributed to your ideas and attitudes.
2. Sort out and evaluate your ideas and attitudes. Put your realization of influence to work for you in a practical way. Examine your ideas and attitudes, even your most cherished ones. Ask, for example, what your political philosophy is. (That question, of course, means more than "Are you a Democrat or a Republican?" It includes your views on the proper role of government, and citizens' responsibility in a democracy.) Ask, as well, about your views on religion, race, nationality, marriage, morality, and law. Compare your ideas and attitudes with others. Make your beliefs prove themselves, not on the basis of their familiarity or their compatibility with other ideas, but on their merit.
3. Choose the best ones. Decide as objectively as you can which ideas deserve your endorsement and which attitudes are worth striving to acquire. Remember that you are never being more an individual than

when you resist the pressure of habit—and change the way you think about a subject or issue because the evidence prompts you to do so.

Real individuality, of course, cannot be attained in a single sitting, or even in a hundred sittings. It is an ongoing task, the occupation of a lifetime. But it is a task that everyone wanting to be a good thinker must undertake. Self-knowledge, as Socrates said, is the beginning of wisdom.

HABITS THAT HINDER THINKING

In your effort to become more of an individual, it is important to identify any habits of mind interfering with clear thinking. Some of these habits will be peculiar to your own situation and depend on your unique background and experience. But there are a number of habits that victimize everyone to some extent. The most significant deserve close attention. They are the mine-is-better habit, face saving, resistance to change, conformity, stereotyping, and self-deception.

The Mine-Is-Better Habit

This habit is natural enough. It begins in early childhood. As children we all said, "My bike is better than your bike," "My Dad is stronger than your Dad," "My Mom is prettier than your Mom." We believed what we said, too. Whatever we associated with was an extension of ourselves. Asserting its superiority was an expression of ego.

The habit does not go away easily as we grow up. "In later life," writes Rowland Jepson, "we are apt to think that the world in which we grew up was the best of all possible worlds, and to regard the customs and notions which helped to mould our own selves as the acme of wisdom and sound sense, never reached before or since."[9] And we tend to regard our present ideas, values, groups, and political and religious affiliations as superior, too.

Mine-is-better is undoubtedly as old as mankind. Primitive societies tend to regard those who are different—foreigners, criminals, the mentally deranged, the physically or emotionally handicapped, other races, other religions, and other social classes—as lesser beings. "The creature who does not 'belong' to the tribe, clan, caste or parish," they reason, "is not really human; he only aspires or pretends to be 'like us.' "[10] From that, it is but a short step to the decision that such "different people," being subhuman, have no human rights, as some cultures have decided.[11]

We are appalled at such a view, yet our mine-is-better habit leads us to similar (if considerably less extreme) conclusions. If a friend proposes a change, we call him a reformer; if an enemy proposes a change, we call him a troublemaker or a fanatic. Likewise, the differences between a traitor and a defector, a religious denomination and a cult, a politician and a statesman depend on how close the person or subject is to us and our view.

The mine-is-better habit hinders our thinking. It destroys objectivity and prompts us to prefer self-flattering errors to unpleasant realities. If you wish to be a good thinker, you must learn to control this habit and keep your ego from interfering with your search for truth.

Face Saving

Like the mine-is-better habit, face saving is a natural tendency arising from our ego. Unlike mine-is-better, it occurs *after* we have said or done something that threatens to disturb our self-image or the image others have of us. Psychologists call face saving a defense mechanism, meaning it is a strategy we use to protect our image.

One common form of face saving is the "It wasn't my fault—he made me do it" or "It wasn't my fault—I had no alternative" excuse most children (and many adults) employ at one time or another. This excuse, though an obstacle to good thinking, at least has the virtue of acknowledging that something wrong or undesirable has occurred. The dishonesty lies in pointing the finger away from ourselves.

A more dangerous form of face saving is called rationalizing. Rationalizing is a dishonest substitute for reasoning. We set out "to defend our ideas rather than to find out the truth about the matters concerned."[12] Let's say, for example, that you are a heavy smoker. As the evidence linking smoking to serious diseases mounts, you begin to realize that your habit harms you. You feel like a fool. But instead of admitting that smoking is harmful (or at least examining the evidence and deciding whether it is valid), you say, "The case against smoking isn't conclusive," and "The relaxing of tension smoking achieves for me more than balances any minor harm it may cause me." That's rationalizing.

Although rationalizing sometimes resembles honest reasoning, there is a simple way to tell the difference between them. You are reasoning if your belief follows the evidence—that is, if you examine the evidence first and then make up your mind. You are rationalizing if the evidence follows your belief—if you first decide what you'll believe, and then select and interpret evidence to justify it.[13]

The process of face saving and its effect on thinking are effectively summed up by Rowland Jepson. He writes

> When we have once adopted an opinion, our pride makes us [reluctant] to admit that we are wrong. When objections are made to our views, we are more concerned with discovering how to combat them than how much truth or sound sense there may be in them; we are at pains rather to find fresh support for our own views, than to face frankly any new facts that appear to contradict them. We all know how easy it is to become annoyed at the suggestion that we have made a mistake; that our first feeling is that we would rather do anything than admit it, and our first thought is "How can I explain it away?"[14]

It is not quite enough to want to *have* a good image—you should want to *deserve* it. Make that your goal, and remember this adage: He who makes a mistake and refuses to admit it is thereby making another mistake. Keeping those two things in mind, you should find it possible to control your face-saving tendencies.

Resistance to Change

Resistance to change is the tendency to reject new ideas and new ways of seeing or doing without examining them fairly. It has been the recurrent reaction to creativity throughout the ages. Galileo came close to losing his life when he suggested the sun, not the earth, was the center of the solar system. It was resistance to change that caused people to scoff at the first plow, the umbrella, the automobile, and the airplane. This trait was responsible for opposition to using anesthetics during surgery, performing autopsies to determine the cause of deaths, and extending voting rights to women. Even the ending of child labor, which we now regard as obviously reasonable, was initially greeted by this same resistance. (Critics of the abolition of child labor called it a "Russian move in the direction of nationalizing American children.")[15]

One cause of our tendency to resist change is simple laziness. Having gotten used to things one way, we resent being asked to regard them another way. It makes us break our routine. Still another reason is excessive regard for tradition. The old ways must be best, we believe, because our parents and grandparents used them. New ideas and approaches seem an affront to our ancestors.

But what is tradition, really? Is it the best way of seeing or doing? In some cases it surely is. But in others, it is more like the path in the following verse:

One day through the primeval wood
A calf walked home as good calves should;
But made a trail all bent askew,
A crooked trail as all calves do.

Since then three hundred years have fled,
And I infer the calf is dead.
But still he left behind his trail,
And thereby hangs my moral tale.
The trail was taken up next day
By a lone dog that passed that way;
And then a wise bellwether sheep
Pursued the trail o'er hill and glade
Through those old woods a path was made.

And many men wound in and out
And dodged and turned and bent about
And uttered words of righteous wrath
Because 'twas such a crooked path;
But still they followed—do not laugh—
The first migrations of that calf,

And through this winding wood-way stalked
Because he wobbled when he walked.

This forest path became a lane
That bent and turned and turned again;
This crooked lane became a road,
Where many a poor horse with his load
Toiled on beneath the burning sun,
And traveled some three miles in one.
And thus a century and a half
They trod the footsteps of that calf.

The years passed on in swiftness fleet,
The road became a village street;
And thus, before men were aware,
A city's crowded thoroughfare.
And soon the central street was this
Of a renowned metropolis;
And men two centuries and a half
Trod in the footsteps of that calf.

Each day a hundred thousand rout
Followed this zigzag calf about
And o'er his crooked journey went
The traffic of a continent.

A hundred thousand men were led
By one calf near three centuries dead.
They followed still his crooked way,
And lost one hundred years a day;
For thus such reverence is lent
To well-established precedent.[16]

In situations where tradition is nothing more than "well-established precedent" or following in the footsteps of those that have gone before, it is more of
an insult to our ancestors to follow than to explore new paths.

But there is yet another, more significant reason for resisting change—
insecurity. Our concepts and habitual ways provide a certain stability to our
uncertain life. Change threatens to make new and strange demands on us, demands we fear we may not be equal to meeting. Our imaginations conjure up a
hundred apprehensions, all of them more frightening for being nameless. And so,
unsure of our ability to cope, we choose to resist rather than to welcome the new.

Unfortunately, if we are resistant to change, we are resistant to discovery,
invention, creativity, progress. Each of these, after all, comes to the world first
as a new idea. *To resist change is to set our minds against our own best and most
worthwhile ideas.*

We must not embrace every new idea uncritically. Many new ideas prove,
on examination, to be worthless or unworkable. But we must be open to any idea,

willing to suspend judgment long enough to test it, and ready to accept it—regardless of how strange it seems—if it proves itself.

Conformity

Not all conformity is bad. We put our out-of-town letters in the out-of-town post office slot, say hello instead of goodbye when we answer the phone, try to spell correctly and not violate the rules of grammar, and stop for red lights when driving. Such actions, and thousands of others like them, are a sensible kind of conformity. If we were to try nonconformity in such matters, we would merely waste valuable time, confuse or annoy those around us, or threaten the safety of ourselves and others.

Harmful conformity is what we do instead of thinking, in order to belong to a group or to avoid the risk of being different. Harmful conformity is an act of cowardice, a sacrificing of independence for a lesser good. In time it makes us more concerned about what others think than about what is right and true and sensible. Once we begin to conform, we quickly find ourselves saying and doing not what we believe is best, but what we believe others want or expect us to say and do. That focus dulls our ability to think creatively and critically.

It's not always easy to avoid conforming. Our friends, families, and associates may exert considerable pressure on us. It takes courage to say "I disagree" or "that's wrong" when the group is firm in their view. If you've ever tried it, you know how painful that why-must-you-be-such-a-traitor look can be. That's why so many people give in again and again until they have completely surrendered their individuality. One widely repeated laboratory experiment documented this surrender dramatically. The experiment involved two subjects, who were told they were participating in a memory test. One assumed the role of teacher, the other the role of student. When the student gave a wrong answer, the teacher was supposed to deliver an electric shock. With each wrong answer the shock increased.

The situation, of course, was rigged. There was really no electric shock, and the student was really an actor instructed to say he had a heart condition, to plead with the teacher to stop, and even to claim chest pains. At the highest level of shock, he remained silent, and, since he was in another room, the teacher must have considered the possibility that the shock killed him.

The result of the experiment? Fully 65 percent of the teachers administered the shocks up to the highest level. Most protested to the experimenter that they didn't want to inflict pain on the student, but when the experimenter insisted, they obeyed.[17]

Perhaps we would behave differently in that experiment. Perhaps not. In any case, the effects of conformity are all around us. Abraham Maslow observed:

Too many people do not make up their own minds, but have their minds made up for them by salesmen, advertisers, parents, propagandists, TV, newspapers and so on. They are pawns to be moved by others rather than self-determining individuals. Therefore they are apt to feel helpless, weak, and totally determined; they are prey for predators, flabby whiners rather than self-determining persons.[18]

It would be a mistake to fight conformity by refusing to do as others do, to be different for the sake of being different. That is no more thoughtful than mindless conformity. The right way to fight is choosing for yourself, whether or not your choice agrees with others' choices—having the courage to be different, if that is the correct way.

Stereotyping

Stereotyping is an extreme form of generalizing. Generalizations classify people, places, and ideas according to their common elements. Thus we may say that most basketball players are tall, that doctors study for years before being licensed to practice, that Toyotas get better gas mileage than Corvettes. These are fair and reasonable generalizations. Some generalizations go beyond the boundaries of reasonableness—these are called *over*generalizations. The belief that, for example, city residents are less friendly than people in the country or that students who drink don't do well in their studies, are overgeneralizations.

Stereotyping, however, is a deeper and more serious problem than overgeneralization. A stereotype is a fixed, unbending generalization, irrationally maintained. As Walter Lippmann explains

> Stereotypes are loaded with preference, suffused with affection or dislike, attached to fears, lusts, strong wishes, pride, hope. Whatever invokes the stereotype is judged with the appropriate sentiment. Except where we deliberately keep prejudice in suspense, we do not study a man and judge him to be bad. We see a bad man. We see a . . . sainted priest, a humorless Englishman, a dangerous [communist], a carefree Bohemian, a lazy Hindu, a wily Oriental, a dreaming Slav, a volatile Irishman, a greedy Jew, a 100% American. . . . Neither justice, nor mercy, nor truth, enter into such a judgment, for the judgment has preceded the evidence.[19]

The most common stereotypes are racial, religious, or ethnic. There is the stereotype of the black, the fundamentalist Christian, the Italian. But there are many other types, as well, no less firm for being less common. There are stereotypes of homosexuals, the clergy, college dropouts, feminists, male chauvinists, New York City, singles' bars, motherhood—even *God!*

Stereotyping sets up a nice neat mental warehouse for ideas. Everything has its own compartment. There is no comparing, no sorting, weighing, or selecting, just storage. Everything is presorted, predetermined, prejudged. That is precisely the harm stereotyping does—it impedes the mind's dynamic activity. It forces life's infinite variety, the myriad circumstances and people around us, into ready-made categories.

It's easy to see that the solution is to resist hard classifications. The problem is that we seldom see our stereotypes. We see them instead as accurate descriptions of reality, the way things are, insights. It is never easy to give up a stereotype —but it is important to make the effort. For unless you can make yourself see the uniqueness of each person, place, thing, and circumstance, as well as its similarity to other things, you will never see accurately.

Self-Deception

A boy once went fishing with several friends. Someone suggested they all share whatever fish were caught. It seemed a reasonable idea, so the boy agreed. Then, as the day wore on and he caught more fish than his friends, his attitude began to change. By the end of the day, he was violently opposed to sharing, and objected loudly, arguing that good fishermen shouldn't be penalized for others' incompetence.[20]

That boy engaged in one of the many kinds of self-deception that tempt us all. "One of the most disturbing habits of the human mind," Katherine Anne Porter observed, "is its willful and destructive forgetting of whatever in its past does not flatter or confirm its present point of view."[21]

One of my colleagues often begins his classes in informal logic by asking students to answer this exercise. "Think of the guy or girl you most resented in high school. In a couple of sentences explain why you resented him or her." He has read hundreds of students' answers, and has found that the great majority say, "That guy had the terrible habit of . . ." or "That girl lacked. . . ." Only 1 or 2 out of 10 will say "*I* was jealous (or immature or insecure)." In other words, any resentment is clearly the other's fault and not their own. A similar kind of self-deception occurs when students who get low grades because of missing class, failing to hand in homework, or refusing to prepare for examinations accuse their teachers of favoritism and prejudice.

People with symptoms of serious diseases—cancer, for example—sometimes lie to themselves that the matter is not serious enough for them to see a doctor. Many divorced people deceive themselves about the reasons for the breakup of their marriages. Most alcoholics lie to themselves about their alcohol dependence—"I can stop any time I want" is the common lie. And most dope smokers deceive themselves that they smoke because they want to, rather than as a means of escape from unpleasant experiences and frustrations. If they smoke heavily, they may also persuade themselves that they are not getting burned out, even when the symptoms—loss of memory, listlessness, and confusion, among others—are obvious.

In addition, many people deceive themselves about their competence. Edwin Clarke describes their behavior this way:

> Persons who, for instance, would consider it the height of presumption to advise an engineer how to plan a simple culvert, have no hesitation in speaking with an air of authority on far more complex questions such as Portugese immigration or the nature of a desirable currency, subjects on which their knowledge

is very superficial and only too often derived from inaccurate and biased sources.[22]

They have acquired the habit of pretending they are knowledgeable, and in time come to believe the pretense themselves.

A good thinker must come to terms with the problem of self-deception. If you deceive yourself about your knowledge, you will not be able to decide accurately what information you need to solve a problem. And if you are in the habit of judging dishonestly, you can never hope to judge well.

All six of the habits that hinder thinking—the mine-is-better habit, face saving, resistance to change, conformity, stereotyping, and self-deception—can become deeply ingrained and therefore difficult to overcome. Nevertheless, they can all be overcome with desire and effort. The following section explains how to attack them.

OVERCOMING BAD HABITS

We saw in Chapter 1 how feelings are part blessing and part curse. On the one hand, they can offer intuition and insight, and can motivate us to persevere in difficult work. On the other, they can mislead us. Now, after we have reviewed the habits that hinder thinking, you should appreciate more fully just how vulnerable we all are to the latter tendency.

The key to overcoming the bad habits we have been discussing is to examine your initial feelings about problems and issues, particularly strong feelings prompting you to take a stand immediately, without examining the evidence or weighing competing arguments. By closely examining such feelings you will often be able to determine that a particular bad habit—resistance to change, for example, or stereotyping—is interfering with your thinking, and thereby realize the importance of suspending that feeling until you have examined the evidence.

Let's see how this advice applies to an actual issue. You are reading a magazine article discussing a scientific study concerning the possibility of life after death.[23] You read that the book is a study of 116 people's near-death experiences and their subsequent memories of floating out of their bodies and, in some cases, travelling down a dark tunnel toward a bright light.

You sense a strong feeling rising in you, something more than interest in the subject. You allow it to surface and then examine it closely, critically, and as objectively as you can. If the feeling is positive, the kind that says to you, "Here it is—proof that there's life after death—just what we need to show the skeptics, the doubters, those of little faith," you will undoubtedly find elements of mine-is-better thinking, and perhaps traces of face saving, stereotyping, and conformity.

And if your feeling is negative ("More nonsense from mindless religious quacks who can't face the reality of oblivion"), you will undoubtedly find elements of mine-is-better thinking, and perhaps resistance to change, stereotyping, and conformity.

Aware of your bias and the particular habits that are likely to corrupt your thinking, you read on, making a special effort to receive what is said instead of what you wish were said or expect to be said, and guarding against self-deception.

This is not a perfunctory exercise—these are very real and specific dangers, and must be avoided. If you have failed to control positive feelings, you may miss the fact that, though the author of the study personally believes in life after death, he does not claim his work *proves* its existence. Nor does he offer his findings in support of any particular religious perspective. Without attention to your bias, you may see the researcher as a champion of your personal theology, and even exaggerate that. A day or two later you may be heard in the snack bar proclaiming that the *entire scientific community* has now *conceded* that your religious view of afterlife is *unquestionably* true.

If, on the other hand, you fail to control negative feelings, you may miss the fact that the author is a medical professor, began his study as a skeptic, and conducted his investigations in a thoroughly scientific manner. Thus, you may convince yourself that the book says nothing of value and your refusal to believe in an afterlife is still the most intelligent view of the matter. In fact, you may even make yourself believe that the book's "miserable failure" to make its case somehow reinforces your belief.

The self-deception described here may seem laughable, but it really is not. Self-deception causes people to read and observe without profit, to remain in a state of self-flattering ignorance instead of learning and growing. Self-deceivers substitute what Henshaw Ward termed *thobbing* for considering and evaluating ideas. The term combines the *th* from *thinking,* the *o* from *opinion,* and the *b* from *believing.* Whenever people think the opinion that pleases them and then believe it, they are thobbing.[24] Be sure you guard against it.

WARM-UP EXERCISES

3.1. Decide whether the reasoning behind the following statement is sound or unsound. Write a paragraph or two explaining your judgment.

> Past medical discoveries met with opposition from the medical community. Laetrile (a controversial drug used in cancer treatment) has met with opposition from the medical community. Therefore, laetrilee is a great medical discovery.

3.2. Follow the directions for Exercise 3.1 above.

> Conservatives believe that the role of the federal government should be much more limited than it has been in recent decades. Marvin believes that the role of the federal government should be much more limited than it has been in recent decades. Therefore Marvin is a conservative.

3.3. Your niece, a preschooler, asks you the following question: "Is it possible to remember the future?" Compose an answer simple and clear enough for her to understand.

APPLICATIONS

3.1. Read the following dialogue carefully, looking for flaws in thinking. If you find one, identify it and explain what is wrong in sufficient detail to persuade someone who has read the passage but sees no flaw. If you find two or more flaws, identify and explain your thinking about each.

> EDNA: Professor, I don't like to complain, but I don't feel I'm getting as much out of this composition course as I should be getting.
>
> PROFESSOR: Really? Where do you think the problem lies?
>
> EDNA: Well, you've got us writing just about every other day if we include the brief responses to the readings as well as the longer compositions. Yet so much of the writing seems wasted—you only correct about half the assignments.

3.2. Look back at the exercises for Chapters 1 and 2. Recall your responses. Decide whether those responses were influenced by any of the bad habits discussed in this chapter. Discuss your findings. (Note: In doing this assignment you should expect yourself to resist admitting such influences. Overcoming that resistance is a mark of thinking effectively.)

3.3. In the interest of highway safety a number of states raised their legal drinking age, and others are considering doing so. Evaluate the idea of having a uniform legal drinking age in all states.

3.4. In Pompano Beach, Florida undercover police agents borrowed a warehouse and stored a large quantity of confiscated marijuana there. Then they passed the word that the supply was available for sale to dealers. When dealers arrived and purchased the marijuana, they were arrested for marijuana conspiracy and trafficking.[25] Do you approve of the police agents' behavior in this case? Explain your position in some detail.

3.5. When Rae Landau and Isaac Perlstein were divorced, Ms. Landau won custody of their 8-year-old son. The boy's observance of Jewish dietary laws was one provision of the divorce agreement. Ms. Landau admittedly failed to honor that provision for a period of 5 years. As a result, a New York Supreme Court justice ruled that Ms. Landau must surrender custody of the boy to his father.[26] Do you agree with the judge's ruling? Explain your position.

3.6. In 1978, in Skokie, Illinois a federal judge decided that the community had no right to prohibit the American Nazi party from holding a parade and rally in Skokie's streets and public square. The community, which numbers many former Nazi concentration camp inmates among its citizens, had objected to the march because it represented advocacy of a dangerous and antidemocratic philosophy.[27] Do you agree with the judge's ruling? Explain your position.

3.7. A homosexual minister was granted permanent adoption of a 13-year-old boy by a Family Court judge in Catskill, New York. The boy will live with the minister and his male companion.[28] Do you believe the judge should have disapproved the adoption because of the minister's homosexuality? Explain your thinking.

3.8. An 18-year-old San Francisco resident sued the high school from which he graduated, contending that the faculty were responsible for his inability to read and write adequately.[29] Do you think such a suit is reasonable? What factors would you consider if you were responsible for judging its merits?

3.9. It is common for high school coaches to forbid their players to drink alcohol. If a coach has such a rule and catches a player drinking, is it reasonable for him to dismiss the player from the team for the rest of the season? Should he treat the team's star player differently than a benchwarmer?

3.10. Apparently a sizeable number of Americans—as many as 32 million, according to one poll[30]—believe in astrology, and think the stars govern their lives. How reasonable is this view? Explain your thinking.

3.11. In November 1981, a San Francisco publisher paid two Jewish businesspeople $1500 in an out-of-court settlement. Their lawsuit had charged him with discriminatory business practices. He published *The Christian Yellow Pages,* a directory of businesses operated by born-again Christians. (The publisher required advertisers to sign a pledge that they accepted Jesus as their savior.)[31] Do you believe the publisher was guilty of discrimination? Explain.

3.12. A minister in Pontiac, Michigan was arrested and charged with practicing medicine without a license—a felony—after he sprinkled blood from a freshly killed rooster on an ailing person. The minister said the authorities were stifling his constitutional rights. Do you agree with him? Explain your position.[32]

chapter 4

Rekindle Your Curiosity

Curiosity is perhaps childhood's dominant intellectual characteristic—and, interestingly, the philosopher's and creative achiever's dominant characteristic, as well. One researcher recorded all the *why* questions asked by a child slightly under 5 years of age over a 4-day period. Read it carefully—it will help recall your own childhood and the state of mind you felt so comfortable with then. (One asterisk indicates no answer was given; two asterisks, no answer and the question was not repeated. Italics are used for the mother's responses.)

1. Why do you have this box for your feet?
2. Why did they bring the bed down from the attic?
3. *Take your dollies in now, Joyce!* Why?
4. *Fix the rug! You caught your feet under the edge of it!* Why? Why did I?
5. Why did you take two cookies?
6. Why does the watering-pot have two handles?
7. Why did he put the solder in so many places?
8. *The song-sparrow isn't pretty to look at*—Why isn't he pretty?
9. *The bobolink has a brown coat in winter.* Why?* Why?
10. *It was careless of you to lose your shovel.* Why?* Why?
11. *This is your orange juice.* Why?**
12. *You are to sit here, in Daddy's place.* Why?*—Please, Mother, tell me why.
13. Do we have bangs at the back of our heads? *No!* Why?* Why, Mother?
14. *And then he made a mast for his little boat.* Why? Please tell me why he made a mast.
15. Why do you wash the hair off (the razor)?

16. (Putting on bathrobe without putting her arms in the sleeves) Is this good? *No.* Why?*—(impatiently) Why? Speak out! (but then without waiting for an answer) Because it wouldn't stay on. *There, you thought it out for yourself, didn't you?*

17. Why did you stub your toe? *Because I wasn't watching out.* Why?

18. *I will tell you a story about this willow plate—*Why?**

19. *Please hurry, Joyce!* Why?*—Because you want me to wash?* Why didn't you wash first? Because you knew I wanted to go with Daddy?

20. See the little tea things! Why did we buy them? *Why do you think?* Because we might use the others all up.

21. Why did you use both a fork and a spoon in making that cake?

22. Why did you sit in that chair, Mother?

23. *Please don't climb in that chair!* Why?**

24. Why are you putting up that screen?**

25. Why are you opening that window?**

26. Why does the little chicken grow in the shell?

27. *You can't win by jumping up and down!* Why?

28. Jeremiah, Jeremiah. He got into a pit, didn't he? Why did they put him into a pit?

29. *Please be careful not to break the bean-plants.* Why?

30. I saw your blue apron through a crack in the door. I thought it was a spider. *A spider isn't blue, dear!* Why?*—Please, Mother, tell me why a spider isn't blue.

31. *You shouldn't talk about a visitor's beard, Joyce, until he has gone!* Why?* Please tell me why.

32. Why don't you have a beard, Mother?

33. I want to cut my eyebrows in half! *Oh! You wouldn't want to do that!* Why? Because I would look funny?

34. Why do we have eyebrows?

35. Why must I hurry?

36. Why should I wait for candy until after supper?

37. Why did you speak to that man?

38. *Please don't bang the car-door!* Why?*

39. Why did the chickens walk in front of the car?

40. *It is time to go home for dinner now!* Why?*[1]

Some of the questions, of course, are merely designed to get her mother's attention. But judging from both the content of the question and the child's expression when asking it, the researcher believed 13 of the 40 questions were genuine expressions of curiosity. Considering that the list contains only *why* questions, and omits *how, where, who,* and *when* questions, it is clear how marvelous a child's curiosity is.

HOW CURIOSITY IS LOST

Unfortunately, children who at 4 are bombarding parents with questions often lose their curiosity by 14. How this happens is clear enough, at least in broad overview. Their parents grow weary of answering and begin to discourage questions. "Don't ask so many questions," they scold. And they warn, "Curiosity killed the cat." Then the children enter school and find the teacher has little time to answer. There are too many other boys and girls in the room, there is a schedule to be followed and material to be covered, and time is short.

Once children lose the questioning habit, they soon lose the habit of even thinking of questions. Thus, like a muscle that is never exercised, curiosity withers. When this occurs, and it occurs in most of us, thinking loses much of its dynamism.

REGAINING YOUR CURIOSITY

At first thought it may seem impossible to regain your childhood curiosity. Yet it is possible. Many people have done so. In fact, without realizing it, you have already taken the first important step in regaining yours. You have learned that disinterest and the tendency to take everything for granted are not natural, but acquired characteristics, and that lack of curiosity is a bad habit that can and should be broken.

A number of years ago, as a young industrial engineer, I had the privilege of working for a man who realized this and shared his realization with his subordinates. The first day I arrived on the job, this man, the chief industrial engineer, gave me these instructions: "For the next week I want you to do nothing but walk around the plant (a large mail-order company), question everything you see, and keep a record of your questions. Screen nothing out, record even the silliest and most obvious questions. At the end of each day I'd like to meet with you for half an hour and have you share those questions with me."

At first I thought the direction strange. "What good can come from this?" I wondered. But I obeyed. I walked through the various departments—shipping and receiving, accounting, merchandising, order filling. And I wrote down my questions.

As the week passed my list grew, and each day's conversation with the chief engineer increased my understanding of my assignment. He wanted me (and every new engineer) to develop a special work style—to see things with heightened curiosity as if through a child's eyes, so that I might think more effectively about what I saw.

"What is being done in this operation? Is it all necessary? If so, in what other ways might it be done? Are any of those ways simpler, quicker, safer, more economical? Who is doing it? Could a less highly paid employee do it? How might the work of several people be reduced to the work of one? Is it done at the right time, in the best place, with the most appropriate materials and equipment?" The four years I spent as an engineer were filled with such questions. (And the answers saved the company tens of thousands of dollars.) Yet they all proceeded from that first strange lesson in regaining my curiosity.

You can regain your curiosity, too. It will take effort, just as it takes time and practice to rebuild muscles that have fallen into disuse. But whatever the effort, the payoff in effective thinking is worth it. That payoff will not be only in personal satisfaction and better grades. It will also be in increased career effectiveness. Whatever your field of study, an efficient, inquiring mind will improve your performance.

SIX HELPFUL TECHNIQUES

Fortunately, it isn't necessary to pretend you are a child again and go about asking a child's kind of questions. (If you were to try it, your friends would probably report you to the campus psychologist.) Nor is it necessary to adopt an industrial engineer's approach—though it works well in that context, it might not fit your situation. There is a better approach. This approach fits a wide variety of situations. It is composed of six specific techniques:

1. Be observant
2. Look for the imperfections in things
3. Regard dissatisfaction as a challenge
4. Search for causes
5. Be sensitive to implications
6. Recognize the opportunity in controversy

Be Observant

Some people are oblivious to what is going on around them. They are so involved in their own internal reverie that they miss much of what is happening. Subtle hints are wasted on them; they never really learn much from experience. How can they? They aren't really in touch with it.

Even if you are not such a person, chances are your powers of observation can stand improvement. Here's a little test to help you decide how observant you are.

1. Does your instructor wear a wedding band?
2. What color are your mother's eyes?
3. How many gas stations are there in your hometown (or neighborhood)?
4. How many steps are there on your front porch at home (or on the stairway to your apartment)?
5. How many churches are there in your home town (or neighborhood)? What denominations are they?
6. Are there any trees in your best friend's yard? If so, how many? Are there any flowers? If so, what kind?
7. What color are the walls in your old high school hangout?
8. Can you describe your high school's band uniforms in detail? Can you describe the athletic uniforms (any sport)?

Most people are surprised at how little they know about supposedly familiar people, places, and things. You've probably heard the stories about people who've lived in a city or town all their lives, yet can't give directions to a stranger. It's because they travel the same route over and over in a daze, automatically, like robots.

Begin looking and listening more closely at people, places, and things. Try to pick up details you'd usually miss. See how people behave. For example, next time you are in the cafeteria or dining hall, watch people's actions. Note how many enter alone. Compare the way those alone and those with others behave. How at ease do those alone seem? Do they seem more or less relaxed? Do they seem nervous as they look for a table? What clues do they give about their feelings?

When you are sitting in a group of people discussing something, note the mannerisms of the group. What speech patterns are repeated? How do they look at each other? Do certain people tend to dominate? If so, in what ways? How does their behavior affect the others?

What clues do you get from people you pass in the hall (students, professors, administrators) about their states of mind? How courteous are people to one another? Do people look and speak differently to those they especially like? What manner betrays their attitude?

What excuses do people give for their behavior? How many of your friends accept responsibility as easily as they give it to others? When your friends go to parties, do their personalities seem to change in any way? Do they behave very differently than when they are in the company of professors? What are your friends' prejudices? How do they reveal them (other than by telling you directly)?

The types of observations you can make about people could be extended indefinitely. But remember, too, not just to be observant about other people. Observe yourself as well, the way *you* act, the broad or subtle clues you give about *your* attitudes and values.

Look for Imperfections

This advice will seem at first to contradict what most parents teach their children. "Don't expect things to be perfect," they say. "Learn to accept things as they are and be happy they aren't worse." But there is no real contradiction. Seeking imperfections does not mean being chronically dissatisfied, a complainer about life. It means realizing where improvements can be made.

Research suggests that productive thinkers and creative people have a keen sense of imperfection, and that this sense is one of the sources of their achievement. They recognize that all ideas, systems, processes, concepts, and tools are inventions and therefore open to improvement.[2]

In some cases, creative people go out of their way to find imperfections. Walter Chrysler, for example, the mechanical genius who founded Chrysler Corporation, was just a young railroad mechanic on a meager salary when he saved enough money to buy a Pierce Arrow automobile. It cost $5000 (at that time a huge sum of money). His purpose was not to drive around and play the big shot, but to take the car apart bolt by bolt—to see what parts and assembly design he could improve.[3]

Look around you at any man-made object—the classroom blackboard and desks, your dormitory bed, your clothes, your car, the library's cataloging system, the rules governing your favorite sport, our democratic system of government. All of these in their present form evolved from earlier inventions. And every step in their evolution was an attempt to overcome imperfection. Let's trace the broad development of two inventions.

ARTIFICIAL LIGHTING	WRITING IMPLEMENTS
The Torch	The Hammer and Chisel
The Candle	The Stylus
The Oil Lamp	The Quill Pen
The Electric Lamp	The Fountain Pen
The Battery-Powered Lamp	The Ballpoint Pen
The Fluorescent Lamp	The Felt-Tip Pen
The Flashlight	The Hard-Point Flowing Pen

More important than the evolution to the present is evolution beyond the present. Everything is still imperfect. One authority estimates that fully 80 percent of the patents issued by the U.S. Patent Office are not for new inventions, but for improvements in existing ones.[4] There is literally no need to curse the darkness—you can invent a new kind of light.

See Dissatisfaction as a Challenge

Each day brings its share of disappointments and frustrations. There's no way to avoid them. But there is a way to capitalize on them. The common response to such experiences, of course, is anger, resentment, and anxiety. That response is understandable. But many people wallow in it. They let dissatisfaction ruin their days.

Seeing dissatisfaction as a challenge means getting beyond those negative reactions and putting your ingenuity to work. Does your roommate stomp into the room at 3 A.M. when you're asleep? Does your professor give sneak quizzes and catch you unaware? Does your younger sister order you around to make herself look important? Does your car refuse to start whenever you're in a hurry? Instead of getting ruffled, accept the challenge being offered. Ask yourself what the problem is and set about finding a solution.

Search for Causes

The people who make breakthroughs and achieve insights are those who wonder. And their wondering extends to the *causes* of things, how they got to be the way they are, how they work.

For example, it was known for years that the disease called anthrax remained in the soil indefinitely. However, that process was a puzzle to scientists. Then one day, while visiting a farm, Louis Pasteur's curiosity was aroused. He observed that one patch of soil was a different color than the soil around it. He wondered what caused that. When he asked the farmer about it, the farmer explained that he buried some sick sheep there the previous year. Why should that make a difference, Pasteur thought. So he examined the soil more closely, noticed worm castings, and theorized that worms bored deep into the earth and carried the anthrax spores up with them. His later laboratory experiments proved him right.[5]

Similarly, diabetes might still be a mystery if it weren't for the curiosity of a research assistant engaged in unrelated research. When he noticed flies gathering around the urine of one dog used in an experiment, he wondered what about that dog's urine would attract flies. His search for the cause ultimately led to understanding and control of diabetes.[6]

The key to searching for causes is to be alert to any significant situation or event you cannot explain satisfactorily. One especially good time to practice this alertness is while reading the news or watching it on television. For example, if you read the report of the man killing his wife in a dispute over a penny on Valentine's Day, your curiosity would be aroused. (Legally separated, they were meeting to discuss their property division. She refused to give him a valuable Indian-head penny and he shot her to death.)[7] What happens to a person that makes him lose his sense of priorities, you might wonder, and your search for an answer would deepen your understanding of human behavior.

Be Sensitive to Implications

As a child you probably enjoyed throwing pebbles in a still pond and watching the ripples reach out farther and farther until they touched the shore. Through those ripples the tiniest pebble exerts an influence out of all proportion to its size. So it is with ideas. Every discovery, every invention, every new perspective or interpretation makes an impact whose extent is seldom fully realized at first. Good thinkers usually recognize that impact before others because they are sensitive to implications. Several examples will illustrate this sensitivity.

In August 1981, the Kinsey Institute released a study of homosexuality that challenged the traditional theories about its cause. The researchers concluded that homosexuality seemed to derive from a deep-seated predisposition that may be biological.[8] The report immediately stirred controversy, so no careful thinker would leap to the conclusion that it was the final word in the matter. Yet a person sensitive to implications would quickly realize that, if the report proves correct —if homosexuality is determined by biology—then homosexuality cannot fairly be considered immoral behavior because homosexuals have little or no choice in the matter.

In January 1982, newspapers reported that new research suggests that in about one-third of all cases, shyness is caused by a genetic predisposition rather than by environmental factors, and that in those cases it is especially difficult to overcome.[9] The person sensitive to implications would consider where shyness affects performance and immediately think of school and career. That would raise, among other questions, the question of whether it is fair to judge students on class participation and whether career guidance should be offered at much earlier ages than at present.

At about the same time, another study demonstrated that some people have a genetic predisposition to commit crimes, and that measurements of brain waves, heart rates, and the skin's electrical properties can predict the onset of criminal behavior as early as 10 years in advance. (The study also made clear that it is possible to overcome such a predisposition and avoid criminal behavior.)[10] One serious implication was immediately recognized by the legal profession—the question of whether testing for evidence of criminal tendencies (in the schools, for example) would constitute a violation of the test subjects' rights.

One final example. The Georgia Supreme Court decided a convicted murderer engaging in a hunger strike while in prison had a legal right to starve himself to death.[11] One interesting, if subtle, implication of this decision concerns the question of suicide. Traditionally, suicide has been considered a crime. (Technically, a person attempting suicide and failing can be legally charged for the attempt.) The Georgia decision implies that one has a right to take one's own life, thereby challenging the traditional view.

Recognize the Opportunity in Controversy

Many people simply foam at the mouth when a controversial issue is mentioned, nothing more. They rant on about the wisdom of their side, and damn those who disagree. If they were a little less rabid and a little more curious, their thinking would be considerably more productive.

What, after all, is a controversial issue? It is a matter about which informed people disagree. Not just any people, mind you, but *informed* people, people who have examined the matter carefully. If such people disagree, there must be *some* basis for disagreement. Either the facts are open to more than a single interpretation, or there must be two or more competing values, each making a persuasive demand for endorsement.

In light of this, *it is probable that neither side in a controversy possesses the total truth; each side has a part of it. Therefore the best answer is the one embracing the truth of both sides.* This is not the same thing as a compromise, where each disputing party gives up something to achieve a settlement. It is, rather, an acknowledgment that neither side has the whole answer, that each needs the other to solve the problem.

This sensible view does not mean seeing every issue as a 50-50 proposition, with each side possessing exactly half the truth. That is no more reasonable than believing one side possesses the total truth and the other nothing. The proportion may be 51-49, 60-40, or 90-10. Start out with *no* assumptions about exactly how much truth is on each side. Leave that question open until you have examined the issue.

A single example illustrates the value of this balanced view. The abortion issue continues to rage after at least a quarter century of intense debate. And how much progress has been made? Virtually none. The pro-choice side continue to believe the pro-life people are fascists who would impose their morality on others. And the pro-life side continues to believe the pro-choice people are morally insensitive baby killers. It seldom occurs to either side that the other has a valid point. The argument that the fetus ought to enjoy some legal rights and the argument that a woman should have some say over what happens in her body are *both* worthy arguments. If both sides recognized this, name calling might stop and cooperation might begin. And out of that cooperation might come, in time, a genuine solution.

Recognizing the opportunity in controversy means, first, willingness to reconsider any issue from a more balanced perspective. That includes issues you feel strongly about, issues you regard as closed. New discoveries and inventions sometimes force us to reappraise even "closed" issues. Most scientists, for example, considered the age of the universe uncontroversial. It was believed to be 20 billion years old. But in early 1982 a team of astronomers produced new data, announcing that the universe is really closer to 10 billion years old.[12] The controversy is alive again and scientists must reexamine the issue.

Secondly, recognizing the opportunity in controversy means making an effort to bridge different viewpoints. You must resist the tendency to join one side of an issue. In situations where you have already taken one side, you must set aside that view and see the issue with fresh eyes. Then you should list the evidence for each side and decide what interpretation is the most balanced and accurate. It is something like putting together a picture puzzle—to do it correctly you cannot ignore any pieces, but must fit them together in the proper places.

Consider whether technology has had a positive or negative effect. (This issue has been around for decades.) In your listing of evidence, you would undoubtedly include the following points:

POSITIVE EFFECT ARGUMENTS	NEGATIVE EFFECT ARGUMENTS
Has shortened the work week, creating more leisure time for workers.	Has made many jobs very routine, increasing workers' boredom.
Has increased the variety of goods and services available.	Has decreased the quality of goods and services in many cases.
Has created many new skilled occupations.	Has eliminated many unskilled jobs.
Has increased the monetary reward to both employers and employees.	Has caused many workers to hate what they do for a living.
Has created the need for new kinds of education—vocational and technical.	Has undermined the role of the liberal arts in education.

Though your list would, of course, be longer and include specific information as well as general points, the above list illustrates how the very act of recording the evidence for both sides of the issue can help you be more objective, and lead to a more enlightened position.

WARM-UP EXERCISES

4.1. Read the following dialogue carefully. Then decide what you would say next if you were Veronica. Make your response so clear and effective that the matter would be settled.

> PERRY: The only book a person ever needs to read is the Bible.
> VERONICA: I don't agree. Other books surely have something to offer.
> PERRY: Let me show you how wrong that is. If other books agree with the Bible, they are unnecessary. And if they disagree, then they are irreligious and should be avoided.

4.2. Answer for Kenneth as you did for Veronica in Exercise 4.1 above.

> KENNETH: Every circle has an inside and an outside.
> KARL: I'll bet you can't prove that statement.
> KENNETH: Sure I can. . . .
> KARL: Remember, you said *every* circle. That's what you've got to prove.

4.3. You have just heard a friend make the following statement. Decide whether his reasoning is sound or unsound. Then write a paragraph or two explaining your judgment.

I would vote this year if I could be reasonably sure any of the candidates would do a good job. But I have no way to be sure, so it's a waste of time to vote.

APPLICATIONS

4.1. Spend some time in the dining hall, snack bar, or some other place where people congregate, and practice observing their behavior. Look for things you have not noticed before, particularly things that reveal attitudes and values. Keep a record of your observations.

4.2. Identify as many things as you can that you often use with a less than perfect performance or design. (Any item from a shoe horn to a car.) Describe their imperfections and, if you can, suggest specific improvements.

4.3. Think of as many experiences as you can that caused you to be dissatisfied or frustrated, experiences that posed a challenge to your ingenuity, but that you were too aggravated to see. Describe the experiences and state the challenges you now see.

4.4. In each of the following situations the causes of behavior are not self-evident. Speculate about those causes, first listing as many possible explanations as you can think of, and then deciding which explanation seems most reasonable in each case. Explain your choices.

a. In Tampa, Florida a 30-year-old man threw a 6-week-old cocker spaniel puppy 30 feet out into a lake. (A photographer caught the incident on film and the Associated Press wired the sad picture to newspapers around the country.)[13] The puppy drowned trying to swim back to shore.

b. Four hundred employers of young people in 5 major cities were studied. The study drew this conclusion: "When recruiting young employees, employers consider in order of importance: appearance and dress, language and speech mannerisms, references and previous work experience. They rely primarily on appearance even though lack of reliability, not lack of proper appearance, is their major complaint about youthful employees."[14] Why would employers place so much importance on dress?

c. Three high school students doing research on shoplifting entered a large drug store in an upper middle class neighborhood and (with the knowledge of the owner) walked up and down aisles stuffing their pockets with large and small items—candy, magazines, watch bands, perfume, a hair dryer, and more. More than 100 shoppers were in the store, and at least 50 of them saw what was happening. Yet every one of the shoppers either walked away or turned their head.[15] How do you explain their reaction?

d. Thirty-eight apartment dwellers in Kew Gardens, New York, watched out their windows while a killer stabbed a woman, was frightened away, returned again, was frightened away again, and returned a third time, finally killing her. The attacks took place over a 35-minute period, yet not one of the 38 people either went to the woman's aid or even called the police.[16]

4.5. Each of the following cases is (or could be viewed as) a controversy as defined in the chapter. Examine each carefully, decide whether you agree or disagree with the action that was taken, and explain your view. In addition, identify any implications suggested by each case, and any connections with other issues.

a. Through most of their 10-year marriage, Mark Sullivan was training to be a doctor, and Janet Sullivan was working to support them. Shortly after he got his degree and set up practice, they were divorced. As part of the divorce settlement, Janet claimed a partial financial interest in Mark's medical degree. The court agreed that her investment in his education entitled her to part of its value. (The exact amount was not decided by the court, but was scheduled for later determination.)[17] Some people argue that the decision is unfair, that she really has no right to any part of his medical degree's value. Others say her share should be at least half. And still others say she should merely be repaid for the money she spent supporting Mark while he was in medical school.

b. Fire raged through the Cicero, New York home of Richard and Meloni Galavotti, taking the lives of the couple and two of their four children. Investigation revealed that a faulty heat-dispersal fireplace caused the blaze—there were at least six flaws in its installation. Because of these flaws, the installing contractor was charged with criminally negligent homicide. The case is unusual because faulty workmanship had previously been the basis of civil lawsuits, but never of *criminal* charges. In effect, the faulty fireplace unit was regarded as a deadly weapon.[18] Many feel that criminal charges are inappropriate in this case.

c. Kathy York Rodriquez was convicted of severely beating her 8-year-old daughter in what police believe was an attempt to exorcise the devil. At her trial in Bartow, Florida, the judge sentenced Rodriquez to 10 years' probation, then added the stipulation that she not become pregnant during that time or marry a man with children. (If she ignored the stipulation, her probation could be revoked and she could be jailed.) Her attorney believes such a stipulation is improper.[19]

d. There has been a tendency in recent years for unmarried pregnant teenagers to have and keep their babies, rather than giving them up for adoption. (One study indicated that 96 percent of all unmarried teenagers fit into this category.)[20] Some people believe the decision to raise a child alone is a sign of maturity and responsibility. Others believe otherwise, and argue that it creates many problems.

e. In December 1981, the U. S. Supreme Court decided that any university permitting secular student groups to meet on campus must also permit students to meet for worship and religious study. Eight justices joined in the majority opinion; one dissented.[21]

f. Robert L. Race of Toddsville, New York believes the state has no authority to require that everyone have a driver's license, so he turned in his license and publicly announced his intention to drive without it. In his view driving is not a privilege, but a right.[22] Many would disagree with his view.

g. Anthony Broussard raped and murdered his girl friend, then threw her body into a ravine. Later, before the crime was discovered by authorities, he bragged about it to friends and took some of them to the ravine to see the body. One friend, 16-year-old Kirk Rasmussen, kicked leaves over the body. After the crime was discovered and Broussard was arrested, Rasmussen was charged with being an accessory after the fact. He was found guilty and sentenced to three years in a reformatory.[23] Many would argue that Rasmussen's sentence was excessive. Some would say he shouldn't even have been charged.

h. In early 1982, when the U.S. government was supporting government forces in El Salvador against leftist guerrillas, several prominent American actors, including Ed Asner, publicly attacked the government's policy and contributed over $25,000 for medical aid to the leftist rebels.[24] Many people regarded that action as irresponsible and un-American.

i. A resident of Washington state named Colbard asked his friend Churches for permission to drive his car to a drinking party with another friend. Churches knew that Colbard was in the habit of getting drunk. Later that night Colbard, drunk, drove the car at a reckless speed and collided with Mitchell's car. Mitchell sued *both* Colbard and Churches for damages and won. Churches appealed the jury's verdict to the Washington Supreme Court. That court upheld the lower court's verdict.[25] Some would hold that Churches was done an injustice; a person should not be held responsible for an act he did not himself commit.

chapter 5

Sharpen Your Analytical Skills

A lively curiosity, as we have seen, can help you become a better thinker by revealing the challenges and opportunities around you. To be successful in meeting those challenges, however, you need more than curiosity. You need analytical skills. These skills enable you to understand and evaluate any ideas you encounter. Undoubtedly you have some of them already. (If you did not have at least rudimentary analytical skill, your education would not have proceeded this far.) But since analysis is not usually taught systematically in American education, you probably learned it haphazardly and use it sporadically, unconsciously, and inefficiently. This chapter will help you use your analytical skills more effectively.

IMPROVING YOUR READING

The term *reading* is used here in the broad sense, covering not only printed material, but all received ideas, including those you get from listening. Almost 400 years ago, Francis Bacon warned about the danger of reading the wrong way. He advised people as they read not to dispute the author's view, nor to accept it uncritically, but to "weigh and consider" it. In the nineteenth century, British statesman Edmund Burke expressed the same view in more dramatic terms. "To read without reflection," he said, "is like eating without digesting."

The definition of reading these men had in mind is best explained as follows:

There is one key idea which contains, in itself, the very essence of effective reading, and on which the improvement of reading depends: *Reading is reasoning*. When you read properly, you are not merely assimilating. You are not automatically transferring into your head what your eyes pick up on the page. What you see on the page sets your mind at work, collating, criticizing, intepreting, questioning, comprehending, comparing. When this process goes on well, you read well. When it goes on ill, you read badly.[1]

Reading with the mind, and not just with the eyes, is not equally intense during every reading occasion. A bus schedule or a menu, for example, can be read well with little or no reasoning. But even the smallest reading challenges involve considerably more reasoning than we realize at the time. Consider the following sentences:

He who hesitates is lost. (Proverb)

We never step into the same river twice. (Heraclitus)

The girl who can't dance says the band can't play. (Yiddish
    proverb)

The first one, of course, is familiar enough that you may be unaware you are reasoning when you read it. But consider the first time you encountered it (probably as a small child). You undoubtedly wondered, "Just who does 'he' refer to in this sentence? And what does 'lost' mean here?" In time, when you considered and tested some possible meanings, you reasoned out the meaning.

The other two sentences are even more challenging. The key to the Heraclitus line is the relationship between *same* and *river.* Only when you perceive that, and grasp the idea that the river is constantly changing, can you be said to have read the line. And you can understand the Yiddish proverb only when you see that the message is not just about girls and bands, but about anyone who can't do something and resorts to face saving.

The kind of reading Bacon and Burke had in mind, and which concerns us here, is not a passive process, but an active, dynamic one. It consists of examining ideas and deciding what they mean and whether they make sense, rather than merely receiving and accepting them. Unfortunately, most of the reading done in grade school and high school consists of getting the facts—and remembering them for the examination. Not only do the teachers expect that—the textbooks offer no real alternative to it. They are filled with facts to be accepted, rather than ideas to weigh and consider. If your school experience has been similar, you are bound to be a little uncomfortable with critical reading. More specifically, you are apt to be confused by long or complex passages, and nervous about reaching conclusions.

Such reactions are completely understandable. But it is important to realize that any difficulty you experience while mastering this chapter's approaches is a result of the material's newness, not of your lack of capacity. Thinking, remember, is largely a matter of acquiring the right skills and the habit of using them.

MAKING IMPORTANT DISTINCTIONS

One of the best ways to overcome confusion about ideas is to make important distinctions—that is, to avoid lumping all considerations together indiscriminately. Here are the distinctions that are most often overlooked. Keep them in mind whenever you are reading (or listening):

Distinctions Between the Person and the Idea

Your reaction to a sentence beginning "Adolf Hitler said . . ." would likely be very different from your reaction to one beginning "Winston Churchill said. . . ." In the first instance you might not even continue reading. At very least you would read with great suspicion—you'd be ready to reject what was said.

There's nothing strange about that. You've learned things about Hitler and Churchill, and it's difficult to set them aside. In one sense, you *shouldn't* set them aside. Yet in another sense, you *must* set them aside to be a good thinker. After all, even a lunatic can have a good idea, and even a genius will, on occasion, be wrong.

If you do not check your tendency to accept or reject ideas on the basis of who expresses them, your analysis of everything you read and hear is certain to be distorted. You will judge arguments on whether the speaker is of your race, religion, or political affiliation, or whether you like her hair style. And so you might embrace nonsense and reject wisdom. Aristotle's contemporaries tell us he had very thin legs and small eyes, favored conspicuous dress and jewelry, and was fastidious in the way he combed his hair.[2] It's not hard to imagine some Athenian ignoramus muttering to his fellows the ancient Greek equivalent of "Don't pay any attention to what Aristotle says—he's a wimp."

To guard against confusing the person and the idea, be aware of your reactions to people and try compensating for them. That is, listen very carefully to those you are inclined to dislike and very critically to those you are inclined to like. Judge the arguments as harshly as you wish, but only on their merits *as* arguments.

Distinctions Between Matters of Taste and Matters of Judgment

In Chapter 2, we saw that there are two broad types of opinion: taste and judgment. They differ significantly. In matters of taste we may express our personal preferences without defending them. In matters of judgment, however, we have an obligation to provide evidence.

Many people confuse taste and judgment. They believe their right to hold an opinion is a guarantee of the opinion's rightness. This confusion often causes people to offer inadequate support (or no support at all) for views that demand support. For example, they express judgments on such controversial issues as abortion, capital punishment, the teaching of evolution in the schools, mercy killing, hiring discrimination, and laws concerning rape as if they were matters of taste rather than matters of judgment.

Keep in mind that whenever someone presents an opinion about the truth of an issue or the wisdom of an action—that is, whenever someone presents a judgment—you not only have a right to judge his view by the evidence. You have an *obligation* to do so.

Distinctions Between Fact and Interpretation

A fact is something known with certainty, something either objectively verified or demonstrable. An interpretation is an explanation of meaning or significance. In much writing, facts and interpretations are intertwined. It is not always obvious where one leaves off and the other begins. Here is an example of such intertwining:

The Writer's Interpretation (Note that merely calling interpretation fact *does not make it so.)*	People don't seem to care much about family life any more. A recent study has made that unfortunate fact very clear. The study, in which 1596 Americans were surveyed, was conducted for Psychology Today *magazine in March, 1982, by Potomac Associates.*[3] *It revealed that Americans are more concerned about the standard of living, personal health, economic stability, and employment than about family concerns. William Watts, president of Potomac Associates, commented as follows: "Traditionally, when asked to talk about their most
The Writer's Interpretation (Both the classification of the trend as a "moral decline" and the assertion about its cause are interpretive.)	important hopes and fears, Americans have ranked family concerns near the top of the list . . . Americans now talk less in interviews about the happiness and health of their families." The cause of this moral decline is without question the emphasis on the self that has dominated our culture for the past two decades.

Fact.

The danger in failing to distinguish between fact and interpretation is that you will regard assumptions that ought to be questioned and contrasted with other views as unquestionable. If the habit of confusing the two is strong enough, it can paralyze your critical sense.

Distinctions Between Literal and Ironic Statements

Not everything a writer says is intended literally. Sometimes a writer makes his point by saying the exact opposite of what he means—that is, by using irony or satire. Suppose, for example, you encountered this passage in your reading:

> The present administration is right in reducing the taxes of the wealthy more than those of the working classes. After all, wealthy people not only pay more into the treasury, but they also have a higher standard of living to maintain. If the cost of soybeans has risen, so also has the cost of caviar; if the subway fare has increased, so has the maintenance cost of a Rolls-Royce and a Lear jet. If the government listens to the minor grumbling and whining of the unemployed, it surely should be responsive to the plight of the affluent.

On the surface, this certainly looks like a plea on behalf of the rich. But on closer inspection it will be seen as a *mockery* of that plea. The clues are subtle, to be sure—the reference to the higher standard of living, the comparison of travel by Rolls-Royce or jet with travel by subway, the reference to the "plight" of the rich. Yet the clues are undeniable.

Such tongue-in-cheek writing can be more biting and therefore more effective than a direct attack. Yet you must be alert to the subtlety and not misread it, or the message you receive will be very different from the writer's intention.

Distinctions Between an Idea's Validity and the Quality of Its Expression

A thought's expression can deceive us about its validity. This is why a mad leader like Hitler won a large popular following even among intelligent and responsible people, and why Jim Jones' followers killed their children and committed suicide in Guyana. Impassioned, eloquent expression tends to excite a favorable response, just as lifeless, inarticulate, error-filled expression prompts a negative response. Compare these two passages:

> A man's gotta love his Momma and Daddy more then he love a stranger. If he don't do right by his kin, he can't never be a righteous man.

> To achieve success in a competitive world, you must honor the first principle of success—treat well those people who can benefit you and ignore the others.

The first passage is less appealing than the second. And yet it contains an idea most philosophers would enthusiastically endorse, while the second contains an idea most find reprehensible. The careful thinker is able to appraise them correctly because she is aware that expression can deceive. Careful thinkers make a special effort to separate form from content before judging. (The careful writer strives for clarity and correctness of form for exactly the same reason.) Thus he is able to say "This idea is poorly expressed, but profound" and "This idea is well expressed, but shallow."

EVALUATING AN ARGUMENT

Analyzing a long piece of writing line by line is probably a frightening idea. You picture yourself gathering dust while scrutinizing each word and pondering its relationship with every other word. "If that's what analytical thinking is all about," you say, "count me out." Here's some good news—most scholars feel the same way. They know that such an approach would not only be boring; it would also be inefficient. They'd never get anything done if they worked that way. And so they develop *shortcuts*.

Particular shortcuts, of course, vary from scholar to scholar. But one common approach is reducing a book or article to manageable proportions before they begin analyzing. In other words, they analyze it in miniature. By applying three simple steps, you can master this approach quickly and easily.

Step 1 After reading the book or article carefully, summarize its essential argument and the evidence presented in support of that argument.

Step 2 Evaluate the essential argument and evidence. (In cases where you are not qualified to judge, of course, postpone your evaluation until you do the necessary research.)

Step 3 Draw your conclusion about the validity of the argument. (In other words, decide whether you accept it, accept it in part, or reject it.)

We'll discuss each of these steps more closely and see their workings in an actual case, but first let's clarify the terms *essential argument* and *evidence*.

Essential Argument. The essential argument is the central or controlling idea in analytical writing, the idea the writer wishes to present as the most reasonable conclusion. In any well-written article or book, the essential argument is expressed directly and given prominence. (Not every article or book, unfortunately, is well written. Whenever you encounter an essential argument not expressed directly, or expressed unclearly, you have to construct the argument on the basis of probability—that is, you have to decide what essential argument is suggested by the overall presentation.) The argument may be expressed in one place. In an article, that place is usually right after the introduction. Or, if the argument is complex, it may be expressed in several parts at different points in the presentation. In any case, it is usually kept in clear focus throughout the material and reinforced in the conclusion, so it is clear and recognizable to the careful reader.

Evidence. Evidence is any material used to support the essential argument, thereby demonstrating the validity of the writer's judgment. There are four broad categories of evidence—confirmed details or statistics, the writer's own experience and observation, the judgment of authorities, and other people's experience and observation. Evidence may take a variety of forms—factual details, examples, cases in point, anecdotes, quotations, comparisons, descriptions, and definitions. The author's reasoning about supporting material is also evidence.

There is a difference between evidence and *proof*. It is proper to speak of proof only when the evidence is sufficient in amount and kind to remove all reasonable doubt and establish certainty. Such a situation is rare, even though all writers strive for it—and sometimes decide prematurely that they have it.

With these important terms clarified, let's return to the three steps in evaluating an argument and look at them more closely.

Step 1: Summarizing

After you've read the article or book carefully, look back at the author's divisions of the work. In an article, look at the subheadings; in a book, at the chapter titles and the subheadings. These will provide valuable clues to the relationships the author sees among his ideas. Next, underline the key sentences or paragraphs in the work.* For an article, limit yourself to one sentence in every few paragraphs; for a book, to a few sentences in every chapter.

When you have finished underlining key sentences, review your work and consider how many sentences can be combined without changing the author's meaning. Using the underlined sentences as a guide, write out the essential argument in complete sentences, keeping to the original phrasing and the original order of presentation as much as possible to avoid distortion. Then briefly list the kind and amount of evidence offered in support of the writer's argument. (Do not attempt to write out the evidence as he presented it—it will make your summary too long to be manageable.)

If you've summarized effectively, you should now have a brief version of the original work that is faithful in content, yet much easier to analyze. A whole book can be reduced to several paragraphs in this way, a full-length magazine article to seven or eight sentences, a short article to two or three sentences. Whenever you summarize, however, keep in mind the danger of distortion and oversimplification. It does little good to criticize an author for something he did *not* say.

Step 2: Evaluating

Read your summary of the essential argument over several times, asking these questions:

- How clear is the author's position? Is any important part of it vague or ambiguous—that is, open to more than one meaning? If you identify any vagueness or ambiguity, consider all reasonable interpretations.
- What challenges would a challenger raise about the author's ideas? Go through each sentence of your summary, asking all the questions you can think of and noting all the responses a critic would probably offer.

Next, look over your list of evidence, asking these questions:

- Is all the evidence relevant to the issue? If any isn't note it and be prepared to explain why not.
- Are the sources cited still current? There is nothing necessarily wrong with old sources. Something written in 1800 may still be valid today. But later findings may have discredited older views.
- Are the sources cited authoritative and reliable? The fact of being well known does not make anyone an authority. A Nobel Prize winner in physics may be totally incompetent in psychology or government. And even if a person is an authority in the field in question, his view is open to question if he has been guilty of unreliability (professional dishonesty, for example) in the past.
- Are the examples and cases offered as evidence typical and comprehen-

---

*It is a common practice to underline while reading. The problem is that you may tend to underline too much, which defeats your purpose in summarizing. Unless you can restrict your underlining to key passages *only,* it is better to underline after you have read.

sive? The author's citation of some examples and cases in point does not necessarily establish the argument's validity. If the cases are extraordinary—exceptions rather than typical instances—they are worth very little. Similarly, if they represent one narrow aspect of the issue rather than all aspects, they may not adequately support the argument.

- Is any significant evidence omitted? Often the weakness in an argument lies in what the author does *not* say. For example, let's say someone told you that an American engineer and his wife visited the Congo in September 1981, trying to find evidence of a dinosaur-like creature reportedly living there. They returned with a picture that documented their sighting of the creature. Everything she told you is correct.[4] However, one important detail is missing—the picture was "severely underexposed" and therefore worthless as documentation. The only defense against such omissions is to be as well informed as you can about any issue.

Step 3: Judging

The final step in analyzing an argument is to decide whether you agree with it, and if so, to what extent. If you have performed the second step carefully and evaluated your evidence thoughtfully, this step should pose little difficulty. You will simply decide whether the author's view is more reasonable than any other in light of the evidence he presented and any additional evidence you considered. In some cases, you will find the author's argument to be most reasonable in every detail. In other cases, you will find it to be completely unreasonable in every detail. Far more often, however, you will accept some parts of an author's argument, reject others, and perhaps be uncertain about still others. In such cases, follow the guidelines below:

- If you agree in part and disagree in part, explain exactly what your position is and support it carefully. Remember that good thinkers judge your arguments as closely as you judge other people's.
- If some vagueness or ambiguity in the author's argument prevents you from giving a flat answer, don't attempt one. Rather, say "it depends" and go on to explain. The if-then approach is very helpful in such cases. Here's how it works. Suppose someone had written "man is an animal." You might respond as follows:

It depends on what you mean by *animal.* If you mean man is included in the broad classification *animal,* as opposed to *vegetable* or *mineral,* then I agree. But if you mean man has nothing more than an animal nature, no intellect and will that distinguish him from other members of the animal kingdom, then I disagree. I believe that. . . .

- If you must deal with conflicting testimony and cannot decide your position with certainty, identify the conflict and explain why you cannot be certain. If you believe that circumstances *seem* somewhat in favor of one side, explain those circumstances and why you are inclined to judge them as you do.

One example of conflicting testimony occurred in the highly publicized trial of Jack Henry Abbott. Abbott, who had spent 24 of his 37 years behind prison bars, was paroled in 1981 after Norman Mailer arranged for Abbott's book, *In the Belly of the Beast,* to be published. Six weeks after his parole, Abbott stabbed a waiter in a dispute over the use of a restroom. Abbott testified that he thought the waiter pulled a knife first, and that he lunged forward with his knife in self-protection. A passerby, however, witnessed the incident and testified that the waiter had made what appeared to be a "conciliatory gesture," and turned to walk away when Abbott raced after him, reached over his shoulder and stabbed him with "terrible ferocity," then taunted him as he lay dying.[5]

In this case, you might reasonably say that, though you cannot be certain which testimony is correct, circumstances seem to favor the witness' testimony. You would go on to explain that Abbott's testimony was more likely to be colored by emotion and self-interest than the witness'.

The above guidelines for dealing with ambiguity and conflicting testimony may seem to encourage evasion, straddling the fence. They are not intended to do so and should not be used for that purpose. Apply them when reasonableness demands a qualified answer, not in situations where timidity prompts you to avoid answering.

A SAMPLE ARGUMENT

Let's see how this approach works in an actual case. You read a magazine article arguing that "inferior" people should be sterilized at puberty. You summarize it as follows (for reference purposes, the sentences and items of evidence are numbered):

> 1) A serious world population problem exists today. 2) The ideal solution is for everyone to be responsible in deciding whether he should reproduce. 3) However, few people make that decision rationally—emotion overwhelms logic. 4) Moreover, the least talented and least intelligent are likely to have the most children. 5) In time, this tendency may set the process of evolution in reverse. 6) The best and most practical solution is to identify inferior people and force them to be sterilized at puberty.

Evidence presented in support of the argument:

7. U.N. statistics on world population.
8. Selected U.N. statistics on world poverty, illiteracy, and disease.
9. A research study showing that more affluent, better educated, higher-IQ couples tend to have fewer children.
10. Quotations from geneticists showing the favorable genetic effects that would occur if only higher-IQ individuals were to reproduce.
11. Quotations from medical authorities showing the benefit that would accrue to world health if people with hereditary diseases did not reproduce.

Your evaluation of the argument and evidence would probably look like this (parenthetical numbers refer to the preceding statements and evidence):

Concerning the clarity of the argument: Several terms are ambiguous. Do *talented* and *intelligent* refer to the broad range of abilities or to some specific ones? Mildly retarded people often possess considerable talent and intelligence, measured by a broad definition of the terms. Does "the process of evolution" (5) mean survival of the physically fit or the perpetuation of culture as we know it? And does "inferior people" (6) mean those with hereditary diseases, the mentally retarded, neurotics, nonconformists, or all of these?

Concerning the questions critics might raise: These are the most probable ones. Isn't it possible forcible sterilization might pose even worse dangers to civilization than a reversing of evolution (5)? Might it not lead to totalitarianism? Wouldn't a better and more practical solution (6) be to improve the distribution of wealth among nations, to find cures for disease, to share technology, and to expand educational opportunity (including education in birth control methods)?

Concerning the kind and quality of the evidence presented: One significant question about some of the evidence (10,11) concerns how typical and comprehensive it is. Is the view expressed in the quotations one that is shared by most geneticists and medical authorities, or is it a minority position? An even more important question concerns the evidence that is *omitted.* Surely psychologists, sociologists, and historians must contribute to this issue. Some of the questions they could answer are these: What psychological effects would forced sterilization have in those subjected to it? A feeling of worthlessness, perhaps, or rage? What social behavior would be likely to result from such effects? Violence? Revolution? What historical precedents are there to help us measure the probable effects?

In light of these considerations, you might conclude that, though the world population problem and the related concerns of poverty, illiteracy, and disease are serious and should be addressed, the idea of forced sterilization should be opposed—at least until its advocates clarify their terms and answer the important critical questions. If you were to make a formal response to the argument in an analytical paper or article, you would develop your ideas thoroughly, meeting the same standards you expect of others. (For a discussion of the principles and approaches used in analytical writing, see Appendix A.)

WARM-UP EXERCISES

5.1. Decide whether the reasoning behind the following statement is sound or unsound. Write a paragraph or two stating and explaining your judgment.

Unicorns must exist because no one has ever been able to prove that they don't.

5.2. Follow the directions for Exercise 5.1.

Some Cubans are fanatics. All of Castro's followers are Cubans. Therefore, some of Castro's followers must be fanatics.

5.3. Follow the directions for Exercise 5.1.

> I could understand the teacher failing me in the course if I didn't hand in my homework. But I did hand it in, faithfully. Therefore, I didn't deserve to fail.

APPLICATIONS

5.1. Read the following dialogue carefully. Decide which statements are reasonable and which are not. Provide a brief explanation why you consider any statement unreasonable.

[Scene: a college dormitory room. A bull session is in progress. George and Ed, freshmen at Proudly Tech, are discussing academic affairs with their sophomore roommate, Jake.]

GEORGE: When I arrived on campus last month, I went to see my advisor to get my freshman English course waived. I didn't get to first base with him. "Everyone takes freshman English," he said. "Everyone!" I'll bet he's got that line taped and just plays it whenever a student raises the question. It really burns me having to take that course. I can see it as a requirement for most students. But I earned straight B's in high school English. Why should I spend more time on that stuff in college?

ED: You're right, George. This place is like home—everybody's on your back making you do things you don't want to do. I should have gone to Bloomville State instead of to this dump.

JAKE: What's so great about Bloomville State?

ED: They let you take whatever courses you want. No required courses at all.

JAKE: Look, my uncle went there after the Korean War. He told me a lot about his college days. But he never mentioned that.

ED: It's true. Listen, there was this guy I was talking to at the bar in the train station when I was coming up here. He goes to Bloomville and he told me they had no required courses.

GEORGE: That really bugs me. Straight B's. And still I've got to take this crappy course. . . .

JAKE: Listen, pal. You're lucky you were born talented in writing. I wish I had that gift. For me, nothing but D's and F's. Hopeless.

ED: Who'd you have for English, Jake?

JAKE: Crawford. An OK guy, I guess, but sort of scholarly. Talks over everybody's head, always quoting some writer or other.

ED: I've got Mr. Schwartz. What's the word on him?

JAKE: You've lucked out, boy. Three of my friends had him last year and two got B's and one a B+. A guy who grades like that has got to be a winner.

GEORGE: I'm glad somebody's luck held. Mine certainly didn't. For the two comps I've written so far, I've gotten a D+ and a C−.

JAKE: Who have you got?

GEORGE: Mr. Stiletto.

JAKE: He wasn't here last year.

GEORGE: I'll bet he's just out of graduate school. Or maybe he never went. At any rate, he sure has it in for me. Maybe he's prejudiced against Germans.

ED: Maybe you picked the wrong side of the issue to write on—you know, the one he disagrees with.

GEORGE: Hey, you may be right. The first topic was birth control and I'm sure he's Catholic because I saw a little statue of Jesus on his car dashboard when his wife dropped him off outside the building last week. I wrote in favor of birth control. Wow. What a jerk I am. Hey, and come to think of it that second comp. . . .

JAKE: I should have taken him for comp. I'm Catholic.

GEORGE: That second comp was on civil rights. And I know he's against blacks. The guy who sits next to me is black and Stiletto really cut him down just because he was late a few times. And there's a black girl he always calls on for the tough questions. No wonder I got a C—.

JAKE: Wait till you guys take Psych next year. I don't know if I'll be able to last till the end of the term. It's the boringest subject ever thought up by man. Professor Clifford walks in, opens his book, and begins reading from his notes in a low mumble. "mmmm . . . Freud says . . . mmm mmm . . . Oedipus complex . . . repression . . . mmmmm." Deadliest stuff you ever heard. I'm glad I don't need another social science course. Those guys are really out of it.

ED: Doesn't he ever let you discuss what you read?

JAKE: Yeah, once in a while. Yesterday, for example, we were talking about some guy named Frankl and Clifford said that according to this Frankl, boredom causes people more problems than distress does. Some kids in the class gave examples of how that's so —you know, there are always some guys looking to agree with the prof to make some points. . . .

ED AND
GEORGE: Yeah.

JAKE: . . . And so I raised my hand and said that that guy Frankl was all wet, that everybody knows that distress causes more problems than boredom. I told him that my own experience proved it because five years ago when my father lost his job, my family really had to struggle for more than a year. We had problems, believe me; and they weren't caused by *boredom!*

GEORGE: What did he say to that?

JAKE: Well, he mumbled something about Frankl not meaning that. And then he started tossing around a lot of statistics and examples to try to get me confused. He couldn't corner me, though. I finally said, "Frankl's entitled to his opinion: I've got my own."

GEORGE: Hey, that's great. I bet he cursed you out under his breath. You really socked it to him.

JAKE: Yeah, I guess I did. When I get mad, I can argue pretty good. Now I've just got to be careful he doesn't take it out on me in my grade.

ED: Say, fellas, I've got to cut out. I'm going to the library and prepare for tomorrow's English class.

GEORGE: What's your assignment?

ED: Oh, a piece by Orwell. We just have to read it and be ready to discuss it. I've read it five times already, but I can't find anything wrong with it, nothing to disagree with. I'll just have to read it again. Be seeing you.

5.2. Follow the directions for Application 5.1. In addition, decide what action you would recommend if you were a school board member. Explain why you think that action best.

[Scene: The Alertia, Indiana, town hall. The members of the Alertia school board are meeting with a group of parents concerned about the school's new sex education program for seventh and eighth graders.]

BOARD
CHAIRMAN: I'd like to welcome the guests of the board to our regular meeting. As you all know, the Board agreed to Mrs. Jackson's request for an opportunity for those who wished to present their views on the school's new program in sex education. As we know, sex was around for quite a while before this program began, heh, heh. . . . [silence]

MRS.
SCHULTZ: It's exactly that sort of levity about this dangerous program that worries me.

BOARD
CHAIRMAN: I'm sorry, Mrs. Schultz. I only meant that as a little joke.

MRS.
SCHULTZ: Well, there's nothing funny about a program that introduces raw sex into the minds of innocent young children.

MRS.
JACKSON: The reason we asked for this meeting is that we feel what is taking place in sex education class goes beyond the bounds of decency.

BOARD
CHAIRMAN: Could you be more specific please. Just what is taking place?

MRS.
JACKSON: Someone told me that Miss Babette encouraged the students to touch each other freely to overcome any inhibitions they might have about sex. Can you deny that such encouragement goes beyond the bounds of decency?

BOARD CHAIRMAN:	No, I certainly wouldn't deny that. But. . . .
MRS. BROWN:	I heard that last week she asked two students to come to the front of the room and demonstrate what petting means.
MRS. GREEN:	That doesn't surprise me a bit. She *does* have that hippie manner, you know. Those micro-mini skirts, that long hair. The way she talks to men is most provocative. Positively lewd. If my daughter dressed and acted like that, I'd feel I had failed as a parent.
BOARD CHAIRMAN:	Ladies, please. We've got to have a little more order. Mr. Lessrow has had his hand up for some time.
MR. LESSROW:	Thank you, Mr. Chairman. Of course, I agree with the good ladies who have spoken thus far. But with all respect to them, I think they may be missing the real nature of this threat to the morals of our young people. We must not forget that those young people are the United States citizens of tomorrow. And let me ask you, just who will stand to profit if they are corrupted, if their preoccupation with the flesh stays them from their duties and obligations as citizens? Let me ask. . . .
FIRST BOARD MEMBER:	Who *will* stand to profit, Mr. Lessrow?
MR. LESSROW:	I was getting to that point, sir. Who else but the *communists.*
FIRST BOARD MEMBER:	Are you suggesting that the communists are in some way *responsible* for sex education in American schools, for the course in our school?
MR. LESSROW:	I am saying precisely that. Sex education is a plot to lure our children into lives of lustful hedonism. It is a plot designed and supported by the international communist conspiracy. All a person needs to do is a little reading, have a little concern for the truth, and not be like these hothouse liberals who believe the communists are our "brothers." The charges have been made, clearly and forcefully, against the national organization that publishes the filth used in these courses—at best, they're a lot of misguided, uninformed dupes; at worst, conscious agents of the conspiracy.
SECOND BOARD MEMBER:	Now that's surely a very extreme interpretation of. . . .

MR. LESSROW: It's an extreme *plot!* Extreme situations demand extreme responses.

SECOND
BOARD
MEMBER: As I started to say, it's an extreme interpretation of a very complex issue. Surely we should be a little less quick to jump at every charge we read in the newspapers, be a little more open-minded.

MRS.
SCHULTZ: A person should be open-minded while he is searching for the truth. When he has found it, he should embrace it.

MRS.
JACKSON: I just can't understand how people can resist common sense. It should be clear enough to everybody—even to the teachers of this school—that when you bring sex into the classroom, you dignify it. When you encourage the young to talk about it openly in school, they'll talk about it openly out of school. And talking is a very short step away from *acting.* I for one don't want my teenagers to become promiscuous just because some so-called educators in this town persist in denying the obvious.

MRS.
OVERLOOK: I don't see the need for a sex education course in the first place. Surely if parents know enough to raise their children in other respects, they are qualified to teach them about sex. Sex is a moral matter—and the school has no business butting into the moral upbringing of the young. The school should stick to the three R's and leave moral and spiritual matters to the home and church.

MRS.
SCHULTZ: If the school were as anxious to guard the innocence of the young as it is to fill their heads with sex ideas, perhaps our society wouldn't be slipping so badly today.

SECOND
BOARD
MEMBER: I'd like to go back to something Mrs. Jackson said a few minutes ago, about promiscuity. Mrs. Jackson, no one wants to make teenagers promiscuous. The whole effect of the program in sex education, as I understand it, may be to prevent just that development. There is a great deal of emphasis on sex in advertising today, and an increasing tendency toward frankness in the arts. The Board had only a brief explanation of the objectives and approaches of this course, but we were told by the principal that the faculty committee that developed the course consulted numerous

statistical studies, and every one showed that most young people receive very little direct, honest, and accurate information about sex. Despite appearances, he said, they're woefully ignorant, in many cases, about the facts of life. That is what the course and its teacher, Miss Babette, are trying to overcome—misinformation and ignorance.

MRS. GREEN
[TURNING TO
MRS. BROWN
AND
WHISPERING]: It's obvious why he speaks that way. I've seen the way he looks at Miss Babette. Those bachelors and their filthy minds.

MRS.
SCHULTZ: A course in sex education is a strange way of decreasing promiscuity. How come since courses like this have been added to curricula around the country, the incidence of rape, out-of-wedlock pregnancy, and venereal disease has risen so dramatically?

SECOND
BOARD
MEMBER: I'm not sure I understand the point you are making. Are you suggesting that. . . .

MRS.
SCHULTZ: I'm suggesting that I'm in favor of ridding our society of its preoccupation with sex. I confess I don't know quite how to do that. But I do know where to start. Right here in Alertia—by ridding our school of that course.

MR. LESSROW
[APPLAUDING
VIGOROUSLY]: My sentiments exactly. If we're not going to defeat the communists abroad or in Washington, at least we can stop their insidious campaign against our youth at home. Mr. Chairman, I voted for you for the school board—probably most of us in this room did. We had confidence in your ability to act wisely, do the right thing. You now know the facts in this matter. It's time to act on them. You can justify our confidence in you by demanding that that course be discontinued immediately.

BOARD CHAIR-
MAN [AFTER
A MINUTE OR
TWO OF
SILENCE]: Well, I believe the Board has a good idea of the nature of your concern about this course. If there are no more com-

ments at this time, I'd like to thank you ladies and gentlemen for coming out tonight, and to assure you that we will give your position our careful consideration. If the Board members will remain, we'll continue with our meeting in a few minutes.

5.3. Read the following dialogue carefully. Then evaluate both Bart's and Bernie's positions on freedom. Decide whom you agree with, or whether you disagree with both. State your judgment and support it thoroughly.

BERNIE: Have you been reading about the way Nixon used the FBI to intimidate people? He had them investigate anyone who spoke out against his policies. They kept a file on such people.

BART: I heard something about it, but I didn't give it much thought. What's wrong with his doing that?

BERNIE: What's *wrong* with it? You must be kidding. It was just a threat to everyone's freedom of speech, that's all. When the secret police spy and pry into people's business so that a president can take them to court just because they denounce his insane behavior, we'd damn sure better worry.

BART: You're overreacting. The government just wanted to be sure that people don't abuse their freedom. After all, you can't just say anything you want to say any time you want to.

BERNIE: Wow, man, you're too much. Don't you realize you can't parcel out freedom? You can't fence in someone's basic rights. "Here is your freedom, kiddies, and here are its boundaries." No way. The minute you say that, you're taking freedom away.

BART: Come on. You're not taking it away by limiting it. It's still there, isn't it? I mean, if you're 82 percent free, that's not zero percent.

BERNIE: That's the government line. You've swallowed the whole poisoned lie. Gulp. Burp. Down it goes. Think about it a minute. Freedom isn't something that can be measured. With a steak you can trim off an ounce of fat here and a few ounces of bone there and still have a steak left. But with freedom it's different. It's all or nothing. You can't be somewhat free, any more than you can be a little bit alive. You're either alive or dead. And you're either free or not free. That's all there is to it.

5.4. Evaluate the argument in the following letter to the editor using the approach explained in this chapter. State your judgment and support it thoroughly.

Dear Editor:
    I enjoyed your recent series of articles on religious views. I believe religious values occupy the central place in one's being. Today an increasing number of young people are giving up their religion because of the vocal skepticism of those who find re-

ligious values too restrictive. If more of us who do
believe were as vocal, the young would surely see the
relevance of religion and not be so easily deceived by
those who wish to mislead them.

It is fashionable today among so-called "human-
ists" to place man's reason above religious faith.
They say a man must follow his own lights, affirm what
he believes is true. But are they really so open-
minded and humble as that view makes them seem? I
think not. For underneath that view lies the fact that
they exalt their own judgment. When they accept the
word of an authority, it is only because they agree
with that authority. And they do not accept one authority without, by that very acceptance, rejecting
other authorities. In short, they are super-egotists
who refuse to accept what transcends their understanding, and who try to fit God into their understanding. Their efforts are in vain; for God will not
fit into the finite mind. A god who can be understood by
man is no God at all, but a poor imitation.

I do not believe that any intelligent, honest person can place his confidence in human intelligence
and reason. Human learning is too sparse and fragmen-
tary to warrant such trust. Human knowledge and understanding change all too quickly. Yesterday's
theories gather dust in the attics of libraries. And
history judges all things mercilessly. But the Bible,
God's own word, remains. It stands as an immutable
beacon to all who love the truth. One need only put
aside his probing and questioning and doubting, become like the little children, and accept it.

                                        Sincerely yours,
                                        Mrs. Joan Truly

5.5. The following letter appeared in the *New York Times Magazine.* [6] Evaluate the argument it presents using the approach explained in the chapter. State your judgment
and support it thoroughly.

To the Editor:
As a man whose past is considerably peppered with
the buckshot of imprisonment including four years at
Attica prison I am in a position to state that William
R. Coons's article, "An Attica Graduate Tells His
Story," (Oct. 10), is equipped with built-in blin-
ders. The reader can look in only one direction: at the
brutal guards, the butcher doctors, the unfeeling,
unconscionable warden, etc. A cartoon, therefore,
forms in the mind of the reader. He sees a huge, hairy

monster, frothing fangs bared, labeled "Penal System" and crushing the life out of a ragged, pity-evoking figure labeled "Defenseless Convict."

I wonder why Mr. Coons omitted the worst handicap facing the inmate who is sincerely interested in rehabilitation—his own "brothers" in gray?

Contrary to what Mr. Coons would have the reader believe, prison populations are not made up solely of misunderstood, slightly tarnished angels unjustly sentenced to hundreds of years for merely stealing wormy apples.

Many—let me lean on that word—*many* convicts are incorrigible scum whose sole purpose in life closely parallels that of a demented crocodile. They wouldn't lead an honest life if guaranteed a thousand dollars per week and half of God's throne in the hereafter.

They are the ones who steal from their fellow inmates, who collect "protection money" from the weak and frightened, who force others with "shanks" pressed to their throats to commit homosexual acts, whose roaring animal voices fill the cell blocks until your brains vibrate from the obscene cacaphony and you couldn't write your own name without misspelling it. They are the ones who will grip prison reform by the throat and choke it, exploit it, mangle and tramp on it until, in disgust, the administration rescinds it.

The first step toward *lasting* prison reform is to collect all the incorrigible scum, the human cockroaches who infest prison populations and place them in separate institutions. Let them prey on each other. Let them, if it comes to it, kill each other off . . . incurable cancers devouring each other.

Unless this step is taken, prison reform, however great and shining, will fade into the limbo of things that might have worked.

Name Withheld.

5.6. Evaluate the argument presented in the following brief essay using the approach explained in this chapter. State your judgment and support it thoroughly.

Each year hundreds of thousands of animals are killed in research experiments. These include not only rats and mice, but also rabbits, monkeys, dogs, cats, and birds. The deaths are considered justified because the research is necessary to save human lives. But this reasoning reflects a complete disregard of animals' rights.

Animals' rights? The idea may seem strange if you've never heard it before. But it is not a new idea. Eighteenth-century French philosopher Voltaire reasoned that because animals have feelings and can understand, at least in a primitive way, they therefore have rights. Albert Schweitzer, the famous jungle doctor and humanitarian, believed that "reverence for life" applied not just to humans, but to all living creatures.

More recently Dr. Thomas Regan, professor of philosophy at North Carolina State University, argues persuasively for such rights in his book *Animal Rights and Human Obligations.* He believes that people resist the idea that animals have rights largely because they think of the world as belonging exclusively to humans. They see dogs and cats and even more exotic animals like dolphins and apes as objects rather than creatures, as things to be *owned* and *used.* He concludes that "it's not crazy to believe, as some Eastern cultures do, that animals have rights. Our aim is to break some standard patterns of thought about animals that are held in Western society."

A number of people have begun to speak out on this issue. For example, the group that organized a petition-signing drive in Ann Arbor to save the lives of six gorillas scheduled to be used (and probably maimed or killed) in a University of Michigan automobile accident research project. And the man in Honolulu who freed two dolphins from a University of Hawaii laboratory where, though they were not being harmed, they were wrongfully imprisoned. Such people may be scorned and derided as fanatics today, but they will one day be regarded as heroes.

Such praiseworthy actions, unfortunately, are too limited to make much of a difference. What is desperately needed is legislation that will grant animals exactly the same rights that humans enjoy, and that will prohibit the use of any animal in any research experiment that will cause it suffering, regardless of the supposed value of the research. All sensitive and caring people will support such legislation and urge their legislators to enact it without delay.

two

BE CREATIVE

chapter 6

The Creative Process

The human mind, as we have seen, has two phases. It both produces ideas and judges them. These phases are intertwined—that is, we move back and forth between them many times in the course of dealing with a problem, sometimes several times in the span of a few seconds. To study the art of thinking in its most dynamic form would be difficult at best. It is much easier to study each part separately. For this reason, we will focus first on the production of ideas (Chapters 6–9), and then turn to the judgment of ideas.*

Although everyone produces and judges ideas, the quality of the effort varies greatly from person to person. One individual produces a single common or shallow idea for each problem or issue, and approves it uncritically, while another produces an assortment of ideas, some of them original and profound, and examines them critically, refining the best ones to make them even better. The terms *creative thinking* and *critical thinking,* as we will use them throughout the remaining chapters, refer to the latter kind of effort.

KEY FACTS ABOUT CREATIVITY

Before the mid-1950s, creativity received little scholarly interest. Then one researcher examined over 121,000 listings of articles recorded in *Psychological Abstracts* during the previous 23 years. He found that only 186 articles—less than two-tenths of 1 percent of the total—had any direct concern with creativity.[1] Since that finding, however, interest in creativity has increased considerably.

---

*Because it is impossible to separate the two completely, there will be minor elements on judging in our treatment of creativity, and vice versa.

Many books have been published on the subject.[2] And researchers have examined the lives of creative achievers, probed the creative process, and tested creative performance in every conceivable circumstance and at every age level.

Researchers' efforts have helped deepen our understanding of creativity and overcome the many misconceptions that for so long went unchallenged. You have undoubtedly been exposed to some of these misconceptions and therefore have developed some false impressions about what creativity is and how it works. Replacing those false impressions with facts is an important first step in developing your creative potential. The facts listed below are the most important ones. Some we mentioned in passing in Chapter 1; all are worth returning to and reflecting on from time to time.

"Doing your own thing" is not necessarily a mark of creativity. "For many people," George Kneller observes, "being creative seems to imply nothing more than releasing impulses or relaxing tensions. . . . Yet an uninhibited swiveling at the hips is hardly creative dancing, nor is hurling colors at a canvas creative painting."[3] Creativity does involve a willingness to break away from established patterns and try new directions, but it does not mean being different for the sake of being different or an exercise in self-indulgence. It is as much a mistake to ignore the accumulated knowledge of the past as it is to be limited by it. As Alfred North Whitehead warned, "Fools act on imagination without knowledge; pedants act on knowledge without imagination."[4] Being creative means *combining* knowledge and imagination.

Creativity does not require special intellectual talent or a high IQ. The idea that highly creative people have some special intellectual ability lacking in the general population has enjoyed popularity for centuries. When the IQ test was devised, that idea was given new currency, and anyone who achieved less than a genius level score (135 and above) was considered to have little or no chance for creative intellectual achievement.

However, when researchers began studying the lives of creative people and comparing IQ test performance with creativity test performance, they made two discoveries. They found that creativity depends not on the possession of special talents, but on the *use* of talents virtually everyone has, but most never learned to use. In addition, they found that the IQ test was not designed to measure creativity, so a high score is no indication of creative ability and a low score no indication of its absence. In fact, they found the great majority of creative achievers fell significantly below the genius level.[5]

The use of drugs hinders creativity. Although many people seem determined to resist this fact, it has long been acknowledged by those who have studied creativity. If liquor and other drugs have been such a boon to original thought, one researcher asks, then why hasn't the corner saloon produced more creative achievers? No one, as yet, has answered this question satisfactorily. Nor is anyone likely to. The reason drugs harm creativity, Brewster Ghiselin explains, is that "their action reduces judgment, and the activities they provoke are hallucinatory rather than illuminating." What is needed, he argues, is not artificial stimulation of the mind, but increased control and direction.[6]

The use of drugs and liquor as stimulants is sometimes part of a larger misconception that might be termed the *bohemian mystique.* This misconception is the notion that a dissipated life-style somehow casts off intellectual restraints and opens the mind to new ideas. Eliot Hutchinson offers an assessment of this that most researchers would endorse: "Narrow streets, shabby studios, undisciplined living, and artistic ballyhoo about local color may all have their place in pseudo artistry, but they have little to do with genuine creation. Nor is the necessary creative freedom clearly associated with them at all . . . Bohemianism squanders its freedom, returns from its hours of dissipation less effective. Creative discipline capitalizes its leisure, returns refreshed, reinvigorated, eager."[7]

Creativity is an expression of mental health. One common image of the creative person is reinforced by a number of low-budget horror films. That image depicts a mad scientist, shuffling nervously around his laboratory (pronounced lab-or´-a-try in such films), rubbing his hands together evilly, a wild look in his eyes, and drool slipping out of the corner of his mouth. Many people really believe the image—they view *creative person* and *lunatic* as near-synonyms. They are wrong.

Harold Anderson summarizes a leading psychological view concerning the relative sanity of creative people in the following passage. (The group includes such respected thinkers as Erich Fromm, Rollo May, Carl Rogers, Abraham Maslow, J. P. Guilford, and Ernest Hilgard.)

> The consensus of these authors is that creativity is an expression of a mentally or psychologically healthy person, that creativity is associated with wholeness, unity, honesty, integrity, personal involvement, enthusiasm, high motivation, and action.
>
> There is also agreement that neurosis either accompanies or causes a degraded quality of one's creativity. For neurotic persons and persons with other forms of mental disease [who are, at the same time, creative] such assumptions as the following are offered: that these persons are creative in spite of their disease; that they are producing below the achievements they would show without the disease; that they are on the downgrade, or that they are pseudo creative, that is, they may have brilliant original ideas which, because of the neurosis, they do not communicate.[8]

CHARACTERISTICS OF CREATIVE PEOPLE

Studies of people who have developed their creative potential have identified a number of characteristics they share.[9] The following characteristics are among the most prominent.

Creative People Are Dynamic

Unlike most people, creative people do not allow their minds to become passive, accepting, unquestioning. They manage to keep their curiosity burning, or at least to rekindle it. One aspect of this intellectual dynamism is *playfulness.* Like little children with building blocks, creative people love to toy with ideas, arranging them in new combinations, looking at them from different perspectives. It was such activity Isaac Newton was referring to when he wrote "I do not know what I may appear to the world; but to myself I seem to have been only like a boy playing on the seashore, and diverting myself in now and then finding . . . a smoother pebble or a prettier shell than ordinary whilst the great ocean of truth lay all undiscovered before me."[10]

Einstein was willing to speculate further. He saw such playfulness as "the essential feature in productive thought."[11] But whatever the place of playfulness among the characteristics of creative people, one thing is certain—it, and the dynamism it is a part of, provide those people a richer and more varied assortment of ideas than the average person enjoys.

Creative People Are Daring

Thinking for creators is an adventure. And they go about it with what Carl Rogers calls "openness to experience," which is the very opposite of defensiveness.[12] Free of preconceived notions and prejudiced views, creative people are less inclined to accept prevailing views, less narrow in their perspectives, less apt to conform with the thinking of those around them. They are bold in their conceptions, willing to entertain unpopular ideas and zany, even outrageous possibilities. Therefore, like Galileo and Columbus, Edison and the Wright brothers, they are more open than others to creative ideas.

Their daring has an additional benefit. It makes them less susceptible to face saving than others. They are willing to face unpleasant experiences, apply their curiosity, and learn from those experiences. As a result, they are less likely than others to repeat their failures.

Creative People Are Resourceful

Resourcefulness is the ability to act effectively and conceptualize the approach that solves the problem—even when the problem stymies others, and even when the resources at hand are meager. This ability is not measured by IQ tests, yet it is one of the most important aspects of practical intelligence. One dramatic example of this quality was reported in *Scientific American* half a century ago. A prisoner in a western state penitentiary escaped, but was recaptured after a few weeks. The prison officials grilled him for days. "Where did you get the saw to cut through the bars?" they demanded. In time he broke down and confessed how he had managed to cut the bars. He had picked up bits of twine in the machine shop, dipped them in glue and then in emory, and smuggled them back to his cell. Night after night for three months he had "sawed" the one inch thick steel bars. They accepted his explanation, locked him up, and made sure he never visited the machine shop again.

That, however, is not the end of the story. One dark night about three and a half years later, the man escaped again, and the prison officials found the bars cut in exactly the same manner. Though he was never recaptured, the way he escaped is legendary in the underworld. He hadn't used anything from the machine shop either time. He had been much more resourceful than that. He had used woolen strings from his socks, moistened them with spit, and rubbed them in dirt on his cell floor.[13]

Creative People Are Hardworking

"All problems," states William Gordon, "present themselves to the mind as threats of failure." Only people who are unwilling to be intimidated by the prospect of failure, and who are determined to succeed no matter what effort is required, have a chance to succeed. (Even for them, of course, there is no *guarantee* of success.) Creative people are willing to make the necessary commitment. It was that commitment Thomas Edison had in mind when he said, "Genius is 99 percent perspiration and 1 percent inspiration;" so did George Bernard Shaw when he explained "When I was a young man I observed that 9 out of 10 things I did were failures. I didn't want to be a failure, so I did 10 times more work."

Part of creative people's industriousness is due to their ability to be thoroughly absorbed in a problem and to give it their undivided attention. But it is due, as well, to their competitiveness, which is unlike most people's in that it is not directed toward other people, but toward ideas. They take the challenge of ideas *personally.* Lester Pfister was such a person. He got the idea of inbreeding stalks of corn to eliminate weaker strains. He began with 50,000 stalks and worked by hand, season after season. After five years he had only four stalks left, and he was destitute. But he had perfected the strain.[14] Where others would have succumbed to frustration and disappointment, he persevered because he was unwilling to accept defeat.

Creative People Are Independent

Every new idea we think of separates us from others, and expressing the idea increases the separation tenfold. Such separation is frightening, especially to those who draw their strength from association with others and who depend on others for their identity. Such people are not likely to feel comfortable entertaining, let alone expressing, new ideas. They fear rejection too much.

Creative people are different. This is not to say that they don't enjoy having the acceptance and support of others, or that the possibility of losing friends doesn't bother them. It means that, however much they may *want* acceptance and support and friendship, they don't *need* them the way others do. Instead of looking to others for approval of their ideas, they look within themselves.[15] For this reason they are less afraid of appearing eccentric or odd, are more self-confident, and are more free to speak and act independently.

Knowing these five characteristics can help you develop your creative potential if you are willing to make the effort to acquire them—or, if you already possess them, to reinforce them. It is never an easy task—old habits resist replacement. But even modest progress will make a difference in the quality of your thinking.

FINDING OPPORTUNITIES FOR CREATIVITY

The essence of creativity is identifying a need or challenge and meeting it in an imaginative, original, and effective way. The need or challenge, however, need not be obvious. It may be so subtle as to go unrecognized until a creative person wonders "What can I do that no one else has done to achieve success and make a name for myself?" Such wondering is very different from waiting for needs and challenges to present themselves—it is *actively seeking opportunities to be creative.* Here are some examples of where it can lead:

> William Ricktor got the idea of gift packaging Idaho potatoes. The package, called "Awesome Potatoes," contains four large potatoes nestled in wood chips in a mahogany-veneered box. It costs $9.95, plus shipping costs, and is selling well.

> Henry O. Dormann got the idea of publishing a high-quality magazine exclusively for top executives and leaders. The magazine, *Leaders,* is not sold, but sent free to over 100,000 people—all of them either leaders of nations, international companies, world religions, or uncommonly distinguished contributors to education, science, or the arts. Dormann's profit comes from advertising. (Advertisers are delighted to pay premium rates to reach such an audience.)

> Milton Zelman got the idea of publishing a newsletter for chocolate lovers. Called *Chocolate News,* and printed on brown, chocolate-scented paper, it reports on news concerning chocolate from around the world. The newsletter has 15,000 subscribers at $9.95 per year.

> Lucy's Canvas, a Boston firm, got the idea of making shoelaces a style item by imprinting them with rainbows, hearts, stars, and other designs. The firm has sold over 6 million pair, selling from $1.50 to $2.00 each.

> Some creative person got the idea of making a calendar serve an educational purpose, and produced The 365 New-Words-a-Year Calendar. The desk calendar presents a new word, together with pronunciation and definition, on each leaf, and sells for $5.95.

APPLYING CREATIVITY TO PROBLEMS AND ISSUES

The two broad applications of creativity that are of special concern to us are solving problems and resolving controversial issues. The terms *problem* and *issue* overlap considerably. Both refer to disagreeable situations that challenge our ingenuity, situations that have no readily apparent satisfactory remedy. But an *issue* has an additional characteristic. It tends to divide people into opposing camps, each sure that it is right and the opposition wrong.

There are four ways to apply creativity to problems and issues. They are taking a novel approach, inventing a new product or service, finding new uses for existing things, and inventing a concept. Let's look more closely at each.

Taking a Novel Approach

This method of applying creativity may involve a simple action or a more complex process or procedure.

For example, Humane Society inspectors who found two dogs in a closed car in brutal 92 degree heat used a novel approach in dealing with the dogs' owners. They offered them an alternative to being charged with cruelty to animals —spend an hour inside the closed car themselves in the same heat the dogs endured, while the dogs spent the hour in the air-conditioned Humane Society building.[16]

A judge in a Michigan divorce court took a novel approach to the issues of custody and the right to live in the family home. He awarded the house to the *children* until the youngest reaches 18. The parents take turns living in the house and paying the bills. (Since both parents live in the area, their housing is no problem during the time they are not occupying the children's house.)[17]

A novel approach can also be used to invent or modify a complex process or system, such as the procedure required to obtain a driver's license or to gain admission to college. For example, a fascinating dental process, developed within recent decades, may make it possible for you to keep your teeth throughout your life. That process is periodontal surgery, in which diseased gums are operated on and plaque formations scraped from the teeth, thus preventing the plaque from causing teeth to loosen and fall out.

Inventing a New Product or Service

In 1845 a man needed money quickly, to pay a debt. "What can I invent to raise some money?" he thought. Three hours later he had invented the safety pin. He later sold the idea for $400. Virtually all the products we use every day have similar, though perhaps less dramatic, stories. The hammer, the fork, the alarm clock, the electric blanket, the toothpaste tube, the matchbook—these and thousands of other products first occurred as ideas in a creative mind. And new ideas are occurring every day. Two relatively recent ones you may not have heard of are Graffiti Gobbler, a chemical compound that can remove ink or paint from wood, brick, or steel,[18] and the Moto-Stand—a three-wheeled, upholstered, motorized truck invented by a man paralyzed from the chest down. The vehicle permits him to maneuver around the house in a standing position.[19]

The laundromat, the car wash, and the rent-a-car agency are examples of successful services that have been invented. When the rent-a-car service became quite expensive, some enterprising people invented rental services providing older, high-mileage cars in good working condition. (One such agency is called Rent-a-Wreck; another, Rent-a-Heap.). A public-spirited psychiatrist invented a service for insomniacs. Called Sleepline, it offers an eight-minute recorded message ("Sleep is coming . . . slower . . . deeper . . .") to help people sleep.[20]

Finding New Uses for Existing Things

No matter how old something is, there are always new uses that can be devised for it. Consider how many kinds of nails, nuts, bolts, and brushes have been developed from the original ideas. Even the waterbed, a relatively new variation on the old bed, has been given a new use—to simulate the warmth and protection of the womb for premature babies.[21] In some cases, apparently useless objects can be put to good use. For example, a St. Louis barber combines hair clippings with peat and other substances to form an unusually rich potting soil, which he believes may help restore drought-ravaged soil in parts of Asia and Africa. And at least one college student devised a use for empty beer cans—he punched holes in the top and bottom, ran heavy cord through them and hung the cans in close rows as window curtains.

Inventing a New Concept

We tend to regard the many concepts that help us think and deal with reality as fixed and eternal. Yet that is not so. Concepts are invented, just as products and services are. The concepts of taxation and punishing criminals, for example, may be very old, but they were once new. Numerous other concepts are relatively recent. It is hard to imagine how mathematics could even be used without the concept of zero. Yet that concept was invented by a Hindu around A.D. 500. Similarly, the concept of a corporation originated in the sixteenth century, and our ideas of progress and worldly success in the seventeenth. Even the concept of the zip code is very recent.

STAGES IN THE CREATIVE PROCESS

Being creative means more than *having* certain traits. It means *behaving creatively,* addressing the challenges we encounter with imagination and originality. In short, it means demonstrating skill in applying the creative process. Although authorities disagree over the number of stages in this process—some say three, others four, five, or seven—the disagreement is not over substantive matters. It is merely over whether to combine activities under one heading or several. There is no real disagreement about the basic activities involved.[22]

For ease in remembering and convenience of application, we will view the creative process as having three stages—identifying the problem or issue, investigating the problem or issue, and producing a range of solutions. Each of these stages will be the subject of a separate chapter. But a brief overview of the process will enable you to begin using it right away.

The First Stage: Identifying the Problem or Issue

This stage's objective is to find the most helpful expression of the problem, the one that will yield the best solution. You should see and express a given problem in as many different ways as you can, and then, if possible, select the best expression of it. Many problems are not solved because people see them in one way only. As a result, they close off all other avenues of solution, sometimes the best ones. "A problem properly stated," notes Henry Hazlitt, "is partly solved."

Consider the prisoner deciding how to escape from prison. His first formulation of the problem was probably something like "How can I get a gun and shoot my way out of here?" or "How can I trick the guards into opening my cell so I can overpower them?" If he had settled for that formulation, he would still be there. His ingenious escape plan could only have been devised as a response to the question, "How can I cut through those bars without a hacksaw?"

In some cases, after you have expressed the problem in a number of ways, you will be unable to decide which expression is best. Whenever that happens, postpone deciding for a time, until your work in the second and third stages of the process enables you to decide.

The Second Stage: Investigating the Problem or Issue

The objective of this stage is to obtain the information necessary to deal effectively with the issue. In some cases this will mean merely searching your past experience and observation for appropriate material and bringing it to bear on the current problem. In others, it will mean obtaining new information through fresh experience and observation, interviews with knowledgeable people, or research in the library. (In the case of the prisoner, it meant closely observing all the accessible places and items in the prison.)

The Third Stage: Producing a Range of Solutions

This stage's objective is to generate an ample supply of possible solutions, from which to choose the best solution to the problem. (The approaches used in making such choices will be discussed in this book's third section "Be Critical.") In this stage you face two obstacles to proficiency. The first is the often unconscious tendency to limit your ideas to common, familiar responses and to block out different, unusual, "inappropriate" ones. Fight that tendency by keeping in mind that it is precisely in the latter responses that your chance to be creative lies.

The second obstacle is the temptation to stop producing ideas too soon. As we will see in a later chapter, research has made clear that the longer you continue producing ideas, the greater your chances of producing *creative* ideas. Or, as one writer put it, "The more you fish, the more likely you are to get a strike."

There is one final matter to be clarified before you will be ready to begin practicing the creative process—How will you know when you get a creative idea? By what characteristics will you be able to distinguish it from other ideas? A creative idea is an idea that is both imaginative and effective. That second quality is as important as the first. It's not enough for an idea to be unusual. If it were, then the weirdest, most bizarre ideas would be the most creative. No, to be creative an idea must work, must solve the problem it responds to. A creative idea must not just be uncommon—it must be *uncommonly good.*

WARM-UP EXERCISES

6.1. Most high school athletic teams have rather predictable, uncreative names—Bull-dogs, Indians, Warriors, and so on. Think of as many creative names as you can for high school teams, names you have never heard used before. Be sure to guard against setting unconscious restrictions on your thinking, and to resist the temptation to settle for too few ideas.

6.2. How many uses can you think of for old socks, stockings, or pantyhose? Observe the cautions in Exercise 6.1 above.

6.3. Every change of season brings a new clothing fashion for men, women, or children. Invent as many new fashions as you can. (If you wish, you may include out-of-date fashions in your list, as long as they have not been popular in recent years.) Observe the cautions in Exercise 6.1 above.

APPLICATIONS

6.1 Four friends have a large garden in the shape below. They want to divide it into four little gardens the same size and shape, but they don't know quite how. Show them.

6.2. Divide the circle shown below into as many parts as you can using four straight lines.

6.3. For each of the following problems, apply the three stages of the creative process. Record all your thoughts as they occur, and be prepared to submit them to your instructor. When you have finished with the third stage, state which of your solutions is best and briefly explain why.

   a. Barney has early classes five days a week. Yet he has attended few of them because he just can't seem to wake up in the morning. If he doesn't find a solution to his problem soon, he'll surely fail out of college.

   b. Olaf was recently in a motorcycle accident that gashed the calf of his right leg and required 10 stitches. The doctor told him not to get the wound wet for at least a week. "Do you mean I can't bathe for a week?" Olaf asked. The doctor shrugged his shoulders.

   c. The campus library has been losing articles from magazines and even pages from expensive books. Irresponsible students just tear them out, hide them in their bookbags, and walk out of the library. But yesterday a student was caught leaving with ripped-out pages. Some of the library staff favor making an example of her by expelling her from school and pressing criminal charges against her. Others favor merely charging her for the mutilated books.

d. "What do you do with a frozen elephant?" may sound like a joke, but it wasn't when Jackson Township, New Jersey officials asked it. A 5-ton elephant which was being kept in a drafty barn by a former circus employee, had caught pneumonia and died. And so it lay in the barn, frozen solid.[23]

e. Virtually every building with a public bathroom has a graffiti problem. Even when the messages are not offensive, they create maintenance problems.

f. The cost of arresting crime suspects and trying their cases in court is high. The financial burden of the police and court system, unfortunately, is carried by the taxpayers, most of whom are law abiding. In these financially troubled times, many communities are unable to bear this burden.

g. Arnold is the president of a small toy-manufacturing company. His business has been declining over the past few years. Traditional toys and games just don't seem to be as attractive to the public as they used to be.

h. Shoplifting cuts deeply into storeowners' profits. Owners and managers would welcome a solution to this problem.

i. Many elderly and handicapped people live lonely lives. No longer active in careers, they are often forgotten by former associates and neglected by family and friends. Many lack transportation to community affairs.

6.4. Think of the most unpleasant task you ever had to do. Use your creativity to make it more pleasant. Follow the directions given at the beginning of Application 6.3.

6.5. Think of your biggest pet peeve about other people, the thing they do that aggravates you most. Use your creativity to reduce or eliminate that aggravation. Follow the directions given at the beginning of Application 6.3.

chapter 7

Identify the Problem or Issue

This first stage in the creative process is the one most often neglected. The reason is not that people decide to be pig headed and to proceed without having identified the best expression of the problem or issue. Rather, it is that they are convinced that the problem is self-evident, and that it would be a waste of their valuable time to consider alternative ways of formulating it.

These people are wrong! Like our first impressions of people, our initial perspectives on problems and issues are apt to be narrow or superficial. We see no more than what we have been conditioned to see—and stereotyped notions block clear vision and crowd out imagination. Most importantly, this happens without any alarms sounding, so we never realize it is occurring.

Have you ever looked closely at the wheels on a railroad train? They are flanged. That is, they have a lip on the inside to prevent them from sliding off the track. Originally train wheels were not flanged—instead, the railroad *tracks* were. Because the problem of railroad safety had been expressed as "How can the tracks be made safer for trains to ride on?" hundreds of thousands of miles of railroad track were manufactured with an unnecessary steel lip. Only when someone thought to redefine the problem as "How can the wheels be made to grip the track more securely?" was the flanged wheel invented.[1]

BENEFITS OF ALTERNATIVE PERSPECTIVES

The key to identifying problems and issues effectively is to realize that our first perspective is not necessarily the best one, and to refuse to proceed until we have considered a number of alternatives. This approach offers four specific benefits:

It Helps Us Move beyond the Familiar and Habitual

The first perspective that occurs to us is usually slanted heavily toward familiar, habitual ways of seeing and interpreting experiences. Thus it is more likely than later perspectives to reflect bad thinking habits—mine-is-better, face saving, resistance to change, conformity, stereotyping, and self-deception. Creativity is not apt to arise out these habits.

It Keeps Our Thinking Flexible

Once we adopt a perspective, even tentatively, it becomes difficult to entertain a different one. The following exercise will help you appreciate this fact more fully. Look closely at each of these pictures for at least a minute. Then continue reading.

In the left-hand figure, you should be able to see both an old woman and a young girl; in the right-hand figure, both a vase and two faces. In each case, many of us see one image quite readily, but have difficulty seeing the other until it is pointed out to us. (If you still haven't seen both, turn to page 214 for assistance.) Once we have seen both, however, we are able to move back and forth between them freely and quickly. It is much the same with perspectives on problems. If we force ourselves to entertain a variety of perspectives, we are better able to maintain flexibility.

It Opens Many Lines of Thought

Once we have settled on a perspective, we close off all but one line of thought. Certain kinds of ideas occur to us, but only those kinds and no others. For example, if the crippled man who invented the motorized cart had defined his problem as "How to occupy my time while lying in bed" rather than "How to get out of bed and move around the house," he would never have thought of his invention.

It Provides Approaches to Fall Back On

There is no guarantee that we will take a productive approach. One view of a problem will not infrequently seem very promising, but turn out to be unproductive. In such cases, if we begin by considering a number of perspectives, we can simply try another one when our first choice proves unworkable. Having an alternative approach lessens the effect of failure and makes it easier to try again.

The benefits of alternative perspectives are best seen by examining an actual case. In the past 10 years almost 7000 public schools around the country have closed their doors because of declining enrollments, budget cuts, and inflation.[2] With further enrollment declines expected through 1990, school budgets increasingly under attack, and inflation continuing to rise, additional closings can be expected. Here are the various ways this problem might be expressed:

- How can school enrollments be increased?
- What economies can be made to reduce school budgets?
- How can the impact of inflation on education be lessened?
- How can school buildings best be used after the schools are closed down?
- How can the unused space in school buildings be used to generate income so the school will not have to be closed down?
- How can school buildings be used in evenings and on weekends to generate income?

There is room for disagreement about which of the above expressions of the problem is best. But there can be no disagreement that we are in a better position to make that decision, and to produce a creative solution, if we take the time to identify and consider all of the questions.

GUIDELINES FOR IDENTIFYING PROBLEMS

The following guidelines will work for you if you use them. You may be tempted to say "I want to be creative, so I won't use these guidelines—I'll develop my own." That would be a mistake. You would probably experience difficulty doing the applications in this and subsequent chapters, become frustrated, lose confidence, and decide that something is wrong with this book or with your instructor. You might even conclude that creative thinking is just too difficult to learn.

We have noted that conformity is not always bad, that there are situations where it makes more sense to do what others do than to develop our own way. This is just such a situation. Your best approach is to faithfully follow the guidelines presented below, and become proficient in applying them. At that time, if you wish to apply your creativity and develop a different set of guidelines, by all means do so.

Guideline 1: Examine the Situation

The moment you are aware that something you have experienced or read about is bothering you, that you are dissatisfied with or frustrated over some person, object, or situation, examine the situation and try to elevate the problem to the conscious level. Ask yourself, "What is wrong here? Why am I so bothered? Exactly what is the problem?" Try to penetrate the cloud of vagueness surrounding your feelings. Consider the situation from all sides. If you find it difficult to do this, ask yourself how another person, with a different viewpoint than yours, might see it. If you can think of an actual person who you *know* would see it differently, so much the better.

Here's an example of this guideline. You have probably heard of the religious objection Jehovah's Witnesses have to receiving blood transfusions. They believe that transfusions constitute "eating blood," an action condemned in the Bible. For this reason, when faced with the choice of violating their consciences and living, on the one hand, and honoring their consciences and dying, on the other, they often choose the latter. There have been a number of highly publicized cases involving this choice. In some of them the choice has been made by a wife or husband for an unconscious spouse, or by a father or mother for an unconscious child.

Many people, when they read of such cases, feel sadness, anger, or frustration—and either carry that burden silently or mutter in disbelief, "I can't understand how people can be so foolish." In other words, they fail to bring the problem to the conscious level *as a problem.* Not everyone reacts this way, of course. Some people do see it as a problem, but from a single perspective. They say "How can these people be persuaded to give up their narrow view of the biblical injunction against eating blood?" Or, in cases where children or unconscious spouses are involved, "How can these people be prevented from endangering others' lives?" Historically, neither of these expressions of the problem has led to many creative ideas.

But in recent years a few people have looked at the problem from other angles. They have asked "How can Jehovah's Witnesses be operated on without transfusions?" and "How can we avoid giving blood, yet still give transfusions?" Creative solutions to the problem have come from these perspectives. One is the use of techniques that reduce the flow of blood during surgery, such as electrocautery or lowered blood or body temperature. Another is the use of synthetic blood substitutes.[3]

Guideline 2: Express the Problem or Issue

Work out your expression of the problem in words on paper or, if appropriate, in sketches. (You don't have to be an artist to use sketches. Rough outlines and stick figures are just as effective.) There are two very good reasons for recording your thoughts. First, the joining of mental and physical effort to externalize ideas often helps clarify them. Secondly, as any composition teacher will verify, *the very act of writing down ideas has a way of triggering other ideas.* One caution, however —don't worry about correct writing at this time. You are not writing for anyone but yourself. If you take the time to look up words in the dictionary, to ponder proper grammar and so on, you will break your train of thought and slow the flow of ideas.

Whatever form of expression you use, be sure that it *focuses the challenge implicit in the problem.* The best form for verbal expression is the *how-question* form referred to in guideline 1—"How can Jehovah's Witnesses be operated on without transfusions?" Let's see how this is used to express another problem in a variety of ways. We noted earlier how a new successful surgical process can save teeth threatened by gum disease. That process was a response to the question "How can we restore the gums to health and make the teeth more secure in the underlying bone?" But there have been many other ways of looking at this problem. We know, for example, that the ancient Etruscans invented false teeth. That invention was a response to the question "How will we chew our food when our teeth have loosened and fallen out?" (Before that, presumably, someone asked "How can we prepare food to make it edible without teeth?" and thought of pounding it with a rock to grind it into powder or paste.) In the future some creative person may ask and answer the question "How can people's gums be protected from disease?"

Guideline 3: Refine Your Expressions

After you have expressed the problem in rough form in as many ways as you can, refine the expressions. That is, replace vagueness with exactness, and general words with specific. The clearer and more meaningful a question is, the more helpful it is in prompting creative ideas. Be especially careful about making your *verbs* specific. It's much easier to think of using beer cans as window curtains when you ask "How can I *decorate* with them?" than when you merely ask "How can I *use* them?"

Guideline 4: Choose the Best Expression

Often the most promising expression of the problem or issue will stand out clearly from the other expressions. If it does not—if two or three seem equally promising —then postpone choosing until the investigative or idea-producing stage, when you will have a better basis for choosing.

A SAMPLE PROBLEM

A situation that occurred recently in a college town illustrates the approach discussed here. Jean, a middle-aged woman, returned to college after many years to complete her degree. She was living off campus, in an apartment house. Directly below her apartment lived a young woman who played her stereo loud enough to reach Vladivostok with a favorable wind. At least it seemed that way to Jean. The sound and the woman's rudeness infuriated her. She pondered the problem and came up with these expressions of it:

How can I persuade her to turn it down?
How can I compel her to turn it down?

> How can I frighten her into moving?
>
> How can I escape the noise?
>
> How can I bother her as much as she bothers me?

Deciding that the first expression of the problem was the best, Jean investigated how she might approach the woman. She tried to recall similarly difficult situations in the past that she had experienced or heard others tell about. Then she brainstormed the possible approaches she might take. After producing a generous number of ideas, she chose the best one, went to the woman, and tried it. It failed—the music continued to blare.

Disappointed, Jean looked at her list of expressions again and decided, probably because of her anger, that *compelling* might succeed where persuasion hadn't. She investigated again, produced ideas again, then selected and carried out not one, but two of them—reporting the matter to the apartment house's owner and registering a complaint with the police. The result was disheartening. The owner made a feeble appeal to the woman and the police gave her a half-hearted warning. After a day or two of quiet, the music blared again.

Now Jean decided her last expression of the problem was the best of the remaining ones. She gleefully listed dozens of hateful ideas for *bothering* the woman (including boring a hole in the floor and pouring water on the stereo). Then the insight came to her. An athletic woman, Jean loved to play tennis and jog. Why not use exercise as a weapon? So she did. She bought herself a jump rope and every morning, promptly at four A.M., she jumped rope in her bedroom —right over the sleeping woman's head. Wham, whump, thump. How sweet was revenge.

What happened next proved Jean's idea to be even more creative than she had realized. In a few days the woman knocked on Jean's door and explained sheepishly that Jean's jumping was keeping her awake. Jean seized the opportunity and said "I'll tell you what—I'll stop jumping rope if you'll turn the stereo down." The woman agreed, and the problem was solved.

WARM-UP EXERCISES

7.1. Many actors and actresses give up their given names and take stage names that are easy to remember and that project a particular image. Thus the silent screen had Theda Bara (her last name was derived by reversing *Arab*), and modern films have had Tyrone Power, Lana Turner, Victor Mature, Kim Novak, and so on. Think of as many creative stage names as you can. (The image you aim to project may be macho male, female sex symbol, charming child, or any other you wish.)

7.2. Create as many new food recipes as you can. Don't limit yourself unnecessarily. Any recipe you have never seen or heard about before will be acceptable. Include ingredients and preparation instructions.

7.3. Old toothbrushes are usually thrown in the trash. But are they really useless? Think of as many uses as you can for them.

APPLICATIONS

Do each of the following applications in this manner: First identify the problem or issue, using the guidelines explained in this chapter. Then investigate the problem, as necessary, and produce as many solutions as you can. (Record all your thoughts as they occur to you, and be prepared to submit them to your instructor.) Finally, state which of the solutions you believe is best and briefly explain why.

7.1. Gail has always slept well. But lately she has been waking up at about 3:00 A.M. and having trouble getting back to sleep.

7.2. James Cook, president of the Thomas Alva Edison Foundation, notes that the number of patent applications in the United States has declined steadily in recent years, and that a large number of the filed applications come from foreigners. He believes that the main reason for the apparent lack of interest in invention here is the poor image technology enjoys, particularly among young people. He cites a U.N. study of the understanding level and appreciation of technology among the people of 19 industrialized countries. Japan scored first, the United States last.[4]

7.3. Ernest Digweed, a British recluse, died and left an unusual will. He bequeathed 30,000 pounds ($57,000) to Jesus Christ, provided Jesus returns within 80 years. At the end of that time, his bequest, plus all accrued interest, would go to Digweed's closest relatives. The relatives, predictably, are contesting the will, and the matter will be decided by the London High Court.[5]

7.4. Hermione is a college student living in a dormitory room with two other girls. Whenever she is trying to study, it seems, her roommates decide to have company in, talk loudly, dance to the stereo, or do something else distracting. It's not that they *try* to bother Hermione, but the effect is the same.

7.5. The elementary school is located in a residential area of a small city. Lately there have been confirmed reports of strangers offering young children rides as they walk to and from school. Parents and school officials fear that the children may be in danger from one or more sexual deviates.

7.6. One apparent reason for the increase of violent crimes in recent years is that criminals' rights are as carefully protected as victims' rights are. Criminals can break the law with greater boldness, knowing that even if they are caught, the slightest technicality—such as a police officer's failure to read them their rights or to permit them to call an attorney—will result in their case being dismissed.

7.7. As procedures for reporting and investigating child abuse grow more sophisticated, it becomes clear that the extent to which children are physically and emotionally victimized by their parents is much greater than most people realized.

7.8. The statistics per country of the number of people killed by handguns in 1980 include the following: Japan, 48; Great Britain, 8; Canada, 52; Israel, 58; Sweden, 21; West Germany, 42; United States, 10,728.[6] Many U.S. citizens argue that handguns should be banned in this country. But many others, including members of the influential National Rifle Association, respond that such a ban would violate the constitutional right of citizens to own and bear arms. So far the latter group have had their way.

7.9. In recent years there has been increasing concern about the competitiveness of U.S. industry in the world market. The quality of work and of employees' attitudes toward work has been researched and studied. American workers seem to feel less identification with their companies, less concern for increasing productivity, and less concern about the quality of their work than, for example, Japanese workers do. In one Japanese factory researchers found that the average worker submitted 10 suggestions for improving the company per year.[7]

7.10. Rocco is the manager of a movie theater. In recent years a number of competitors have cut into his business, and Home Box Office has reduced the number of moviegoers still further. Rocco desperately needs to get more people to patronize his theater, particularly since he has begun to hear the owners talk of closing it and dismissing him if box office receipts don't improve.

7.11. Many authorities agree that one of the important reasons for the high divorce rate in this country is the naively romantic view of love many people have when they enter marriage.

chapter *8*

Investigate the Problem or Issue

It may seem strange to learn that the investigation of problems is a creative stage. You may think of investigating as a dull, plodding effort involving very little thinking of any kind, let alone creative thinking. In part, that is right. The way many people actually carry out their investigation involves little or no thinking. That is why their investigation is so often unproductive.

Investigation, as we define it, means more than routinely getting the same information as everyone else. It means getting information others overlook, by searching in ways and places that never occur to the uncreative. It means using our resourcefulness and originality, being imaginative in our search.

Not every problem you encounter requires significant investigation. If, for instance, you decide to go beyond grumbling and kicking your gym locker when the string in your sweatpants slips out, you can apply the creative process without using the investigative stage at all. You can identify the problem in a number of ways—"How can I insert the string again easily?" "How can I avoid having it slip out again in the future?" "How can I eliminate the need for a string?"—and then go directly to the third stage of the creative process, producing as many solutions to the problem as you can think of.

In many other cases, however, the investigative stage is a crucial step in the process. The scientists who developed the creative surgical procedure in response to periodontal disease first had to investigate the nature of the disease—that is, its causes, its progress from initial infection to tooth loss, and the various technological methods, medical tools, and approaches available to be used. In the case of unwanted graffiti, the invention of Graffiti Gobbler depended on 1) a knowledge of what techniques had been unsuccessfully tried and 2) a basic understanding of chemistry. "Inspiration," wrote Louis Pasteur, "is the impact of a fact on a well-prepared mind." The investigation stage provides the mental preparation.

Investigation is especially important in complex and controversial issues. In such matters, unless you know all the relevant facts, including the various viewpoints involved and the different lines of reasoning people follow, you are not likely to make sound judgments and develop workable solutions. A. E. Mander makes the point vividly:

> The fewer the facts [one] possesses, the simpler the problem seems to him. If we know only a dozen facts, it is not difficult to find a theory to fit them. But suppose there are five hundred thousand other facts known—but not known to us! Of what value then is our poor little theory which has been designed to fit, and which perhaps fits, only about a dozen of the five hundred thousand known facts![1]

The point is not that you should feel daunted by difficult problems and issues, say "What's the use?" and give up. (That would certainly not help you become a better thinker.) It is that you should appreciate the importance of not rushing in, like the proverbial fool, where angels fear to tread.

THREE SOURCES OF INFORMATION

Most people, if they bother to investigate problems and issues at all, do so unimaginatively. They have a very narrow mind set about information. They know it is contained in libraries, but they aren't sure where else it may be found, or how to go about getting it quickly and efficiently. That is unfortunate because knowing other sources can make handling problems and issues much easier and more enjoyable.

There are three sources of information—*yourself, the people around you,* and *authorities.* Let's look closely at each.

Yourself

The first source to consult in the investigation of any problem or issue is yourself —that is, your own experience and observation. You are literally a knowledge factory. You have been receiving sense impressions every moment of the day and night since birth. (Though sight and, to some extent, taste are dormant at night, hearing, touch, and smell remain active.) Calculated at the rate of 1 impression per second—a modest estimate—if you are now 18 years old, you have over *56 million* perceptions stored in your mind. They include innumerable experiences of your own, and experiences you witnessed or heard about from others. They include, too, all that you have read about or seen on television. In addition to all this information, you have all the ideas you have ever generated, consciously and unconsciously.

If you remind yourself from time to time that you have a wealth of information to draw upon in solving problems, you'll be much more likely to make the effort to tap this priceless resource. And that effort is the first important step toward mastering the investigating stage of the creative process.

The next step is to be ready to receive insights from seemingly unlikely sources. Most of us grow up thinking that every subject, and often every aspect within a subject, is neatly and permanently separated from every other one. We would never dream of finding a scientific insight in a poem, or a clue to an ethical problem in a math book. Yet many of the most creative insights come from just such unexpected places.

The forklift truck, for example, which makes it possible to move the heaviest objects effortlessly, was first conceived when the inventor was standing in a *bakery*. He noticed how the doughnuts were lifted out of the oven on steel "fingers" and thought, "Why shouldn't that same idea work in the warehouse?"[2] Similarly, the idea of the printing press first occurred to Johann Gutenberg while he was watching a winepress operating. He had long pondered how to achieve quicker book production; the current method was to carve words laboriously on blocks and then to rub paper against them. The winepress suggested the idea of transferring an image to paper by pressing an inked lead seal against it.[3]

What connection is there between a secretary's desk and an operating room? Or between the dolphins at Florida's Ocean World and the education of the retarded? "No connection at all," most people would say. And yet creative people have seen a very valuable connection. Surgeons are now using staples in place of sutures to save time and blood loss. And David Nathanson, a professor of psychology at Florida International University, has demonstrated that young victims of Down's syndrome learn to speak more quickly and remember words longer when they are placed in pools with trained dolphins. He got the idea for the experiment when he noticed that retarded children who couldn't sit still and pay attention to a teacher would sit playing with a puppy for a quarter of an hour. Speculating on how this interest in animals could best be used in teaching, he decided to use dolphins.[4]

In addition to searching for connections among ideas you encounter now, you can also search for connections you overlooked in past experiences and observations. You surely have thousands of experiences classified under only one heading that could be classified under several. For example, you may have gone swimming as a child, gotten a little too far from shore, struggled, panicked, and almost drowned, until a friend saved you. That experience and the circumstances surrounding it are probably etched in your mind as *narrow escape from drowning*. But think of the other possible classifications—*effects of fear on performance, importance of children's obedience to parents, role of personal sacrifice in friendship.* By seeing more connections between past experiences and observations, you multiply your store of useful information.

People Around You

The next source of information to consult in investigating a problem is other people. Like you, they are knowledge factories. If you were able to draw on all their perceptions, you would be rich indeed. By adding just nine other people's perceptions to your own, you would increase your total to half a *billion.* Such total acquisition, of course, is out of the question. Nevertheless, you can learn a great deal from others if you approach them skillfully, with questions that stimulate their thinking and assist them in recalling relevant experiences.

Let's say your problem is how to overcome your fear of heights. You could ask a friend, "Have you ever been afraid of high places?" but that wouldn't be the best way to phrase the question. *Any* of her fears might give you helpful information, so your first question should be broader. And you should be ready with subsequent questions to direct her recall in ways that seem helpful to you. Here's how you might proceed:

> YOU: Have you ever had a nagging fear you wanted to overcome?
> FRIEND: I don't know . . . I guess so. Hmmm . . . [trying to remember something specific.]
> YOU [STIMULATING RECALL]: I mean a fear like being closed in or dogs or high places.
> FRIEND: Yeah, when I was about 12 I can remember being terrified of the dogs on my paper route.
> YOU: Tell me about it. How did you feel? . . .

Later in the conversation you would ask how she thought the fear began and, more importantly, how she coped and overcame it. You'd also ask if she ever received any advice from others that proved helpful, if she knows any books and articles that speak to the question of overcoming fear. You might even share *your* fear with her and ask for comments.

Any time you try to draw on other people's experience in this way, keep two points in mind. First, some people are more helpful than others. You'll always do better asking a good thinker rather than a poor thinker; or an open, talkative person rather than a shy, secretive one. Secondly, successful questioning depends not only on your ability to ask the right question at the right time, but also on your willingness to listen at other times, to open yourself to the person's experience and not let other thoughts (even analytical ones) intrude.

It is also a good idea not to rely solely on your memory. Instead, get in the habit of taking notes. In most cases this is better done after the conversation rather than during it, because many people will find your writing while they speak a distraction. It may prevent them from concentrating fully on the questions.

Authorities

Although anyone who has had some experience with the problem you are addressing can be a source of helpful information, the best sources are usually authorities on the subject. Authorities are people who possess expertise—that is, people who have mastered a subject well enough to know not only its principles and practices, but also its areas of dispute. They are also familiar with the various theories and arguments advanced to extend the frontiers of knowledge in the subject.

It would be unwise to expect authorities to be infallible. Being human, they are subject to the same errors as the rest of us. They can, for example, be blinded by personal preferences, cling stubbornly to outmoded views, and suffer lapses in their reasoning. Should we disregard their views because of these imperfections? No. It would be as foolish to do so as it would be to have a bartender diagnose our stomach pains because our physician *might* make a wrong diagnosis.

Good thinkers prefer the views of authorities despite their susceptibility to error simply because authorities are likely to be correct in their views. The odds are with them. There is a way of increasing those odds, of getting the most accurate and helpful information—and that is to consult more than one authority, especially in matters where disagreement exists.

Where do you find authorities? It's common for people to think, "There are no authorities around me. I don't live in New York or Los Angeles or Washington, D.C. And I don't know anyone in Harvard or Stanford. So I really have no access to authorities." That view is mistaken. Not all authorities live in big cities or work at prestigious universities. Many are nearer to you than you imagine. The biggest obstacle to recognizing them is the notion that if you know the person, he can't be an authority; that to possess real expertise he must live at least 100 miles away. (Familiarity, in this sense, unfortunately does breed contempt.)

If you are wrestling with a problem in psychology, why not consult a psychology professor on your campus? He's an authority in the subject. He may even have published an article or book in the area of your concern. Similarly, if the question concerns the availability of jobs in a particular field, you can consult your college placement director. But what about questions in fields not represented at your college—for example, a question about architecture? With only a modest investment of imagination, you can turn to the yellow pages of your local telephone directory and look under "Architects."

And what if you find no such listing? In that case, you turn to your imagination once again and consider what *related* professions might be listed. "Building Contractor" is one example. Many contractors have had one or more courses in architecture. Even those that haven't may work closely with architects. Still other possibilities are state or county public works or highway departments, which usually employ architecturally trained people.

The advantage of this approach is that it offers a valuable bonus—if the people you contact can't answer your questions, they can usually offer suggestions on whom to consult or at least where to look. This is why so many professional writers use this method. If they are researching a story on a medical breakthrough, for example, they often begin by consulting their county or state medical association or a respected local physician.

CONDUCTING AN INTERVIEW

Once you find an authority, the next step is arranging an interview. All interviews have one basic rule: be considerate of your interviewee. He is donating his valuable time, so don't take him for granted. Here are five guidelines to help you observe this rule.

1. Call or write ahead for an appointment. Explain exactly what you wish to discuss and how long you'll take. (Keep the time as brief as you can, preferably under half an hour.) Make yourself available at a time that fits the interviewee's schedule best.
2. Carefully prepare your questions in advance. Make them clear and brief. Try to avoid those that can be answered yes or no—they won't be very helpful. For instance, instead of asking "Do you agree with the governor's position?" ask "What is your reaction to the governor's statement?"
3. Anticipate the responses to your initial questions, and prepare follow-up questions to probe those responses you feel don't go far enough or don't address the points you wish addressed.
4. Arrive on time. When you begin the interview, get right to the point. Keep your questions crisp and clear. Avoid thinking ahead to your next question. Instead, listen carefully to the reply. If any of his comments open an aspect of the issue you did not consider, but is worth pursuing, be sure to pursue it. However, try not to overstay your welcome.
5. If at all possible, don't make the person wait while you take notes. If you can't take shorthand or write rapidly in longhand, consider the possibility of taping the interview. (Always obtain permission to tape an interview. Never merely assume it is acceptable to the other person.)

If the authority you wish to interview lives too far away for you to visit, consider doing a telephone interview. Such an interview is conducted as above, with two additional requirements. First, be sure to call or write in advance to determine when the interview will be most convenient. It is boorish to assume that because you are ready, he is too. Secondly, remember that when conducting a telephone interview, it is especially important to speak clearly and to ask clear, concise questions.

USING THE LIBRARY

Fortunately, you needn't limit your investigation to those authorities available for interviewing. There is a way to consult those who live too far away to call, those who are too busy to receive your call, even those who are dead! It is to use the library. Perhaps you think of the library as a gathering place for dull, strange people, a place of little use to those who are lively and creative. That is a very shallow view. In fact, the library is best seen as *a formal meeting room for interviews with authorities not otherwise available.* That's precisely the way the very best thinkers regard it.

If your aversion to the library is based instead on the fear of lingering too long and gathering unwanted creases in your Calvin Kleins, then you'll be pleased to learn that people who use the library most often—professional writers, speakers, and scholars—have even more reason than you to save time. They often have difficult deadlines to meet. Efficiency is not just a matter of preference with them —it's a dollars and cents concern. Yet they don't avoid the library—they simply use it more effectively.

The first step in using the library as professionals do is to determine all the headings and subheadings that might apply to your subject. Since the information sought may appear under different headings in the library's various sources, this is an important step. Start by giving free rein to your imagination and listing as many headings as you can. For example, for *crime* you may think of the subtopics *homicide, rape, shoplifting, kidnapping, vandalism,* and *burglary.* Next expand your list of headings by consulting two sources available in most college libraries —the index volume of *Encyclopedia Americana,* and the *Thesaurus of Psychological Index Terms,* a companion volume to *Psychological Abstracts.* You'll find such additional headings as *felonies, misdemeanors, antisocial behavior, behavior disorders, psychosexual behavior,* and *infanticide.*

Once you have determined the headings under which the information you are looking for is classified, get the information by using these simple and efficient approaches:

1. Consult a good encyclopedia for a broad overview of your subject. *Encyclopaedia Britannica* and *Encyclopedia Americana* are generally considered to be the best. Note important facts. In addition, note special terms that might be useful in further research.
2. Consult an almanac. An almanac is a collection of miscellaneous facts and statistical information about a wide variety of subjects. On the subject of crime, for example, you can find information under as many as two dozen specific listings. Most almanacs are published once a year. Thus, you can obtain comparative data—say, for 1960, 1970, and 1980 —quickly and easily.
3. Consult the appropriate indexes. Indexes do not present the information you are looking for, but they tell you where to find it, and so save you much time and energy. The following are mong the most generally useful indexes. (Your librarian will be able to suggest others.)

For information in nontechnical periodicals—*The Readers' Guide to Periodical Literature.*

For information in specialized and technical publications—

Applied Science and Technology Index

Book Review Index

Business Periodicals Index

Education Index

General Science Index

Humanities Index

Index to Legal Periodicals

Psychological Abstracts

Social Science Index

For information in newspaper reports—*The New York Times Index.*

For information in government publications—the *Monthly Catalog of*

United States Government Publications and the *Monthly Checklist of State Publications.*

4. Consult the *subject index* of the card catalog for books on your subject. Use broad subject headings as well as narrow ones—often a book that treats a larger subject will have a chapter or two on your subject.
5. Obtain and read the books and articles that are most relevant to your subject. Though the number of books and articles you read will depend on the scope of your project, the first four steps of the process should be followed for all but the very briefest of treatments.

KEEPING CREATIVITY ALIVE

As crucial as the investigation stage is in the solution of many problems, it can threaten creativity. The more information you accumulate, the greater the potential for confusion. To keep creativity alive, you will have to overcome that confusion. Here is how to do so.

Whenever you are confused by the amount or complexity of the information you have obtained, and experience difficulty sorting it out, pause for a moment, look back at your statement of the problem (stage 1), and use that statement to decide what is relevant and what is not.

If you are dealing with an especially difficult problem, you may have to use this approach many times. Even the best and most creative thinkers lose their bearings from time to time. But they don't allow themselves to become discouraged. They just find their bearings again and continue.

A large amount of information can also have a daunting effect on your confidence. The more you probe a problem, the more you are apt to realize its complexity. In time you may find yourself thinking, "I didn't realize it would be this difficult. Maybe there is no solution. If other, more qualified people have been unable to find a solution, what business do I have trying?"

When such thoughts occur, remind yourself that others may not have solved the problem precisely because they gave in to their feelings of apprehension —the ones that at this very moment threaten your creativity. Or because, despite their expertise, they lacked the techniques for unlocking and applying their creativity. (After all, creativity is not a subject taught in most schools and colleges, so it is not surprising that otherwise educated people should be uninformed about it.) Remember, too, that whatever difficulties arise in thinking, there are effective methods for dealing with them, and your resources for producing creative solutions to problems are, as the next chapter will demonstrate, truly formidable.

WARM-UP EXERCISES

8.1. Think of as many creative names as you can for a restaurant. Consider all types of establishments from the fancy, high-priced variety to the lowly coffee shop, and all types of cuisines.

8.2. Old dishwashing liquid containers (the plastic kind that Dawn, Joy, and Ivory liquid come in) are usually discarded when empty. But perhaps they could be put to some use. Think of as many uses as you can for them.

8.3. Most of us complain that we don't have enough closets. Yet we seldom use the closet space we have very efficiently. Redesign your closet at home (or, if you prefer, the one you use at college) to achieve maximum use of the space in it. Do a before and after sketch of the closet.

APPLICATIONS

8.1. Each of the following cases was reported in the news. Most readers undoubtedly viewed them narrowly, believing each was entirely separate from any but the most obvious subject. Yet to someone searching for more than surface connections, each case offers some interesting possibilities. For each of the following cases, list as many implied subjects or issues as you can. Be sure to specify what those implications are.

a. In 1981, a 9-year-old boy known as Robert M. pointed a toy gun at a New York City bank teller and robbed her of $118. He was placed on two years' probation after his attorney argued he was only play acting during the robbery. Then, in 1982, the same boy, with two accomplices, was arrested for stealing a sled from two boys at knifepoint.[5]

b. Three-year-old Chad Chancey was expected to be the youngest trial witness in Oklahoma's history. He was the only person with any knowledge of the events that took place the night his mother and sister were murdered. Chad reportedly heard a loud argument in the next room, women's screams, a sound he described as a loud handclap, then silence. He later identified the man who had been in the apartment that night from a police file photo. The defense attorney expressed concern that the child might be too young to separate fact from fantasy.[6]

c. In 1945 Charles Jamison was found badly wounded on a Boston dock. He carried papers identifying him as a first mate on the USS *Cutty Sark*. Yet no records could be found of the existence of such a ship, and all further investigations about the man revealed nothing. Interviews with him disclosed only that he had no family, had gone to sea at age 13, and believed his ship had been torpedoed. He remained in a Boston hospital until his death 30 years after his discovery on the dock.[7]

d. Dr. Martin Orne, a psychiatrist and expert on memory and hypnosis, and Dr. Elizabeth Loftus, a psychologist and memory expert, presented information to the American Association for the Advancement of Science that suggested using hypnotism to get witnesses to recall details of past events may be ill-advised. Their research showed that memory may be unintentionally altered by the form of the hypnotist's questions. "If the hypnotist has certain beliefs," said Dr. Orne, "he will create memories in the subject's mind."[8]

e. After 60 years of business the American Seed Company closed its doors. In 1981, its fifth straight year of losses, the company lost $600,000. One of the principal reasons for the company's demise was the refusal of the children who sold the seeds to pay the company its share of the money they earned. (The arrangement was fair—the company was to receive 40¢ and the child 20¢ for each packet of seeds sold.) According to the *Wall Street Journal,* when the company appealed to the children's parents, they got little or no cooperation. "Far from lending a helping hand," the *Journal* wrote, "the parents often sided with their outlaw offspring" by saying essentially "You're a big company; you don't need the money and you're only trying to cheat my child."[9]

f. A director of the National Credential Verification Service, a company that checks job applicants' academic backgrounds for employers, reports that *one-third* of its investigations uncover false credentials. College officials corroborate the estimate. Such misrepresentation is not limited to young applicants. Many middle managers also practice deception.[10]

g. Recent studies suggest that the hormone secretion and levels of certain chemicals in a mother's blood may affect an unborn child in more far-reaching ways than ever realized. Not only physical effects, but also *behavioral* effects, are demonstrable. For example, children exposed to progestins before birth turn out to be more independent and self-assured, while those exposed to estrogens are more disposed to group dependency. There is even speculation that transsexuality may be linked to a decrease in testosterone during the fetal period.[11]

h. A human fetus survived to full term after it was extracted from its mother's womb for surgery and then returned to the womb following surgery. The surgery, which took place in the twenty-fourth week of pregnancy, corrected a life-threatening urinary tract obstruction.[12]

8.2. Woebegone College is having a problem with grade inflation. The average grade submitted by many professors is a B+, despite the fact that the average entrance examination score of Woebegone's students has declined steadily over the past decade. It appears that work that would have received a C 10 or 15 years ago is now being given a B or B+. One effect of this has been that 60 percent of the student body are on the Dean's List. Find the best expression of this problem. Then investigate it, as necessary, using the approaches explained in the chapter, and produce as many solutions as you can. (Record all your thoughts as they occur to you, and be prepared to submit them to your instructor.) Finally, state which of your solutions you believe is best and briefly explain why.

8.3. Every so often someone writes an article about the poor state of composition teaching, usually with a title like "Why Dick and Jane Can't Write" or "The Scandal in the English Classroom." The public then gets excited and calls for a study of the problem, and the media explore methods of developing students' language skills. But no lasting creative solution to the problem ever seems to be found. Identify and solve this problem following the directions in Application 8.2, above.

8.4. The recession of the early 1980s caused a bad employment situation to grow much worse. Some people grew pessimistic about this country ever being able to guarantee a job for everyone who wants work, no matter how desirable that goal might be. Identify and solve this problem following the directions in Application 8.2, above.

8.5. Alcohol and drug abuse are associated with crime in the streets, health problems, the breakdown of the family, and poor job performance. Identify and solve this problem following the directions in Application 8.2, above.

8.6. Women and racial and ethnic minorities faced job discrimination for many years in this country. Then in recent years the government instituted affirmative action programs that attempted not only to ensure present fairness but also to compensate for past grievances. The idea was to give some job preference to those who were discriminated against in the past. Yet these programs drew criticism for creating *reverse discrimination*—in other words, for being as unfair as the system they were designed to correct. Identify and solve this problem following the directions in Application 8.2, above.

8.7. In many third world countries, the United States is faced with a difficult choice. We can either support the existing governments and risk alienating the masses of people who are victimized by them, or support rebel groups and drive the existing governments into closer relationships with Moscow and Cuba. Identify and solve this problem following the directions in Application 8.2, above.

8.8. In many states the schools are financed primarily by property taxes. This system, of course, tends to favor wealthy areas over poor areas, and often results in inequality of educational opportunity. Identify and solve this problem following the directions in Application 8.2, above.

8.9. On the one hand, the federal government forbids cigarette advertising on radio and television, and requires health warnings to be printed on every pack of cigarettes sold. On the other hand, the same government heavily subsidizes tobacco farming. Identify and solve this problem following the directions in Application 8.2, above.

chapter 9

Produce Possible Solutions

Imagine a pearl diver on an island in the South Seas. He pushes his canoe off from shore, paddles out into the lagoon, dives deep into the water, picks an oyster off the bottom, surfaces, climbs into his boat, paddles to shore, and opens the shell. Finding nothing but an oyster inside, he pushes his canoe off again, and begins paddling into the lagoon. "Wait a minute," you're probably thinking, "he's wasting an awful lot of time. The right way to do it is not to paddle back to shore with one oyster, but to dive again and again, to fill the canoe with oysters and then return to shore."

You're right. Pearls are rare—a diver must open many oysters before finding one. Only a very foolish diver would waste time and energy making a separate trip for each oyster.[1] *And it's exactly the same with producing ideas.* Foolish people think of a single solution to a problem and then proceed as if that solution *had* to be creative. But creative ideas, like pearls, occur infrequently. So sensible people produce many ideas before expecting to find a creative one.

Researchers have found a clear relationship between the number of ideas produced and the quality of the ideas. The more ideas produced, the better the chances of having one or more good ones.[2] There are two reasons for this. The first is a matter of simple probability. Creative ideas are statistically uncommon. As Alfred North Whitehead explains:

> The probability is that nine hundred and ninety-nine of [our ideas] will come to nothing, either because they are worthless in themselves or because we shall not know how to elicit their value; but we had better entertain them all, however skeptically, for the *thousandth* idea may be the one that will change the world.[3]

The second reason is that initial ideas are usually poorer in quality than later ideas. Just as water must run from a faucet for a while to be clear and free of particles, so thought must flow before it becomes creative. "Early ideas," Herbert Spencer warned, "are not usually true ideas."[4] Exactly why this is so is not known, but one very plausible hypothesis is that familiar and safe responses lie closest to the surface of our consciousness and therefore are naturally thought of first.[5] In any case, success in creative thinking depends on continuing the flow of ideas long enough to purge the common, habitual ones and produce the unusual and imaginative.

STIMULATING YOUR IMAGINATION

Producing a large quantity of ideas is the first way to produce creative solutions, but it is not the only way. Another important one is to stimulate your imagination. Studies confirm that most people behave unimaginatively not because they lack imagination, but because they fear the reaction their ideas will receive. In time they grow used to suppressing ideas that differ from the norm, ideas that might raise eyebrows. They do themselves a great disservice, because creativity depends upon imagination. "No great discovery is ever made without a bold guess," observed Sir Isaac Newton.[6] And Albert Einstein added, "I believe in imagination . . . imagination is more important than knowledge."[7]

It takes more than determination to stimulate your thoughts, of course, particularly if you have gotten into the habit of suppressing them. You'll need some strategies for activating your creative imagination. Here are five effective ones:

1. Force uncommon responses
2. Use free association.
3. Use analogy.
4. Look for unusual combinations.
5. Visualize the solution.

Force Uncommon Responses

We noted that common, familiar ideas tend to come first. Nothing can be done to avoid this pattern. Therefore, your best approach is to expect them, even encourage them, in order to free your mind for more original ideas. Begin by asking yourself what responses most people would think of. Write them all down. When you have produced a number of these, and you can't think of any others, ask yourself what responses others would probably *not* think of. Press yourself for as many as you can produce.

One predictable outcome of this effort is the listing of some outrageous or silly ideas. Chances are you will feel a little uncomfortable with such ideas. "How can they be helpful?" you'll think. "Problem solving is a serious business—no place for foolishness here." *Resist that feeling.* Playfulness, as we saw, is one important characteristic of creative people—it contributes to their dynamism.

There's nothing wrong with writing even the most outrageous ideas down on paper. Listing them is not the same as endorsing them—you can always cross them out later. But don't screen them out now—you might inadvertently discard an original insight in the process.

Don't misunderstand this advice. It doesn't mean you should *try* to be outrageous or ridiculous. It means you should *tolerate* being so when it occurs as a natural consequence of striving for uncommon ideas.

Use Free Association

Free association means letting one idea suggest another. It differs from forced response in that you are not directing your mind at all, but giving it free rein, relaxing your control over it momentarily and observing what ideas, what *associations*, result. Some of them may be quite unexpected, and point out interesting and profitable directions. As with forced responses, you should not screen any associations out as they occur to you. Rather, write them all down for later examination. (Often what seems totally irrelevant when it occurs to you may later prove valuable.)

A word of warning is in order. Though this strategy is helpful when used sparingly, it can easily slide into aimless daydreaming. Be sure you use it as a variation on other strategies and not as a substitute.

Use Analogy

An analogy is a reference to one or more similarities between two otherwise very different things. An analogy might be made, for example, between a football halfback's broken field running and the movements of a jaguar or cheetah. When Gutenberg looked at the winepress and conceived of the printing press, and when the inventor of the forklift got his insight from the doughnut machine, they were using analogy. To use analogy in your thinking, simply ask what the problem is like, what it reminds you of. Where appropriate, you may also ask more specific questions, such as "What does this *look* like (or sound, taste, smell, or feel like)?" or "What does it *function* like?"

Here's how you might have used analogy in Exercise 8.2 (p. 112). "What does a dishwashing liquid container look like?" you'd have asked. "A human body," you'd have replied (among other possible responses). And that analogy might suggest using the container to make dolls.

Look for Unusual Combinations

Sometimes the best solution to a problem will be to combine things not usually combined. The miner's cap (combining a flashlight and a protective hat), the wheelchair, and the clock radio are examples of how combining results in invention. Perhaps the most common example of this kind of invention is the recipe. Every time a cook blends different ingredients to make a dish differently, he is inventing by combination. Thus the first person to put a slice of mozzarella cheese on a veal cutlet invented veal parmigiana, and the ingenious person who couldn't afford veal and substituted a slice of meatloaf invented meatloaf parmigiana.

This same strategy works well in other kinds of creativity as well—finding solutions to social problems, for example. One problem of growing concern today is the increasing cost of our prison system. Someone wrestling with that problem might well consider combining prisons with factories—that is, having convicts work for private industry behind bars, be paid for their efforts, and reimburse the taxpayers for the cost of their imprisonment. (The idea might even come through analogy—by noting that prisons sometimes resemble large factory complexes.)

Visualize the Solution

This strategy consists of imagining the problem solved and visualizing what it would look like then. For example, back in the days before the problem of automobile travel on snow- and ice-covered roads was solved, someone forced to drive in such conditions would have pictured in his mind not the reality of tires mired in snow or spinning on ice, but the condition he *wished for*—wheels turning smoothly, tires biting into the snow and grasping the ice firmly. His imagination thus stimulated, he'd have asked himself, "What would those tires look like if they were able to perform the way I wish?" And he might just have visualized pieces of metal wrapped around the tire (chains), or spikes protruding from the tire to grip the road (studs).

These five strategies will give you significant help in activating your imagination. But don't expect to be able to use them smoothly right away. Give them time to become familiar. If you are inclined to give up after a few tries, remember back to your childhood. Recall the difficulty you had learning to use a fork. It, too, seemed impossible to learn, but you mastered it. Whenever your turning from one strategy to another confuses you, simply look back at your statement of the problem, regain your bearings, and continue producing ideas.

AIMING FOR ORIGINALITY

In the popular view, originality is a kind of genetic endowment. Either you have it or you don't, and if you don't have it, you have no hope of learning it. Research has demolished this idea. Like every other creative skill, *originality can be learned.* If you don't produce original thoughts, it is only because you have acquired the habit of being unoriginal. One study revealed that originality can be stimulated simply by letting a person know it is expected of her.[8]

To achieve originality in your thinking, demand it of yourself. Remind yourself that there is nothing mysterious about originality—it lies just a step or two beyond the commonplace. Don't restrict your ideas to those you have heard or thought of before. Every time you address a problem and try to find solutions, stretch your mind a little, reach for thoughts a little more daring than you have entertained before.

There is one additional method that can help you be more original—*watch your fringe thoughts.* The term *fringe thoughts* was coined by Graham Wallas.[9]

It means thoughts occurring on the edge or fringe of consciousness, much the same way objects appear on the periphery of our vision. When walking down the street or driving a car, we focus our gaze in one direction, but continue to see objects outside that focus. When something unusual or unexpected appears there, we are able to turn our attention to it. Since original ideas often appear first on the fringe of consciousness, the more alert you are to what is happening there, the more original ideas you will discover.

WITHHOLDING JUDGMENT

Judgment is an essential part of thinking. Without it, we wouldn't be able to distinguish between good and bad solutions or select the best and most workable one. But the timing of our judgment can make all the difference. Most people don't time their judgment well: They are impulsive, evaluating ideas as soon as they are produced, sometimes even screening out certain ideas before they are fully conceptualized. At the first inkling of an idea, they say "No, that's no good" or "This is silly" or "That can't be a solution."

Yet often the most creative ideas are the ones that seem silliest at first. Rushing to judgment, therefore, causes some of the best ideas to be discarded— and the least creative ones to be approved without question. Ironically, it assures that people will be uncreative just when they want most to be creative.

Research has documented that thinkers who resist judging ideas during the idea-producing stage, and who extend their effort to produce ideas beyond the point where they are tempted to stop, are rewarded with a greater proportion of good ideas.[10] As you do the applications for this and subsequent chapters, and whenever you look for solutions to problems outside this course, don't allow yourself to judge any idea until after you have produced as many ideas as you can. Don't set artificial limits on the number of your ideas. When you find yourself thinking, "I've got 10 (or 20 or 30) ideas now—that's enough," remember that the best solution to the problem very likely lies 10 or 20 ideas beyond that point. It can only be reached by pressing on. Moreover, just to be sure you are not *unconsciously* setting limits on your thinking, look back occasionally at previous efforts—the applications you did in the last few chapters, for example—and decide whether you stopped producing ideas too soon.

OVERCOMING OBSTACLES

The three most common obstacles to the effective production of a large and varied number of solutions are thinker's block, vagueness and confusion, and inflexibility. Learning how to recognize each, and mastering a few simple responses, can prevent your problem-solving efforts from being frustrated.

Thinker's Block

Like writer's block, which prevents an author from putting words on the page, thinker's block prevents us from producing possible solutions to a problem. It makes us sit idle and grow increasingly nervous, waiting for ideas that do not come. Poor thinkers are not the only ones afflicted with thinker's block. Everyone experiences it from time to time. But good thinkers have learned that they needn't be victimized by it, that there are effective methods for dealing with it.

The best way is to minimize the chance of its occurring by doing something we have already discussed—*developing the habit of withholding judgment while you are producing ideas.* Every time you stop the flow of ideas to make a judgment, even if you stop for only a second or two, you run the risk of not being able to start again. On the other hand, the more you resist the temptation to stop, and instead sustain your idea production, the less trouble thinker's block causes you.

When it occurs despite your best efforts to avoid it, try one or more of the following approaches, in the order they are presented:

1. Look back at the ideas you have written down. Read them carefully, concentrating on each as you read it. Usually one of those ideas will suggest another that you have not written down. As soon as it does, write it down. Now that the ideas are flowing again, don't stop until you have to. It doesn't matter if the first few ideas are off-target. You can gently direct the flow back to the problem.
2. Run through the strategies for stimulating your imagination again. That is, force uncommon responses (however outrageous), use free association and analogy, look for unusual combinations, and visualize solutions. You'll seldom get beyond the first or second strategy before the ideas are flowing again.
3. Copy your list of ideas over again and again, concentrating on each idea as you are writing it. Be alert to the appearance of a new idea on the fringe of your consciousness. This approach keeps you active and prevents frustration and apprehension.
4. Walk away from the problem for a time (an hour, a day, a week). Return to it only when you can take a fresh look at it, unburdened with anxiety.
5. If all else fails, go back to your first-stage work, select a different expression of the problem, and proceed with that.

Vagueness and Confusion

Even the greatest thinkers experience this obstacle to problem solving. Einstein, for example, began considering the problem that led to his relativity theory when he was 16 years old. He struggled with it for seven years before reaching a solution. During that time he experienced vagueness, confusion, and puzzlement to the point of depression and despair.[11]

Whether this obstacle appears during the investigating stage or the idea-producing stage, it is most often caused by losing sight of the problem. The best way to overcome it is the way we noted in Chapter 8—*to look back at your statement of the problem and get your bearings.* In the beginning you may have to stop the flow of ideas to take this backward look, but with a little practice you will be able to do it without stopping the flow. You will merely slow it down a little. It's much like steering a car. A beginning driver often has to come to a complete stop to straighten the car's direction, but very soon he learns to make slight corrections with the steering wheel while maintaining speed.

You will find this kind of mental steering easier to master if you write down your expression of the problem on a card or sheet of paper and keep it handy while working on the problem.

Inflexibility

This obstacle is characterized by too many ideas of one type, with little or no variation. It is caused by unconsciously directing your thinking along one narrow line of thought. Whenever you find this obstacle in your work (a simple glance back over your ideas will reveal whether or not it is present), make a special effort to stimulate your imagination. Any of the six strategies we discussed may be used, but the first two—forcing uncommon responses and using free association—are especially helpful.

HOW INSIGHT OCCURS

The most dramatic experience of the idea-producing stage—indeed, of the entire creative process—is the arrival of an insight. The moment of insight has been described in many ways. One is the *Ahah!* reaction, such as Archimedes experienced when he sat down in a tub of water, noticed the displacement of the water by the mass of his body, and instantly conceptualized the principle of specific gravity. "Eureka! I have found it," he is said to have shouted, as he ran naked through the streets. (Apparently the law against indecent exposure was not well enforced then, or else he ran very fast. In any case, he seems to have escaped arrest.) Another way of describing the moment of insight is an intense feeling of satisfaction, such as we get when we find a missing puzzle part. But perhaps the most common experience is sudden illumination, like the light bulb glowing above the head of the cartoon character.

For some reason many insights come during moments of rest. One of the building blocks of modern science, an idea called "the most brilliant piece of prediction to be found in the whole range of organic chemistry," occurred at such a time. Friedrich August von Kekulé lay dozing by the fire one day in 1865 and suddenly realized that the molecules of certain organic compounds were not open structures, but ring-shaped. Here's how he described the experience:

> I turned my chair to the fire and dozed. . . . Again the atoms were gambolling before my eyes. This time the smaller groups kept modestly in the background. My mental eye, rendered more acute by repeated visions of this kind, could now distinguish larger structures, of manifold conformation; long rows, sometimes more closely fitted together; all twining and twisting in snakelike motion. But look! What was that? One of the snakes had seized hold of its own tail, and the form whirled mockingly before my eyes. As if by a flash of lightning I awoke.[12]

The fact that many imaginative leaps have come during periods of leisure or rest has led to the misconception that insight comes without effort. Authorities on the creative process are in agreement that insight is not associated with idleness. (If it were, then the village loafer would hold the record for creative achievement.) Nor does it arrive during any type of leisure. Rather, it arrives during the leisure that follows periods of intense activity, in which the thinker grapples with the problem, is momentarily defeated by it, and turns away in frustration. Authorities theorize that the conscious mind then turns the problem over to the unconscious, which continues working. Insight comes from that effort.[13]

Insights, like all dramatic experiences, tend to be more widely publicized and more memorable than everyday occurrences. However, the fact is that many, sometimes the vast majority, of creative solutions come about more quietly. They are the result of alertness to details and careful analysis of ideas. Such solutions, though they arrive with no fanfare, are no less valuable for that. And they have one great advantage over insights. We can, to a significant extent, control them, make them happen.

A SAMPLE PROBLEM

You are a bill collector for a magazine. You have wasted countless hours sitting in waiting rooms hoping to see the magazine's debtors. But most secretaries have been instructed to let you wait until you get tired and leave. You examine the problem from all sides and consider a number of expressions. Finally you decide that the best expression is "How can I get to see debtors despite their secretaries' refusal to let me do so?" Here is how your production of ideas might proceed.

You begin listing all your ideas. The first ones are outrageous, but that doesn't bother you. You know you shouldn't stop to evaluate them.

- Carry a shotgun and threaten the secretary
- Threaten to kidnap the debtor's wife and kids
- Bring an attack dog to the office
- Scale the building and climb in the debtor's window
- Tell the secretary you are the boss's brother or sister
- Tie up the secretary and barge into the office

You encounter thinker's block, so you apply one or more of the strategies recommended in the chapter for overcoming this obstacle. The ideas begin to flow again.

- Sweet talk the secretary
- Call and make an appointment first
- Send a letter requesting payment
- Barge right in
- Change jobs
- Take a course in quick thinking

- Cancel the debtor's subscription
- Take legal action
- Sit and wait until the office closes
- Take an attorney with you
- Send someone else to wait in your place

At this point you become confused—you believe you've lost sight of the problem. A glance back at the ideas you've just produced confirms this. They do not address the problem as you expressed it. You reread your expression and begin producing again.

- Bother the secretary
- Give him/her a box of candy
- Take him/her to lunch
- Try bribery
- Beg to see the debtor
- Wait for the secretary to go to lunch and then barge in

You run dry again, so you start once more with the first strategy, looking back over the ideas you have produced. Starting with the most recent, you read "Wait for the secretary to go to lunch . . . beg to see the debtor, bribery. . . ." Suddenly you realize your inflexibility—you have slipped into producing ideas of the same type, with little or no variation. You try to stimulate your imagination, first by forcing uncommon responses. The ideas begin again.

- Pretend to be someone else
- Catch the debtor outside the office
- Bother the other people in the waiting room
- Cause a disturbance
- Be obnoxious

The ideas stop once more, so you stimulate your imagination. When you fail to force uncommon responses, you turn to free association. Several of your ideas suggest a number of associations. Specifically, "pretend to be someone else" suggests:

- A telephone repairer
- A janitor
- A job applicant
- A police officer
- An office-supplies salesperson
- A priest or nun
- An electrician
- A newspaper reporter
- A magazine contest representative (to award a prize)
- A window washer

"Bother the secretary" suggests:

- Ask to be announced every few minutes
- Sit on the secretary's desk
- Talk to her incessantly

"Bother the other people in the waiting room" suggests:

- Talk loudly about your recently contracted contagious disease
- Tell everyone loudly that the debtor has been named in a paternity suit
- Tell them the truth about the debtor's bill

"Cause a disturbance" suggests:

- Fall down and feign a seizure
- Practice the tuba
- Yell "fire"
- Jump up and down on a whoopee cushion
- Sing off-key
- Pitch a tent (literally)
- Make howling noises
- Put up signs saying "This guy doesn't pay his bills"

"Be obnoxious" suggests:

- Put on a horrible mask and fake blood
- Rub your clothing with garlic and onion
- Soak your clothes in skunk spray

At this point you'd have produced enough good ideas, including a number of creative ones, to stop producing and select your best one. Which would that be? A real bill collector, Andy Smulion of London, England, uses the very last one with great success. He soaks his clothes in skunk spray, walks quietly into the debtor's office, and hands the secretary a note saying, "I'll leave when you pay." Needless to say, he doesn't have to wait long.

WARM-UP EXERCISES

9.1. One thing at least is indisputable about rock music—it produces groups with very creative names. But perhaps you can do even better. Think of as many creative names as you can for a rock group. The only requirement here is that the name not have been used before.

9.2. The chain letter is usually associated with dishonesty, superstition, and even illegality. (The mailing of money is illegal in many places.) But it could be used constructively and beneficially. Think of as many such ways as you can to use the chain letter.

9.3. List as many ideas as you can for new products or services—that is, products or services that do not presently exist, but for which there is a need.

APPLICATIONS

For each of the following applications, find the best expression of the problem, investigate the problem as necessary, and then produce as many solutions as you can, applying what you learned in this chapter. (Record all your thoughts as they occur to you, and be prepared to submit them to your instructor.) Finally, state which of your solutions you believe is best and briefly explain why.

9.1. You've entered a snow sculpture contest. The most important judging criterion, according to the organizers of the contest, will be creativity. There is no special theme, nor are there any restrictions on size or form.

9.2. When you read about the creative desk calendar in Chapter 6 (the one offering a new word every day), you said to yourself "That idea is so obvious, such a natural combination of purposes, I should have thought of it myself before reading about it." Since then you've wondered what other creative possibilities calendars present.

9.3. In Chapter 8 we noted that the problem of having the string slip out of your sweatpants can be expressed in a number of ways, but we did not discuss that problem's solution.

9.4. Marian's roommate has developed the habit of borrowing Marian's clothes without permission. On top of that, she is careless with them, more often than not returning them soiled or even torn. Marian has tried speaking to her, but it hasn't seemed to help.

9.5. Newton's friends are a partying crowd. Almost every night they are either having a party themselves, attending a party in someone's dorm room or apartment, or making the rounds of the local bars. Newton wants to do his best academically, and would prefer to drink only on weekends—and even then only moderately. He'd like to explain this to his friends, but he's sure they wouldn't understand—they'd either try to pressure him into conforming or feel he was rejecting them.

9.6. You are the editor of the college newspaper. Your staff consists of two other people who limit their work to a few hours a week. In order to get the paper out each week, you've had to spend many more hours than your course load permits. On several occasions you've stayed up all night and slept through the next morning's classes. You've tried putting ads in the paper to get more staff members, but no one answers them.

9.7. In some cultures, the elderly are greatly respected and made to feel important. Their views are considered especially valuable because they are formed out of a lifetime of experience. In our culture it is quite different. Those over 60 are regarded as having nothing to offer society.

9.8. Many people, notably students, believe that extracurricular activities in high school complement the curriculum and provide valuable opportunities for personal growth and achievement. Yet many communities are finding the cost of financing today's schools an intolerable burden and looking for ways to reduce that cost. Some are deciding, reluctantly, that they must cut extracurricular activities (including varsity sports) from the school budget.

9.9. The welfare program is a financial drain on the country. Many argue for abolishing it. Yet others object that such a move would abandon the poor, the disabled, innocent children, and the elderly to starvation.

9.10. More U.S. citizens have been lost on the nation's highways than on the battlefields of war. Drunk driving is one major cause. The illegality of driving under the influence of alcohol (or drugs) seems not to make much difference.

9.11. A new Pennsylvania gun law has been in effect since June 1982. Among its provisions is a mandatory 5-year prison term for anyone convicted of using a gun in the commission of a crime. Hiram works for a firm hired by the state to create an advertising campaign making the public aware of this tough provision and deterring would-be criminals. Assist Hiram.

9.12. The American Lung Association is looking for ways to warn teenagers about the dangers of cigarette smoking. Assist the association.

9.13. Many parents place intense pressure on children to win in competitive sports. These parents can be seen screaming at, and even hitting, little leaguers when they make a mistake or have a bad day. And, when the children get older and compete at a higher level, the parents are always hovering about, grim-faced, missing no opportunity to cajole, nag, and intimidate them to succeed. Authorities agree that such pressure is harmful to children.

9.14. Going to the hospital for the first time can be a frightening experience, particularly for small children. Think of as many ways as you can to make the children's ward of a hospital a nonthreatening, cheery place.

three

BE CRITICAL

chapter *10*

The Role of Criticism

Gilbert Keith Chesterton once described a poet as a person with his head in the clouds and his feet on the ground. That description also fits good thinkers. They are able to entertain the boldest ideas, the undreamt-of solutions to problems—yet they are also able to fit their ideas to the exacting demands of reality. They are not only imaginative, but practical as well. We have examined the former, creative phase of thinking. Now we will examine the latter, critical phase.

Critical thinking, as we define it here, means the close examination of a proposed problem's or issue's solution to determine both its strengths and its weaknesses. In short, it means evaluation and judgment.

WHY CRITICISM IS NECESSARY

The role of criticism in the overall thinking process is important for two reasons. First, as we have seen, no solution is ever perfect. However creative it may be, there is always room for improvement. Moreover, even the best ideas seldom occur in refined form. Like fine gems, they must be cleaned, cut, and polished before their potential worth is realized. Second, in many cases solutions cannot just be put into effect—they must first be approved by others. Ideas for the improvement of the office or factory, for example, may require the approval of an employer or supervisor. Ideas about overcoming difficulties in family relationships may depend on the cooperation of other family members. And creative solutions to social problems often require the support of government leaders or the endorsement of the voters. In such cases, the best idea in the world is of little value until others are persuaded of its worth.

129

FOCUS ON *YOUR* IDEAS

The focus of this and the following chapters is not on criticism of other people's solutions. It is rather on a much more difficult, even painful criticism—that of *your own* solutions. Like everyone else, you are vulnerable to a variety of errors. You may receive inaccurate reports from others, including the media. In addition, you may misunderstand accurate reports, fall prey to rumor and hearsay, let emotion color your judgment, and suffer lapses in logic. For these reasons the ideas you produce need criticism.

Ironically, though you are undoubtedly ready to criticize others' ideas freely, like most people you are probably blind to the need for criticism of your own thinking. There are several reasons for this. First, your ego is inclined against it. Once you have settled on an idea, you feel a proprietary interest in it. "It is mine," you tell yourself, "so it must be good." And once in that frame of mind, you are ready to defend the idea against all attack, even the attack that *your own good judgment* might mount against it. It's something like a dog with his bone. He will cling to it tenaciously, and growl and snarl when anyone approaches, not because the bone is worth anything (it may long since have been chewed out), but simply because it is his.

Another reason you will be reluctant to evaluate your own ideas is their familiarity makes it difficult to see flaws in them. The longer you work on a problem or issue, the more accustomed you get to its details. And once your effort yields a solution, you have usually gotten so close to the problem that it is difficult to distance yourself from it, to step back mentally and see it objectively.

OVERCOMING OBSTACLES TO CRITICAL THINKING

This blindness toward imperfections in your solutions will make it tempting to approach criticism of your ideas with, at best, a brief look of mock analysis followed by a vigorous nod of approval. There are two ways you can safeguard against this mistake. The first is to say to yourself, before you begin to take a critical look at any solution, "I know this solution is going to look good to me, and that I am going to feel it's pointless to look for flaws. That's natural. I thought of the solution, so I *want* to think it's perfect. *But I'm going to disregard this reaction and force myself to examine it critically.*"

The second safeguard is to turn your ego to advantage. Whenever you find yourself ready to stop evaluating your solution before you really should, reflect for a moment on how it would feel to have a serious flaw pointed out by someone else, particularly by someone you don't care much for. Visualize the situation, imagine yourself squirming with embarrassment and awkwardly offering face-saving excuses. Such a mental picture ought to be enough motivation to continue evaluating your solution.

APPLYING CURIOSITY

We have seen how curiosity increases awareness of problems and issues, enabling us to feel dissatisfactions and annoyances more consciously, and to regard them more productively, as challenges and opportunities. We have seen, too, that curiosity keeps our minds dynamic and contributes to the playfulness Einstein regarded as "the essential feature of productive thought." That same curiosity is also a valuable aid to critical thinking.

Perhaps you've had the experience of adding up a column of figures and getting the same answer—the *wrong* answer—again and again. Psychologists have long recognized that when we travel a particular mental route a second or third time, we often follow our earlier footsteps without realizing that we are doing so. That's what happened when you added up those figures. You had the impression that each new totalling was fresh and independent. In reality, though, you were trapped by your initial miscalculation.

That same kind of mistake can occur when you examine your solutions critically. You can look at an idea again and again and still not see its flaws. For this reason, merely spending a lot of time criticizing is not necessarily effective. You need to examine the solution from different perspectives in order to break out of your first view. That's where curiosity comes in. By approaching criticism inquisitively, asking "How will my solution work when it is applied?" and "How will others react to it?" you will increase your chances of finding the imperfections and complications that need to be addressed.

AVOIDING ASSUMPTIONS

To assume is to take something for granted, to expect that things will be a certain way because they have been that way in the past, or because we *want* them to be that way. It's natural to make assumptions. Everyone makes them continually. You assume, for example, that your professor will be in class when class is scheduled, that the cafeteria will not serve lunch two hours early, that the college will not rent your room to someone else and change the lock on the door, that the bank that has always cashed your checks will continue to do so, and that the elevator is really going up when the indicator says it is. Making such assumptions is reasonable, even if on occasion they later prove incorrect.

Yet while refining problems and issues, it is wise to make no assumptions at all. The reason for this is not only that unexpected outcomes can cause you embarrassment. It is also, and more importantly, that *what you take for granted you do not examine critically.* Assumptions obstruct the refining process.

It would be impossible to list all the assumptions one is tempted to make while problem solving. However, the following assumptions occur often enough, and interfere with critical thinking seriously enough, to warrant special mention:

1. The assumption that others familiar with the problem or issue will share your enthusiasm for your solution. Although this might seem a reasonable expectation, it seldom is. The more familiar people are with a problem or issue, the more likely they are to have their own preferred solutions.

2. The assumption that small imperfections in your solution will not affect people's acceptance of it. When people have their own preferred solutions that differ from yours, they are likely to magnify small imperfections without even realizing it. This is often because, subconsciously, they are looking for an excuse to reject your solution. Those small imperfections may provide that excuse.

3. The assumption that if the solution is clear to you, it will be clear to others. If you've ever sat in a classroom and heard a teacher offer an explanation she understood perfectly, but realized it didn't make the slightest sense to you, then you should appreciate this. *Your* understanding of what you are expressing does not constitute clarity. If you want the solution, and its presentation, to be clear, you must *construct* it to be so and not just assume that it is.

4. The assumption that the people who stand to benefit most from your solution will accept it automatically without any persuasion on your part. This assumption has caused creative people incalculable grief. For example, when Isaac Singer invented the sewing machine, he knew it would be a boon to the garment industry. It would revolutionize garment construction and make the clothing business much more profitable. He may very well have assumed that the mere unveiling of his invention would be sufficient to have the leaders of that industry praising it and him. But reality didn't match that assumption. Singer couldn't get a single American firm interested enough to buy the machine. He was forced to go to England to find a favorable reception. To save yourself considerable disappointment, never assume that the value of your solutions will be universally recognized. Expect to have to persuade everyone.

REFINING YOUR SOLUTIONS

Refining your solutions means making your best ideas even better—that is, making the results of your creative thinking even more effective, more workable, more attractive. Although much of what you will be doing in this stage is finding flaws and complications, the emphasis is not negative, but positive. Your aim is to *improve* your solutions.

Not every solution, of course, requires refinement. With the problem of the string that slips out of your sweatpants, for example, there is little or no need for refinement and no need to present the solution for others' approval. Once you have decided on a solution, you can just implement it. Most of the important problems and issues you will encounter, however, are more demanding.

The two final steps of the problem-solving process, refining the solution and preparing its presentation, will be developed in the chapters that follow. The basic approach presented below will enable you to begin using these steps and developing skill in applying them even while you are studying each in greater depth. The approach consists of asking and answering these four questions:

1. How exactly will your solution be applied? (List all steps and all important details.)
2. What difficulties could arise in application and how would these best be overcome?
3. What reasons might others find for resisting this solution? What modifications could you make to overcome their resistance?
4. Who, specifically, will have to be persuaded of the value of your solution? What kind of presentation would be most likely to persuade them?

PROBLEMS AND ISSUES: AN IMPORTANT DISTINCTION

In Chapter 6 we noted in passing that the terms *problem* and *issue* overlap considerably. They both refer to disagreeable situations that challenge our ingenuity, situations that have no obvious, satisfactory remedy. But an issue, we saw, has an additional characteristic—it tends to divide people into opposing camps, each sure that it is right and the opposition wrong. There was no need to do more at that time than acknowledge that characteristic, because it had little bearing on creative thinking. It does, however, have significant bearing on *critical* thinking, so we will examine it more closely here.

Let's look back at a few of Chapter 9's applications and see whether they are best classified as problems or issues. Application 9.9 concerning the future of the welfare program clearly concerns an issue. It focuses directly on the controversial question of whether welfare helps more than it hinders society. In contrast, Application 9.11 concerning Hiram's advertising campaign for Pennsylvania's new gun law concerns not an issue but a problem. Its focus is not on the question of whether gun control laws are desirable, but merely on public awareness of an existing law.

One way to tell the difference between a problem and an issue is to examine the circumstances. Whenever the circumstances are likely to arouse powerful *partisan* feelings, you are dealing with an issue. Applying this test, we would say that the creative desk calendar case, the case concerning our society's treatment of the elderly, and even the drunken driving case are problems, but that the case concerning the dropping of extracurricular activities is an issue.

Another way to determine whether a situation is best regarded as a problem or an issue is to examine your solution. This way is even more important than the first because *it is possible for a solution to create controversy where none existed.* For example, few things are less controversial than a new desk calendar. Yet several years ago one creative idea for a calendar caused such negative public reaction that publishers were forced to withdraw it. (It was called the Cat-Hater's Calendar, and featured pictures of dead cats.)

Refining an issue's solution is more complicated than refining a problem's. The solution to an issue must overcome not only objections, but also the powerful emotional resistance that exists on both sides of the dispute. (Both sides may sincerely want an end to the controversy, but on opposing terms.) In other words, the solution to an issue must *bridge the controversy.*

This requirement adds one question to the basic four above. That question is "How sound is your argument?" Because your answer may force you to change the solution, it is best asked before the other questions.

A SAMPLE PROBLEM

The following problem was included in Chapter 9's applications.

You are the editor of the college newspaper. Your staff consists of two other people who limit their work to a few hours a week. In order to get the paper out each week, you've had to spend many more hours than your course load permits. On several occasions you've stayed up all night and slept through the next morning's classes. You've tried putting ads in the paper to get more staff members, but no one answers them.

Let's say you identified the problem as "How to reward students for joining the staff." (This is one good expression of the problem, though not, of course, the only one.) Let's say further that, after investigating the problem and producing a number of possible solutions, you chose *giving college credit to those who work on the paper* as the best one. Here is how to apply the critical approach.

1. How exactly will your solution be applied?

Here you'd have to decide and list the requirements for obtaining credit for the work. You'd also have to decide which department would grant credit, how much credit would be granted, and whether it would be elective credit or would fulfill some course requirement.

2. What difficulties could arise in the application and how would these best be overcome?

The most obvious difficulty would involve course requirements and evaluation of student performance. Who would teach the course? Where? (In a classroom? In the newspaper office?) How could one, two, or three time periods per week satisfy the demands of producing the paper? How would the instructor evaluate performance? Would the editor have to meet a different standard than a reporter or layout person? If so, how would the registrar clarify what standard was met on each student's transcript? These and other questions would have to be not only raised, but answered satisfactorily.

3. Why might others resist this solution? What modifications could you make to overcome this resistance?

Here you'd consider such reasons as the inappropriateness of the new course to any curriculum on campus (assuming the campus did not offer a journalism major), the lack of journalistic expertise among campus faculty, and the possible course overload the solution would represent for faculty.

4. Whom would you have to persuade of the solution's value? What kind of presentation would be most likely to persuade them?

You'd surely have to persuade the college administration and the faculty, particularly the faculty of the department you would have teach the course.

A SAMPLE ISSUE

The following issue was included in Chapter 8's applications.

In many third world countries the United States is faced with a difficult choice. We can either support the existing governments and risk alienating the masses of people who are victimized by them, or we can support rebel groups and drive the existing governments into closer relationships with Moscow and Cuba. Identify and solve this problem. . . .

Let's say you identified the issue as "How to support existing governments without alienating the masses of people, but rather winning their friendship and support." (This is a good expression of the problem, but not the only one.) Let's also say that after investigating the problem and producing a number of possible solutions, you chose *giving all aid in the form of technological education and employment opportunities, with the stipulation that the governments end all victimization of the people* as the best one. Here is how you would apply a critical approach.

1. How sound is your argument?

This step involves examining the evidence supporting your solution and the reasoning behind it in the same analytical way you examine other people's arguments. To accomplish this, you would ask whether your evidence is relevant, typical, comprehensive, and obtained from reliable sources. In addition, you'd determine whether your reasoning is free of flaws (for example, errors of narrow perspective, confusion, or carelessness).* Since your reasoning is not formally stated in the solution to this case, you'd first identify it by asking *why* your solution is the best one to the problem. Your answer might be as follows: "The best support of a government is that which reaches the people most directly and helps them become both skilled and independent. The aid (and the stipulation) I propose would accomplish this better than any other aid proposal. Therefore it is the best one." If your examination revealed any weaknesses in your argument, you would correct them and, if necessary, modify your solution.

2. How exactly will your solution be applied?

Here you'd have to detail the kinds of technological education and employment opportunities you have in mind. You'd also have to decide whether the teachers and employers would be sponsored by our government, private enterprise, or a combination of the two. Finally, you'd have to detail any special employment conditions, including wages and benefits.

3. What difficulties could arise in applying your solution?

The most obvious difficulty would be policing the country's government—how would you ensure that the government ended victimization? Another diffi-

---

*The most searching examination of your reasoning will involve considerably more than this general determination. Because of its importance, all of Chapter 12 is devoted to this kind of rumination.

culty would be how to achieve the workers' technological education in a reasonable time, given the problems of illiteracy and disease.

> **4.** What reasons might others find for resisting your solution? What modifications could you make . . . ?

The principal difficulty would undoubtedly be the view that arms aid is the more important need, and that by eliminating it you would endanger the government's stability. (This is a matter you might compromise on.) Another objection might come from those opposing all aid to existing governments and favoring rebel forces. (Here you might compromise by strengthening your check on the government—for example, by proposing that a United Nations task force monitor governmental activities, and by suggesting profit-sharing plans and worker cooperatives to give the lower classes more power. This would overcome some of the issues the rebels are concerned about.)

> **5.** Whom will you have to persuade . . . ?

The problem here, as in all controversial issues, is that any concession to one side of the issue alienates the other side. This is a dilemma that challenges your creativity. In meeting it, be sure to remember that the greater opposition will always come from the side your proposal is less favorable to.

One final suggestion. If you ever become discouraged about imperfections and complications in your work—if you are inclined to say "How can I ever be expected to work out all the flaws I discover? It's an impossible task!"—try this approach: Treat each significant imperfection or complication as a new problem, first finding the best expression, investigating it if necessary, and finally generating as many possible solutions as you can. In short, treat it as a miniature problem. Not every issue warrants such meticulous attention. But the more important ones will. And by using a familiar process to address them, you bolster your confidence as well as stimulate your imagination.

WARM-UP EXERCISES

10.1. Ozzie and Harriet are sitting at the breakfast table, quietly drinking their morning coffee. Ozzie seems deep in thought. Finally, he speaks.

> OZZIE: Anyone who believes what he reads is a fool.
> HARRIET: What an insult to the reader!
> OZZIE: What reader do you mean?
> HARRIET: Any reader.
> OZZIE: What do you mean?
> HARRIET: Think about what you said for a minute and you'll see.

Explain what Harriet means and whether you agree with her.

10.2. A hunter sees a squirrel on the trunk of a tall tree. He approaches quietly, but the squirrel hears him and scampers to the other side of the tree. The hunter follows the squirrel around the tree, but the squirrel is very clever—he keeps moving at the same pace as the hunter. Around and around they move at exactly the same pace, on into the night. The question is: Does the hunter ever go around the squirrel? Explain your answer.

10.3. Zane is sprawled on the dormitory lounge couch, holding forth on various matters of great philosophic import. As you approach, you hear him say the following:

One of the biggest problems in the criminal justice system today is the backlog of cases in the courts. And that backlog gets bigger every day. There's no hope of adding more judges with the economy in the shape that it's in. But there is an answer. It's to abolish trials for suspects who freely confess to crimes.

No one says anything. Zane turns to you and says, "Makes sense, doesn't it?" What do you answer? Be sure to explain your position thoroughly.

APPLICATIONS

10.1. In the Application 7.9 you applied your creativity to a question concerning the quality of American workers' performance and their attitudes toward work. (See page 102.) Refine your best solution to that application using the approach explained in this chapter.

10.2. In the Application 9.9 you applied your creativity to a question concerning drunk driving. (See page 126.) Refine your best solution using the approach explained in this chapter.

10.3. Since you graduated from high school, you've been wondering what single improvement could be made in your school system between kindergarten and twelfth grade that would have the best and most lasting impact on students. Now you've come up with the answer—have the students be taught *how to think,* directly and systematically. Now take that idea and refine it.

10.4. You are a Hollywood film producer. You have just been tried in federal court for agreeing to buy 5 ounces of cocaine. The judge deferred final judgment of your case for a year, but put you on probation and offered you this challenge: "If you put your talents to work fighting drug abuse by children, I will wipe your record clean." You feel remorse for your own drug use and resolve to meet the challenge. Identify and solve this problem, then refine your best solution.

10.5. Tens of thousands of shoplifting arrests are made across the country every year. In many cases the shoplifters have a checkbook, a credit card, or enough cash to pay for what they steal. To jail these offenders costs the taxpayers money. Yet to treat them leniently encourages shoplifting and adds to the cost of consumer goods. Identify and solve this problem, then refine your best solution.

10.6. Your older sister shares this personal problem with you. Her daughter is only a toddler, but before long your sister will have to explain the best advice about being honest in daily life. Yet she herself is confused. Here's how she explains her dilemma to you. "Mom and Dad always told us that 'honesty is the best policy' in every case. Yet every other day, it seems, I read about some worker who reports corruption in his company or in government and then loses his job for his honesty. I want to give my daughter the best advice, and yet I'm not sure what the best advice is." Identify and solve your sister's problem, then refine your best solution.

10.7. There's probably not a home in the land that has managed to avoid wrangling over whether the parents' generation or the children's generation had a more difficult time growing up. Apply your creative and critical thinking to this issue as you did in previous applications.

10.8. Michael is very excited. He has just gotten his first job, delivering newspapers in a residential neighborhood. The only problem is that his route has several large dogs on it and he has been afraid of dogs as long as he can remember. Identify and solve Michael's problem, then refine your best solution.

10.9. For as long as anyone in your town can remember, there has been a manger scene on the village square at Christmastime. But this year a group of civil libertarians and atheists challenged the placing of such scenes on public property, claiming a violation of the constitutional prohibition of the "establishment of religion." There is strong feeling on both sides of the question. Identify and solve this problem, then refine your best solution.

10.10. Approximately 23 million American adults, 1 out of every 5, is functionally illiterate. These people cannot decipher a bus, train, or airline schedule, write a letter, or fill out a job application. Such illiteracy is estimated to cost the United States $6 billion a year in welfare and unemployment payments. With the federal government decreasing its aid to education, that cost is likely to increase.[1] Apply your creative and critical thinking to this problem as you did in previous applications.

10.11. Zeb and Jeb are engaged in a spirited discussion. Read it carefully, identify and resolve the issue, then refine your best solution.

ZEB: There's one thing I don't think belongs in our Constitution.

JEB: What's that?

ZEB: The freedom of religion clause.

JEB: But that's one of the basic freedoms we all enjoy.

ZEB: As I see it, it's a dangerous business allowing people to practice any religion they want with no restrictions. What if people want to worship the devil. Do you think that's right?

JEB: No, I don't personally, but I wouldn't deny others the right to do so.

ZEB: You're just repeating empty formulas you were taught. What if a group made sexual orgies their main ritual. Would you approve that?

JEB: Hey, man. Where do I sign up for that religion?

ZEB: Be serious. There were lots of religions in the past that practiced some pretty weird and disgusting things. Like the sacrifice of young girls to ensure a good harvest and the murdering of servants so some king or queen could be properly attended in the afterlife. Do you approve of that kind of stuff?

JEB: No, I guess not, but . . .

ZEB: Right. The more you think about the issue, the more you've got to agree my fears make good sense. We should change the Constitution.

chapter *11*

Refine Your Solution to the Problem

How might the human voice be carried over distances beyond the normal range of hearing? That was the problem facing Alexander Graham Bell. The solution, as we all know, was the telephone. But how did Bell actually invent it? Most of us probably have the vague notion that once he got his creative idea, he merely retired to his workshop, built a model of the machine, sold it, and became rich and famous. In fact, it wasn't that simple. Although Bell was an expert in sound, he knew virtually nothing about electricity. Before he was able to make his idea a reality, he had to learn all about electricity and then put his knowledge to work and solve the technical problems.

The refinement of solutions to problems does not always demand learning an entirely new field, but it is seldom the easy matter many people assume. As Eliot Hutchinson explains:

> There is nothing trifling, incidental or dilettantish about this business of [refining solutions]. It is work, days and nights of it, months and years of it, the perspiration that is nine-tenths genius. And it tires, discourages, exhausts. . . . The history both of art and of science is largely the history of man's personal endurance, his acceptance of labor as the price of success. To be sure, some men dash off a brilliant piece of work, spread themselves for a time. But 90 per cent of reputable authors, no matter how sure their technique, and well-nigh all reputable scientists revamp their work until what was given in insight is so overlaid with secondary material that it is hardly to be recognized. Elaboration is for the mature only; it is for the rigorous, the exacting, the profound.[1]

THREE STEPS IN REFINING

Because refinement can spell the difference between success and failure, you should approach it very seriously. Yet there is no reason to be frightened by the task. It usually requires no special gift or talent. Rather, it is achievable by anyone willing to work hard and patiently. Three steps are involved: working out the details of the solution, finding imperfections and complications, and making improvements.

Step 1: Working Out the Details

This means determining exactly how your solution will be applied. It's easy to overlook this step or to ignore its significance. After all, most of the things we use every day and take for granted—the concepts, the processes and systems, the products and services—appear to us in refined form. We seldom have occasion even to imagine how they appeared in rough form, or to appreciate the difficult challenges their refinement posed for their creators.

Consider the ballpoint pen. It was first conceived of in the United States in 1888 by John Loud. He even obtained a patent for his idea of using a rotating ball to deliver the ink to the paper. Yet he never was able to refine the pen enough to make it write cleanly. In 1919, Lasalo Biro of Hungary reinvented this pen, but was unable to complete his design and market his idea until 1943—and even then the ink came out in splotches. Finally, Franz Seech of Austria worked out the basic difficulties in 1949 (the key to his pen's performance was fast-drying ink) and marketed his pen successfully. Thus *61 years* elapsed from conception to refinement.[2]

When William Addis, a prisoner in a British jail, got the idea for the first toothbrush in 1870, he faced a number of challenges to his ingenuity. (In case you didn't know, before 1870 people cleaned their teeth by rubbing them with a rag.) What would be the right size for the invention? What shape would be best? What should it be made of? What kind of bristles would work best? How should they be held together? What could be used to contain the bristles? Addis saved a bone from his supper, bored tiny holes in it, obtained some bristles from his prison guard, cut, tied, and glued them together, and inserted them into the bone. When he was released from prison, he marketed his invention and became a business success.[3]

The refinement of the typewriter posed even greater challenges. How to place the keys, how to arrange the keyboard, how to make the keys strike, how to hold the paper, how to make it move so that the keys wouldn't strike the same place over and over, how to move from line to line without turning the carriage by hand, how to ink the keys—these were just some of the details that had to be worked out! In light of the numerous and complex problems, it is perhaps not surprising that before Christopher Sholes and Samuel Soulé completed their first working model in 1867, *51 other inventors* had tried and failed.[4]

We could cite many other examples of the refinement difficulties facing the originators of most new ideas. The point is that even the most creative idea does not become useful until the details of its application are worked out. The following approach will help you work out the details of your solutions more effectively:

> If your solution involves *doing* something (as, for example, in a new process), answer these questions:

- How exactly is it to be done, step by step?
- By whom is it to be done?
- When is it to be done? (According to what timetable?)
- Where is it to be done?
- Who will finance it?
- What tools or materials, if any, are to be used?
- From what source will they be obtained?
- How and by whom will they be transported?
- Where will they be stored?
- What special conditions, if any, will be required for the solution to be carried out?

> If your solution involves *making* something (as in a new product), answer these questions:

- How will it work? Be specific.
- What will it look like? Be specific as to size, shape, color, texture, and any other relevant descriptive details.
- What material will it be made of?
- What will the product cost to make?
- Who will pay for it?
- How exactly will it be used?
- Who will use it? When? Where?
- How will it be packaged?
- How will it be delivered?
- How will it be stored?

Step 2: Finding Imperfections and Complications

After you have worked out the details of your solution, your next step is to examine those details for imperfections. Remember that despite the normal tendency to regard your solution as perfect and to view this step as unnecessary, it is almost certain that your solution, like any other, contains at least minor flaws. Remember, too, that your success in persuading others of your solution's value will depend in no small part on your willingness to improve your idea in any way you can.

Until you are experienced in examining solutions critically, the biggest difficulty you are likely to encounter is knowing what kinds of imperfections and complications to look for, and how to go about looking for them. The following four approaches will prove helpful both in overcoming that initial difficulty and in assuring that your analysis will be comprehensive.

1. Check for common kinds of imperfections The areas listed below are the ones in which imperfections most commonly occur. (Not every one, of course, will apply to every type of solution.) Although the list is not exhaustive, and therefore you should not limit yourself to it, it is an excellent starting point for examining most solutions.

- Clarity—is the solution difficult to understand?
- Safety—Does the solution create any danger for those who use it or those for whom it is used?
- Convenience—Is the solution awkward to use or implement?
- Efficiency—Does using the solution involve significant delays?
- Economy—Is the solution too costly to build or implement?
- Simplicity—Is the solution unnecessarily complex in design or format?
- Comfort—Is the solution uncomfortable to use?
- Durability—Is the solution likely to break or malfunction?
- Beauty—Will most people find the solution ugly or unappealing?
- Compatibility—Does the solution clash with any other product or process it should harmonize with?

2. Compare the solution with competing ones Examine the existing product or process your solution is designed to replace, or study another proposed solution competitive with yours. Determine how the existing product, process, or competing solution has the advantage over yours. (Although your solution should be superior in most major respects, there will often be one or two inferior respects. Any such area should be considered an imperfection.)

3. Consider what changes your solution will cause Ask yourself what will occur if your solution is implemented. Don't overlook even minor changes. Decide which of them, if any, will cause complications.

4. Consider the effects your solution will have on people Look among the physical, moral, emotional, intellectual, and financial areas of life to see how any would be affected. Be sure to consider even the remote effects that might occur to any person or group. Most of the changes you list will undoubtedly be beneficial. But those that are in any way undesirable will often signal imperfections or complications in your solution.

Step 3: Making Improvements

The third and final step in refining your solutions is to make improvements that will eliminate imperfections. Here, classified according to the kinds of solutions they are usually associated with, are the kinds of improvements you will find applicable in most situations.

For a new or revised *concept:*

- Change the terminology—make it simpler, easier to remember, more eye-catching
- Change the way it is explained—use different illustrations, analogies, and so on
- Change the application—use it in other situations or in different ways

For a new or revised *process, system,* or *service:*

- Change the way it is done, the step-by-step approach
- Change who does it
- Change the place it is done in
- Change the tools or materials used
- Change the source from which the tools or materials are obtained
- Change the place the tools or materials will be stored
- Change the conditions required

For a new or modified *product:*

- Change its size, shape, color, texture, and so on
- Change its composition (the material it is made of)
- Change the way it is used
- Change who will use it, or when or where it will be used
- Change the way it is packaged or delivered
- Change the way it is stored

Whenever you address an imperfection and are trying to think of ways to improve your solution, be sure to consider using the approaches for producing possible solutions explained in Chapter 9. Specifically, you should consider *forcing uncommon responses, using free association and analogy, looking for unusual combinations,* and *visualizing the possibilities.* Each imperfection and complication is, after all, a miniproblem in itself and will therefore respond to the creative process much as the larger problem did.

Most importantly, be sure not to settle for the first improvement idea that occurs to you. Instead, extend your effort to produce ideas, and withhold judgment of any one idea until you have produced a generous number of possibilities.

Occasionally you will encounter an imperfection that requires you to return to the second stage of the creative process and investigate the matter more deeply —much as Alexander Graham Bell did when he took time out to master the principles of electricity. In extreme cases you may even find that your solution is too badly flawed to be workable. At such times you will feel as if all your efforts were wasted. But they will not really have been wasted. *To find out what does not work is an important step toward finding out what does.*

TWO SAMPLE PROBLEMS

The First Problem

Now let's apply this approach to some cases and note how it works. The first case concerns Rocco, the manager of the movie theater. His problem was discussed in Application 7.10. "In recent years, a number of competitors have cut into his business, and Home Box Office has reduced the number of moviegoers still further. Rocco desperately needs to get more people to patronize his theater, particularly since he has begun to hear the owners talk of closing it and dismissing him if box office receipts don't improve."

Let's say that after considering several expressions of this problem, you decide that the best is "How to attract moviegoers away from other theaters to Rocco's, and how to attract people that ordinarily don't go to movie theaters." Let's say, further, that after investigating the problem and producing a number of possible solutions, you decide that three ideas, in combination, are the best solution—to present interesting displays, to provide entertainment, and to offer discounts to groups. Here is how you would refine this solution. (Only one or two ideas are provided for each point. You would, of course, consider many more in your analysis.)

Step 1: Working Out the Details

To present interesting displays:

- What displays? Arts and crafts, for example.
- Which artists and craftspeople? There would be no restrictions.
- How would Rocco find people to display their work? He could check with area arts and crafts councils.
- Where would the displays be set up? In the lobby.
- What supplies would be needed and how would they be provided? Tables, chairs, and display shelves. Each displayer would provide his or her own.

To provide entertainment:

- What entertainment? Amateur or professional musicians, performing individually or in small groups.
- How would Rocco find them? He could advertise on posters in the lobby or check with area high school music teachers or the local musicians' union.
- How would he pay them? He could let them pass the hat for donations from theater patrons, or let them put up a sign listing their phone number, so they could get jobs by word of mouth among theater patrons.

To offer discounts to groups:

- Which groups? Senior citizens' organizations, employees of particular businesses in the area, members of a union (any union).

- How would he let people know of this discount? He could highlight the fact in his usual newspaper advertisements.

Steps 2 and 3: Finding and Overcoming Imperfections and Complications
To present interesting displays in the lobby:

- Complication—Such displays might block the flow of traffic in and out of the theater and thus create problems of inconvenience and even a violation of the safety code.
- Improvement—Limit the number of displays provided and put them in an out-of-the-way corner. Change them each week.

To provide entertainment:

- Complication—The musicians' union might object to members working for no pay.
- Improvement—Limit the entertainment to young amateurs (high school students, for example).
- Complication—Amateurs might not want to hire out for other jobs, so advertising their skills might not be an incentive.
- Improvement—Pay them in free admissions, one week free for every night of playing.

To offer discounts to groups:

- Imperfection—Senior citizens might not want to attend at night because they fear street crime.
- Improvement—Offer them discounts for matinees.

The Second Problem

We first encountered the second problem in Application 9.14. It was phrased this way: "Going to the hospital for the first time can be a frightening experience, particularly for small children. Think of as many ways as you can to make the children's ward of a hospital a nonthreatening, cheery place."

Let's say your best solution to this problem was a combination of these ideas —to have the hospital staff dress in colorful outfits, to have children's music playing, and to decorate the lounge appealingly. Here is how you would refine this solution. (As in the previous case, only one or two ideas are provided for each point. You would consider many more in your analysis.)

Step 1: Working Out the Details
To have the staff dress in colorful outfits:

- What would the colors be? Would the uniforms have a design on them? They'd be pastel colors and have pictures of animals, clowns, and nursery rhyme characters on them.

- Who would wear them? Doctors, nurses, aides, secretaries—anyone who worked on the children's ward.
- What kinds of outfits would they be? Lab coats for the doctors, smocks or aprons for the secretaries, nurses, and aides.

To have children's music playing:

- What kind of music? Nursery songs, songs from Disney movies, songs from The Muppet Show, and so on.
- Where would the music be playing? Throughout the children's ward—rooms, halls, and in the lounge.

To decorate the lounge appealingly:

- What decorating ideas would you use? I'd have special furniture made and use wallpaper on the walls.
- What furniture specifically, and what would be special about it? Child-size heavy plastic furniture—chairs, bookcases, a table for games, perhaps a small seesaw. Each piece would be in a bright color and be shaped like an animal. For example, a chair could be shaped like a kangaroo, with the seat where the pouch would be.
- What pattern would you have for the wallpaper? Scenes from Mother Goose.

Steps 2 and 3:   *Finding and Overcoming Imperfections and Complications*
To have colorful outfits:

- Complication—Doctors would be unlikely to want to dress in, say, a Pluto coat. People on other wards might think them strange when they made their hospital rounds. Nurses and others would undoubtedly object to such an unprofessional outfit too, even though they'd be sympathetic to the idea of making the ward cheery.
- Improvement—Let the *children* have colorful gowns and even colorful sheets instead.

To have children's music playing:

- Imperfection—Children's music at the nurses' station might upset the work being done there. And it wouldn't be appropriate in some rooms, either—for example, the rooms with very ill children or those who have just returned from surgery.
- Improvement—Have the music piped into the rooms of those who want it. Also, have it playing quietly in the lounge.

To decorate the lounge appealingly:

- Complication—The cost of such extensive redecorating and refurnishing might be prohibitive for the hospital.

- Improvement—Appeal to a local service organization (Lions, Kiwanis, Rotary, for example) to donate funds.

All the improvements presented overcome the imperfections and complications they address without creating new difficulties. Naturally, not all the improvements you think of will do this. Many will create greater imperfections and complications than the ones they correct. For this reason, you should exercise care in selecting your improvements.

WARM-UP EXERCISES

11.1. Is it possible for you to think of a city or a country that you have never been to? Explain your answer thoroughly.

11.2. In the following dialogue Lily admits she is confused. Perhaps Daisy is too. Clear up the confusion for them.

DAISY: What is the meaning of life?

LILY: There is no one meaning.

DAISY: There's got to be—otherwise everyone makes his own, and that would create chaos.

LILY: No, everyone *decides* his own. Whatever he says, that's it.

DAISY: Do you mean if I say the meaning of life is "Eat, drink, and be merry for tomorrow we die," then that *is* the meaning of life.

LILY: Yes, for *you* it is, though maybe not for me.

DAISY: That would mean no one can be wrong in his view. And if that's the case, why is everyone so concerned about finding the meaning of life?

LILY: I don't know. That's always puzzled me.

11.3. A law student hired a tutor to help him with his law studies, and promised to pay for the tutor's services as soon as he passed his bar exam, set up practice and won his first case. He subsequently passed the exams and set up practice, but a year passed and he still had not won a case. The tutor grew tired of waiting and sued him for payment. The young lawyer then wrote the tutor a letter and said, "If your suit against me goes to court and I win it, I won't have to pay you. And if I lose it, I still won't have to pay you, because the terms of our agreement (my winning my first case) will not have been met." Do you agree with the young lawyer's reasoning? Explain thoroughly.[5]

APPLICATIONS

11.1. The Surgeon General has termed cigarette smoking "the chief preventable cause of death in our society." In addition, cigarette smoking costs as high as $13 billion a year in health care expenses and more than $25 billion in lost production and wages.[6] Yet it continues to be appealing to many people, including teenagers. Identify and solve this problem, then refine your best solution as explained in the chapter.

11.2. According to one estimate, there are 2 million homeless people in the United States.

They include alcoholics, drug addicts, derelicts, and the mentally deficient who were released from institutions but have no place to go. These people live on the streets seeking whatever temporary shelter they can find, and often lack proper food and clothing.[7] Identify and solve this problem, then refine your best solution as explained in the chapter.

11.3. Most experts seem to agree that children from one-parent homes have more problems (including health problems) than children from two-parent homes.[8] Yet one-parent families are on the increase not only because of the high divorce rate; but also because it has become fashionable among some unmarried middle class women to have a child and raise it alone, and among some homosexual males to hire a woman to bear their child so that they can "reproduce themselves." Identify and solve this problem, then refine your best solution as explained in the chapter.

11.4. Several years ago you bought a house for $90,000, about twice the amount you could comfortably afford at the time. Because your business prospects seemed favorable, you expected to be in much better financial shape in a year or two. Unfortunately those prospects did not materialize. Now you'd like to sell the house (you can't afford the mortgage payments much longer), but the interest rates are so high you haven't been able to find a buyer. Identify your problem and solve it, then refine your best solution as explained in the chapter.

11.5. College athletes are supposed to be amateurs. That is, they are not allowed to receive money for performing their sport. The National Collegiate Athletic Association publishes a 322-page rule manual governing the way colleges recruit athletes, the academic requirements athletes must meet to remain eligible for play, and the limitations on financial and other assistance they may receive. But college athletics is big business—national rankings bring lucrative television payments to colleges and help finance costly educational programs. So colleges are tempted to ignore the NCAA rules. In 1982, 17 colleges were on probation for doing so, and 35 investigations were pending. And Notre Dame's well-known basketball coach "Digger" Phelps publicly stated that at least 7 colleges, and probably more, pay their star basketball players $10,000 a year under the table.[9] Identify and solve this problem, then refine your best solution as explained in the chapter.

11.6. According to a Gallup poll of the public's attitudes toward the public schools, 79 percent of those surveyed favor instruction in morals and moral behavior. An even larger percentage of parents of schoolchildren (84 percent) favor such instruction.[10] Any actual plan for moral education would, of course, have to be acceptable in form and content to people of widely varying backgrounds and beliefs. Identify and solve this problem, then refine your best solution as explained in the chapter.

11.7. You are the parent of two children, an 8-year-old daughter and a 6-year-old son. They love to watch television, but you believe that most programs are either a waste of time or promote harmful attitudes and values. Identify and solve this problem, then refine your best solution as explained in the chapter.

11.8. In recent years a great deal has been written about the problem of child abuse. Most people are aware that there are agencies to call to report actual or suspected abuse cases—that is, there are ways to deal with child abuse when it has occurred. But there seems to be no effective way to prevent it from occurring. Identify and solve this problem, then refine your best solution as explained in the chapter.

11.9. The Federal Communications Act of 1927 established in law that the airways belong to the public. Radio and television station licenses are supposedly granted only if the station's programming practices serve the public interest. Yet the practice of interrupting programs every 10 minutes with commercials that all too often assault the senses and insult the minds of viewers is, in the judgment of most people, decidedly not a service to the public. Identify and solve this problem, then refine your best solution as explained in the chapter.

11.10. Professor Danielle Murphy teaches literature at a small liberal arts college. She begins every term hoping to do little lecturing and to devote the larger part of each class period to class discussion. Yet she is invariably disappointed with student response. No matter what the assigned work of literature, only one or two students will volunteer their comments, and discussion quickly fizzles out. The rest of the class sit and stare at their desks, or cast nervous glances at the clock. Identify and solve Professor Murphy's problem, then refine your best solution as explained in the chapter.

chapter *12*

Evaluate Your Argument on the Issue

Evaluating your argument on an issue means looking at the argument critically to determine if it is sound—that is, free from error. There are two broad kinds of error to consider. The first affects the *validity* of the argument, the quality of the reasoning by which the conclusion is reached. The second affects the *truth or relevance* of the argument, the degree to which each statement reflects reality or meets the issue's demands. A sound argument is not only valid, but also true and relevant.

ERRORS AFFECTING VALIDITY

To determine an argument's validity, we must examine the entire argument. It is the relationship between the premises and the conclusion that make an argument valid or invalid. The logical principles governing the validity of arguments are the substance of *formal logic,* the area of logic concerned with the various forms of argument. Since a detailed treatment of formal logic is beyond the scope of this book,* we will focus on an essential error that commonly occurs in controversial issues. That is the *illegitimate conclusion.*

An illegitimate conclusion is one which does not follow logically from the premises preceding it. Before examining an illegitimate conclusion, let's first look at a legitimate one:

---

*For a brief introduction to the basic principles of formal logic, see "The Fundamentals of Logic" in Appendix A.

Anything that shortens people's attention span harms their concentration. Television commercials shorten people's attention span. Therefore television commercials harm people's concentration.

This conclusion is legitimate because if *anything* that shortens people's attention span harms concentration, and if television commercials do shorten that span, they therefore *must* harm people's concentration. Commercials, after all, are *a thing,* so they fit in the *anything* specified in the first premise. When we are checking for the validity of the reasoning, remember, we are not checking for the truth of the premises or conclusion. That concern is a separate matter. Thus even a ludicrous argument could be technically valid. Here is one such variation:

Anything that gives people indigestion harms their concentration. Television commercials give people indigestion. Therefore television commercials harm people's concentration.

Let's now look at some illegitimate conclusions and see what makes them so.

All people who take courses significantly above their level of competency will surely fail. Samantha is taking a course well within her level of competency. Therefore Samantha will surely pass.

Even if it were true that all people who take courses well above their competency level necessarily fail, this would not eliminate the possibility of other reasons for failure, reasons that apply to the competent as well as the incompetent. In other words, the first premise does not imply that *only* the incompetent will fail. Samantha may be extraordinarily proficient and still fail because she cuts classes and does not submit the required work.

Here is another example of an illegitimate conclusion:

People who care about the environment will support the clean air bill now before Congress. Senator Boychik supports the clean air bill. Therefore Senator Boychik cares about the environment.

The first premise of this argument says that people—all people*—who care about the environment will support the bill. However, it does not say that no one else will support the bill. Thus it leaves open the possibility that some who do not care will also support it, perhaps for political reasons. Which group Boychik belongs to is unclear. Therefore the conclusion is illegitimate.

Illegitimate conclusions can also occur in hypothetical (If . . . then) reasoning. Of course, not all hypothetical reasoning is faulty. Here is an example of a valid hypothetical argument:

*Though the premise says *people,* not *all people,* the sense of *all* is clearly conveyed. Usually, when no qualifying word or phrase—such as *some, many, the citizens of Peoria*—is present, then we presume the universal *all* is intended.

> If a person uses a gun in the commission of a crime, <u>then</u> he should be given an additional penalty. Simon used a gun in the commission of a crime. <u>Therefore</u> Simon should be given an additional penalty.

The first premise sets forth the conditions under which the additional penalty should be applied. The second presents a case which fits those conditions. The conclusion that the penalty should apply in that case is legitimate. Here, in contrast, is an illegitimate conclusion:

> If a person uses a gun in the commission of a crime, <u>then</u> he should be given an additional penalty. Simon was given an additional penalty for his crime. <u>Therefore</u> Simon used a gun in the commission of the crime.

Here the first premise sets forth one condition for an additional penalty. It does not *exclude* the possibility of other conditions carrying additional penalties. For this reason, we have no way of knowing whether Simon's additional penalty was for using a gun or for some other reason.

The following is another example of an illegitimate conclusion:

> If a person has great wealth, he can get elected to political office. Governor Mindless got elected to political office. Therefore Governor Mindless has great wealth.

The first premise of this argument specifies one way of getting elected. There may be others. Did Governor Mindless get elected in this or some other way? We can't be sure from the information given, so the conclusion is illegitimate.

Occasionally an illegimate conclusion in hypothetical arguments takes a slightly different form; the reversal of conditions. The following argument illustrates this:

> If the death penalty is reinstated, the crime rate will drop. Therefore, if the rate of crime is reduced, the death penalty will be reinstated.

The error here is reversing what is not necessarily reversible. The clear implication in the first premise is that there is a cause and effect relationship between the reinstatement of the death penalty and a drop in the crime rate. To reverse that relationship makes the effect the cause, and vice versa. Such a reversal does not logically follow.

A SPECIAL PROBLEM: THE HIDDEN PREMISE

An argument's expression in ordinary discussion or writing is not always as precise as our examples seen. The sentence order may vary—the conclusion, for example, may come first. In place of the word *therefore,* a variety of signal words may be used. *So* and *It follows that* are two common substitutes. Sometimes no signal word is used. These variations make the evaluation of an argument a little more time-consuming, but they pose no real difficulty. There is, however, a variation that *can* cause real difficulty—the *hidden premise*. A hidden premise, known in formal logic as an *enthymeme,* is a premise implied but not stated. Here is an example of an argument with a hidden premise:

ARGUMENT WITH PREMISE HIDDEN	SAME ARGUMENT, PREMISE EXPRESSED
Liberty means responsibility. That is why most men dread it.	Liberty means responsibility. Most men dread responsibility. Therefore most men dread liberty.

There is nothing necessarily wrong with having a hidden premise. It is not an error. In the above case, the hidden premise argument is from the writing of George Bernard Shaw. In either of the forms shown, the argument is perfectly valid. The only problem with hidden premises is that they obscure the reasoning behind the argument and make evaluation difficult. Accordingly, whenever a premise is hidden, it should be identified and expressed before the argument is evaluated.

Here are several more examples of hidden premise arguments. Note how much easier it is to grasp the reasoning when the hidden premise is expressed.

PREMISE HIDDEN	PREMISE EXPRESSED
Prostitution is immoral, so it should be illegal.	Everything immoral should be illegal. Prostitution is immoral. Therefore, it should be illegal.
Newspapers are a threat to democracy because they have too much power.	All agencies that have too much power are a threat to democracy. Newspapers have too much power. Therefore newspapers are a threat to democracy.
If Brewster Bland is a good family man, then he'll make a good senator.	If a person is a good family man, he'll make a good senator. Brewster Bland is a good family man. Therefore Brewster Bland will make a good senator.

EVALUATING COMPLEX ARGUMENTS

Not all arguments can be expressed in two premises and one conclusion. Many are complex, involving a network of premises and conclusions. Moreover, some of these may be unexpressed, like the hidden premises we have discussed. Consider, for example, this argument:

> People who lack control over their sexual urges are a threat to society, so homosexuals should be banned from the teaching profession.

At first glance, only one premise may seem to be missing from this argument. Actually it is a complex argument and much more is missing. Here is how it would be expressed if nothing were omitted:

> People who lack control over their sex urges are a threat to society. Homosexuals lack control over their sex urges. Therefore homosexuals are a threat to society. Furthermore, people who are a threat to society should be banned from the teaching profession. Homosexuals are a threat to society. Therefore homosexuals should be banned from the teaching profession.

In a world of complex realities, a world of controversial issues with no simple solutions, complex arguments are often unavoidable. Yet such arguments are likely to be flawed precisely because of their complexity. For this reason, we must exercise special care in identifying all the premises and conclusions our arguments contain.

ERRORS AFFECTING TRUTH OR RELEVANCE

Unlike validity errors, errors affecting truth or relevance are not necessarily found in the relationship between premises and conclusion. In fact, in many cases these errors are confined to a single premise. That fact, however, does not make them less harmful to an argument. (Remember that for an argument to be sound, it must not only be valid, but true and relevant as well.) It merely means that they are usually found by testing the accuracy of the premises and the conclusion *as individual statements,* rather than by examining the reasoning that links them.

There are numerous errors affecting truth and relevance. The first and most obvious error of this kind is simple factual inaccuracy. If we have investigated the issue properly and have taken care to verify our evidence wherever possible, such errors should be eliminated. We will therefore limit our consideration to the more subtle errors. They are as follows:

- Either/Or Thinking
- Avoiding the Issue
- Overgeneralizing
- Oversimplifying
- Double Standard
- Shifting the Burden of Proof
- Irrelevant Appeal

Either/Or Thinking

This error consists of believing that only two choices are possible in situations where there are more than two choices. A common example of either/or thinking occurs in the creationism versus evolution debate. Both sides are often guilty of the error. "The biblical story of creation and scientific evolution cannot both be right," they say. "It must be either one or the other." They are mistaken. There is a third possibility—that there is a God who created everything, but did so through evolution. Whether this position is the best one may, of course, be disputed. But it is an error to ignore its existence.

Either/or thinking undoubtedly occurs because in controversy the spotlight is usually on the most obvious positions, those most clearly in conflict. Any other position, particularly a subtle one, is ignored. Such thinking is best overcome by conscientiously searching out all possible views before choosing one. If you find either/or thinking in your position on an issue, ask yourself "Why must it be one view or the other? Why not both or neither?"

Avoiding the Issue

The attorney was just beginning to try the case in court when his associate learned that their key witness had changed his mind about testifying. The associate handed the attorney this note, "Have no case—abuse the other side." That is the form avoiding the issue often takes—deliberately attacking the person in the hope that the issue will be forgotten. It happens with lamentable frequency in politics. The issue being debated may be, for example, a particular proposal for tax reform. One candidate will say, "The reason my opponent supports this proposal is clear —it is a popular position to take. His record is filled with examples of jumping on the bandwagon to gain voter approval. . . ." And so on. Of course, what she says may be true of the opponent, and if it is, then it would surely be relevant to the issue of whether the opponent deserves to to be elected. But it is not relevant to the issue at hand, the tax reform proposal.

Avoiding the issue may not necessarily be motivated by deceit, as the above errors are. It may occur because of unintentional misunderstanding or because of an unconscious slip to something irrelevant. But it is still error, regardless of its innocence. To check your reasoning, look closely at each issue and ask if your solution really responds to it. If it doesn't, make it do so.

Overgeneralizing

Overgeneralizing means taking a valid idea and extending it beyond the limits of reasonableness. Here are some examples of overgeneralizations:

- Women who have abortions are poor and unmarried.
- Convicted criminals must be imprisoned or the public safety will be threatened.

- Women are athletically inferior to men and more emotional than rational.
- Men are coarse and insensitive, inept at cooking and cleaning, and unable to give affection freely.

Each of the above statements could be true at times. That is, we could find examples of poor, unmarried women who have had abortions, convicted criminals whose release would endanger the public, and so on. Yet in each case we could also find examples that do not fit the assertion. That is what makes these statements overgeneralizations. (The fact that your overgeneralizations do not take the most extreme form, stereotypes, which we discussed in Chapter 3, should not make you complacent about correcting them. They still mar your reasoning, usually significantly.)

To find overgeneralizations in your reasoning, be alert to any idea in which *all* or *none* is stated or *implied*. (That is the case in each of the four examples given above.) Occasionally you will find a situation in which *all* or *none* is justified, but in the great majority of cases critical evaluation will reveal it is not valid. To correct overgeneralizations, decide what level of generalization is appropriate and modify your reasoning accordingly. For example, in the four cases discussed, you would consider these possibilities:

Some
Many
Most   . . . of women who have abortions are poor and
All   unmarried.
A specific
  number

Some
Many
Most   . . . of convicted criminals must be imprisoned
All   or the public safety will be threatened.
Certain types

Some
Many
Most   . . . women are athletically inferior to men and
All   more emotional than rational.
In certain cultural
  conditions

Some
Many
Most   . . . men are coarse and insensitive, inept
All   at cooking and cleaning, and unable
In certain cultural   to give affection freely.
  conditions

Oversimplifying

There is nothing wrong with simplifying a complex reality in order to understand it better or to communicate it more clearly to others. Teachers simplify all the time, especially in grade school. Simplification is only a problem when it goes too far—when it goes beyond making complex matters clear and begins to distort them. At that point it ceases to represent reality and *mis*represents it. Such oversimplification is perhaps most often found in reasoning about causes and effects. Here are three examples of this error:

- The cause of the economic recession in the early 1980s was excessive welfare spending.
- The American Nazi party has a beneficial effect on the intellectual life of the country. It reminds people of the constitutional rights of free speech and assembly.
- A return to public executions, shown on prime time television, would make crime less glamorous and thus in time make us a less brutal, more civilized society.

These statements contain an element of truth (many authorities would say a very small element). Yet they do not fairly or accurately represent the reality described. They focus on one cause or effect as if it were the only one. In fact there are others, some of them significant.

To find oversimplifications in your reasoning, ask what important aspects of the issue it ignores. To correct oversimplifications, decide what expression of the matter best reflects the reality without distorting it.

Double Standard

Applying a double standard means judging the same action or point of view differently depending on who does or holds it. It can often be recognized by the use of sharply contrasting terms of description or classification. Thus we may attack a government assistance program as a welfare handout if the money goes to people we don't know or don't identify with, or defend it as a necessary subsidy if it goes to our friends. Similarly, if one country crosses another's border with a military force we may approve the action as a "securing of borders" or condemn it as "naked aggression," depending on our feelings toward the countries involved.

Be careful not to confuse the double standard with legitimate judging of cases according to their circumstances. It is never an error to acknowledge real differences. Accordingly, if you find you have judged a particular case differently from other cases of the same kind, look closely at the circumstances. If they warrant the unusual judgment, you have not been guilty of applying a double standard. However, if they do not warrant it—if your reasoning shows partiality toward one side—you have committed the error and should revise your judgment to make it fair.

Shifting the Burden of Proof

This error consists of making an assertion and then demanding the opposition prove it false. This is an unreasonable demand. The person making the assertion has the burden of supporting it. Though the opposing side may accept the challenge of disproving it, they have no obligation to do so. Suppose, for example, you said to a friend, "Mermaids must exist," your friend disputed you, and you responded, "Unless you can disprove their existence, I am justified in believing in them." You shifted the burden of proof. You made the assertion about mermaids, so it was your responsibility to support it. To overcome this error in your reasoning, identify all the assertions you have made but not supported, and provide adequate support for them. (If you find you cannot support an assertion, withdraw it.)

Irrelevant Appeal

This error bases your position on an appeal not relevant to the particular issue in question. Among the most common forms of irrelevant appeal are the appeal to *common practice* ("Everyone does it"), the appeal to *tradition* ("It has been accepted for a long time"), and the appeal to *fear* ("Awful things could happen"). There is nothing wrong with claiming that an activity is common practice, or that an idea is a tradition, or discussing matters that could trigger fear in your audience. It is only when these are a substitute for substantive reasoning, when they are used to persuade an audience emotionally *rather than* through their minds, that they are misused. To correct irrelevant appeals, refocus your argument on your solution's specific merits.

STEPS IN EVALUATING AN ARGUMENT

The following four steps are an efficient way to apply what you learned in this chapter—in other words, to evaluate your argument and overcome any errors in validity, truth, or relevance it may contain.

1. State your argument fully, as clearly as you can. Be sure to identify any hidden premises and, if the argument is complex, to express all parts of it.
2. Examine your argument for validity errors; consider the reasoning that occurs from premises to conclusion. Determine whether your conclusion is legitimate or illegitimate.
3. Examine each part of your argument for errors affecting truth or relevance. Note any instances of either/or thinking, avoiding the issue, overgeneralizing, oversimplifying, double standard, shifting the burden of proof, or irrelevant appeal.
4. Revise your argument to eliminate any errors you find.

The changes you will have to make in your argument will depend on the kinds of errors you find. Sometimes only minor revision is called for—the adding of a simple qualification, for example, or the substitution of a relevant appeal for an irrelevant one. Occasionally, however, the change required is more dramatic. You may, for example, find your argument so flawed that the only appropriate action is to abandon it altogether and embrace a different argument. On those occasions, you may be tempted to pretend your argument is sound and hope no one will notice the errors. Resist that hope. It is foolish to invest time in refining a solution that you know is based on unsound reasoning.

WARM-UP EXERCISES

12.1. Your little niece looks puzzled. You ask her what's wrong and she says, "It doesn't make sense—we blow on our hands to warm them when they're cold, but we blow on our food to cool it when it's hot. How can blowing make things both hot and cold?" Construct a clear and meaningful reply.

12.2. Oscar and Felix are having a discussion:

OSCAR: I'll prove to you there's no such thing as a pile of sand.

FELIX: That's ridiculous. You can't do it.

OSCAR: Oh yeah. Listen carefully. A single grain of sand is not a pile, right?

FELIX: Right, so what?

OSCAR: If we add another grain of sand, that's still not a pile, right?

FELIX: OK, OK. Get on with it.

OSCAR: If we add another grain, and another, up to 10 million, we'd never reach a point where *no pile of sand* is converted to *pile of sand*. So there's no such thing as a pile of sand.

What should Felix say next to prove Oscar wrong?

12.3. As soon as you enter the room, your roommate challenges you. "You're taking a course in thinking, answer me this—if perfection in anything is beyond human attainment, what's the point in striving to be better in anything?" What do you reply?

APPLICATIONS

12.1. Check each of the following arguments to be sure that it contains no hidden premises and, if it is a complex argument, that all parts are expressed. Revise each, as necessary, to make the expression complete. Then evaluate the argument and decide whether it is sound. Explain your judgment.

a. No one who ever attended this college achieved distinction after graduation. Marvin attends this college. Therefore Marvin will not achieve distinction after graduation.

b. Drug dealing should not be a crime because it does not directly harm others or force them to harm themselves.

c. A mature person is self-directing, so parents who make all their children's decisions for them are doing their offspring a disservice.

d. There's no point in attending Professor Drone's class—all he does is lecture in a boring monotone.

e. Power must be evil because it can corrupt people.

f. If the theory of evolution is true, as scientific evidence overwhelmingly suggests, then man is nothing more than an ape.

g. Rock musicians are contributing to the decline of language by singing in a slurred, mumbling manner.

h. If emphasis on error paralyzes effort, then this college is paying my English professor to make it impossible for me to learn English.

i. Nuclear power is a threat to world peace. Nuclear energy stations generate nuclear power. So nuclear energy stations are a threat to world peace.

j. Lew Fairman is the best candidate for governor because he is in favor of the death penalty.

k. All religious authorities are concerned about the dangers of nuclear war. All statesmen are concerned about the dangers of nuclear war. Therefore all statesmen are religious authorities.

l. The government should undertake a comprehensive censorship program because censorship eliminates undesirable books and films from the market.

m. If the social security system is further weakened, the elderly will have to fear poverty. Therefore if the social security system is not further weakened, the elderly will not have to fear poverty.

n. Challenging other people's opinions is a sign of intolerance, so debating courses have no place on a college campus.

o. It's ridiculous to think that there will be fewer deaths if we ban handguns. Handguns don't kill people—*people* kill people.

p. The antiabortionists say that the fetus is human, but they have not proved it. Therefore they have no reasonable basis for opposing abortion.

q. We must either defeat communism or be defeated by it. To be defeated by communism is unthinkable. Therefore we must defeat communism.

r. There is no way that anyone can ever *deserve* to live better than his neighbors, so capitalism is an immoral economic system.

s. If an expectant mother drinks, smokes, takes drugs, or fails to get proper rest, she may damage her unborn child. Therefore if an expectant mother does these things and her child is born with a defect or ailment that can be traced to them, the mother should face criminal charges.

t. Custom is a form of folk wisdom. In some parts of the world it is customary for "bride buyers" to buy (or sometimes kidnap) young women from their parents and sell them to men looking for wives. Even though we might find this practice distasteful, it would be morally wrong for us to object to others practicing it.

12.2. Identify, investigate (as necessary), and resolve each of the following issues. Be sure you do not just accept your reasoning uncritically. Evaluate it using the approach explained at the end of this chapter. Then decide how you can best overcome difficulties and apply your solution, what modifications in your solution would most effectively overcome resistance, and what kind of presentation would be most persuasive.

a. London test-tube baby pioneer Dr. Robert Edwards and a colleague have announced that they plan to freeze spare embryos and donate them to infertile women. They explain that their test-tube technique involves the removal of eggs from a woman's ovary, fertilization with the husband's sperm, and reimplantation of one of the many embryos that result. Instead of destroying the unused embryos, they propose to offer them (with the mother's permission) to infertile women at a later time. Freezing the embryos will permit implantation at the best moment in the woman's menstrual cycle. A controversy has arisen over the legal and moral implications of the plan.[1]

b. The inclusion of religion in school curricula is not as widely publicized as the issue of prayer in the schools, but it is almost as controversial. Some people are very much in favor of formal religion courses. Others strongly oppose giving religion any place in school activities.

c. A number of states and many foreign countries have programs forcing alcoholics to receive treatment. A person arrested for drunken driving, for example, is required to receive treatment as a stipulation of probation. Or a welfare recipient will be threatened with loss of benefits if he does not comply. The programs range from individual therapy to group therapy to the taking of such drugs as Antabuse (which can make a person violently ill if he drinks within three days after ingesting it). There is sharp disagreement over such programs. Many feel they are a violation of civil rights.[2]

d. Many military authorities say the United States should develop an up-to-date arsenal of chemical warfare weapons to maintain parity with the Soviet Union. Many critics of this view oppose all research and development in chemical warfare.

e. In the past decade thousands of aliens, including many illegal aliens, have come to the United States. The numbers from Mexico, Cuba, and Latin America have been especially great. The traditional attitude in this country has been to accept anyone who wishes to flee poverty or oppression abroad and build a new life here. Many still feel that way. Yet others believe that stricter limits should be imposed, particularly because today's immigrants often come from an entirely different culture and tend to resist assimilation.

f. Pac-Man is a popular entertainer, but he is not welcome everywhere. At least one college administration banned the game from campus out of fear that students would take too much time from their studies to play it.[3] Many people, of course, regard that administration's decision as unreasonable.

chapter 13

Refine Your Solution to the Issue

Evaluating your argument is an important *preliminary* to refining your solution, but it is not the same as refining it. A solution may be based on a sound argument and still contain imperfections and complications. To see the relationship between evaluation and refinement, let's look closely at an actual issue. Peggy Ward, a high school majorette, was declared overweight by her twirling advisor and prevented from twirling her baton at athletic events and other school functions. (Though Peggy's case received an unusual amount of publicity, the problem is fairly common—many high schools around the country have written or unwritten weight standards for majorettes and cheerleaders.) She had tried to meet the standard, which for her at 5 feet 4 inches was a maximum of 126 pounds. But despite severe dieting she tipped the scales at 127.5, so she was benched.[1]

Let's say you identify the issue here as "How can parents and students gain assurance that twirlers will be judged on the basis of ability and not on other, irrelevant bases?" After investigating the issue and producing a number of possible solutions, you decide the best one is to devise a scoring system to be used in the selection process that includes specific twirling skills and marching maneuvers; and to have the selection process monitored by an impartial panel selected by the Parent-Teachers Association.

Next, you evaluate the argument behind your solution. You express that argument as follows:

Skill criteria are the only criteria that should be used in selecting a high school majorette. Weight is not a skill criterion. Therefore weight should not be used as a criterion in the selection of a high school majorette.

You decide that the argument is valid, but that the first premise oversimplifies the matter. Reasonableness demands adding two other criteria to skill criteria—willingness to accept direction in learning and performing twirling routines, and a spirit of cooperation with the other twirlers. You revise your argument to eliminate the oversimplification.

> The criteria of skill in twirling, willingness to accept direction while learning and performing twirling routines, and a spirit of cooperation are the only criteria that should be used in selecting a high school majorette. Weight is not a skill criterion and is not related to learning or cooperation. Therefore weight should not be used as a criterion in the selection of a high school majorette.

Now you are ready to refine your solution. To do this you must address two important questions—How can your solution most effectively bridge any controversy? and What improvements can be made in the details of its application? We will discuss what is entailed in answering each of these questions for controversial issues in general, and then return to our discussion of this case.

BRIDGING THE CONTROVERSY

We have noted that the one great difference between a problem and an issue is that an issue divides people—that is, informed and reasonable people can be found on either side of an issue. Issues are controversial. They create dilemmas, situations where one side or the other will not be completely satisfied no matter what is done. As we saw in Chapter 10, there is no resolution of an issue unless the dilemma is addressed and, to some measurable extent, creatively responded to. In other words, there is no resolution of an issue unless the controversy is bridged.

To bridge a controversy, first recall the particular aspect or aspects of the issue that people disagree most sharply about. State them in their most extreme form. Next remind yourself that, since almost every side possesses some validity, the most reasonable position, the best solution, will usually be found *somewhere between* the two extremes. Remind yourself, too, that in most issues there are not just two sides or three (a neutral one in the middle) to choose from, but many possibilities. You may find it helpful to make these points visual. Here's how you'd do so if the issue were abortion:

Extreme pro position		Extreme con position
Abortion is justified in all cases. A woman may, at any time before delivery, terminate her pregnancy for any reason at all	Neutrality	Abortion is never justified. A woman may never, at any time after conception, terminate her pregnancy for any reason

Next decide where in the scale between the extremes your solution fits. You should be aware that if it is at one of the extremes, the clear implication is that you believe the issue is really not controversial at all, and therefore that the opposing view has not the slightest validity. Likewise, if it is exactly between the extremes, the implication is that the opposing arguments are in exact balance, with neither having the slightest advantage over the other. In either case—if your solution is at one of the extremes or at the point of neutrality—you will need to examine it critically.

Note that last sentence very carefully. It does not say there is anything necessarily wrong with concluding that one side of a controversial issue is completely right and the other completely wrong, or with concluding that the weight of their positions is exactly equal. It says you should look very closely at such a conclusion. The reason for this is that *it seldom bridges the controversy.* If after examining your conclusion you determine that it does not reflect closed mindedness or a desire to evade the issue, if you believe it is the most sensible one, then by all means endorse it. To do otherwise would be intellectually dishonest. But if there is any way you can modify your solution, even slightly, to bridge the controversy more effectively without compromising good sense or honesty, by all means do so.

Finally, determine what negative effects your solution creates or fails to overcome. One effective way of doing this is to imagine the various kinds of cases your solution would have to fit or the various situations that might arise when it is implemented. Use your imagination here. If you have researched the issue well, you should be able to think of a number of cases and situations. They should, of course, be plausible, but don't limit them to the usual and predictable. Often the unusual case reveals negative effects most clearly.

MAKING IMPROVEMENTS

Make whatever revisions in the solution are suggested by your evaluation and your effort to bridge the controversy. Begin by examining the various kinds of situations you felt might arise. Wherever those situations produce a negative effect, consider as many modifications of your solution as you can to overcome it. Next ask which of the following changes associated with solution refinement (and discussed in Chapter 11) are applicable to your solution:

If your solution presents a new or revised *concept,* consider:

- Changing the terminology, making it simpler, easier to remember, more eye catching
- Changing the way it is explained, using different illustrations, analogies, and so on.
- Changing the application, using it in other situations or in different ways.

If your solution presents a new or revised *process, system,* or *service,* consider:

- Changing the way it is done, the step-by-step approach.
- Changing who does it.

- Changing the place it is done in.
- Changing the tools or materials used.
- Changing the source of the tools or materials.
- Changing the place the tools or materials will be stored.
- Changing the required conditions.

If your solution presents a new or modified *product,* consider:

- Changing its size, shape, color, texture, and so on.
- Changing its composition (the material comprising it).
- Changing the way it is used.
- Changing who will use it, or when or where it will be used.
- Changing the way it is packaged or delivered.
- Changing the way it is stored.

THE CASE OF THE MAJORETTE

Now we can proceed with our discussion of the case of the "overweight" majorette. How well does the solution we specified earlier bridge the controversy? That solution, remember, was to devise a scoring system to be used in the selection process, and to monitor that process through an impartial panel. The scoring system would evaluate twirling skills and marching maneuvers, but not a majorette's weight. To decide where this solution fits between the two extreme positions that might be taken on this issue, you'd make the following diagram:

Extreme pro position		Extreme con position
Weight is very relevant; enough to be cause for dismissal from the squad	Neutrality	Weight is totally irrelevant to the selection of a majorette and her continued membership on the squad

You'd look closely at your solution (and at the assumptions behind it), and note that it is on the extreme anti-weight-requirement side. It concedes nothing at all to the opposing side. In effect, it says that there is no basis for controversy. Fortunately, in this case it is possible to modify your position, thereby bridging the controversy. And you can do so without comprising your essential argument. Acknowledge that a *seriously* overweight majorette is not likely to perform her best, nor to look very attractive in the abbreviated costume a majorette wears. (In fact, her appearance could make herself and the rest of the squad the object of derision.) You can agree, further, that there is nothing wrong with encouraging majorettes (or other students) to strive for sensible weight control through good nutrition and regular exercise.

Next, you'd consider any possible negative effects this solution created or failed to overcome. One of the most significant would be the possibility that the squad in general might lose interest in weight control.

Finally, you'd make the improvements in your solution suggested by your evaluation, your effort to bridge the controversy, and your consideration of the common changes that occur in refining solutions. They are as follows:

Evaluation of your argument   Your evaluation led you to add two criteria to the selection process—willingness to accept direction in learning and performing routines, and a spirit of cooperation. But these criteria are difficult to measure and could allow unfairness to enter the selection process. (For example, a judge might cite unwillingness or uncooperativeness when the real decision was made on the majorette's weight.) To overcome this problem, you might specify that these two criteria are not to be judged by the special panel, but by three teachers who have had the candidates in class.

Bridging the controversy   Your effort to bridge the controversy led you to acknowledge that it is better for majorettes not to be seriously overweight. You have no objection to *encouragement* to strive for sensible weight control. Here you'd consider how such encouragement might be given without coercing the majorettes. Your answer might be to have nutrition instruction and weight control added to all twirling classes in junior and senior high school. In addition, you might urge that appropriate exercises be included in those classes.

Consideration of common changes   Not all the possible changes associated with refining solutions are applicable to this problem, but some of those listed under "A New or Revised Process, System, or Service," above, are. Thus you would decide exactly what instruction would be given in nutrition and weight control; who would give it (the twirling instructor? a health teacher? the school nurse? a local doctor?); and what specific materials would be used (for example, a particular pamphlet or book).

THE CASE OF THE RETARDED GIRLS

Let's now turn to another, very different case and see how we would refine it using this approach. We encountered this one in Application 2.7h. The parents of three severely retarded girls, you may remember, brought court action seeking the legal right to make the decision to sterilize the girls. The larger issue here continues to be controversial. Briefly stated, that issue centers around the question "Should anyone have the right to make a significant decision for another person?" Some argue that in cases of retardation, another definitely should have that right. Others believe that such a right endangers personal freedom.

Let's say you define the issue as "How can parents or guardians be allowed the right of determination in extreme cases, such as the case of severe retardation, while at the same time guaranteeing that the right will not be misused?" (This is not the only expression of the problem. It could, for example, be expressed "How can pregnancy in the retarded be prevented without resorting to sterilization?") After investigating the issue and producing a number of possible solutions, you decide that the best answer is to allow parents or guardians the right to make the decision about sterilization for their son or daughter in early childhood, as long as a qualified doctor certifies that there is no reasonable hope that the child will ever be able to meet the responsibilities of parenthood.

Next, you evaluate the argument that underlies your solution. You express that argument as follows:

Those who have the child's interest at heart can be expected to judge wisely if they are properly informed. Most parents or guardians have the child's interest at heart. Therefore most parents or guardians can be expected to judge wisely if they are properly informed. Furthermore, knowing whether the child will ever be able to meet the responsibilities of parenthood constitutes being properly informed. A qualified doctor can tell parents or guardians whether the child will ever be able to meet the responsibilities of parenthood. Therefore a qualified doctor can properly inform parents.

You'd note that the argument (a complex one that cannot be expressed adequately in two premises and a conclusion) is valid and seems both true and relevant. So you'd proceed with your refinement and check how well your solution bridges any controversy. To determine where it fits between the extreme positions on the issue, make the following diagram:

Extreme pro position   Extreme con position

Parents should be | | | | Neutrality | | | | Parents should never
granted the right in   be granted the right
all cases, without
exception

You'd note that your position is on the pro side, but not at the extreme. It includes two important restrictions. The right to sterilize can only be allowed in cases where the child will never be able to meet the responsibilities of parenthood, and a qualified doctor must certify that the criterion is met. Therefore it represents a reasonable effort to bridge the controversy.

Now you'd consider the possible negative effects your solution would create or fail to overcome. You'd imagine a variety of situations that might arise if your solution were implemented. Among them might be the following:

1. The parents have strange notions about sexuality and are obsessed with the fear that their child will bring shame on them. They pressure the doctor to certify that their child will never be able to fulfill parental responsibilities even though that is not really the case. The doctor is qualified, but unscrupulous—as long as his fee is paid, he is willing to certify anything.
2. The parents are responsible and the doctor is not only qualified, but above reproach morally. The decision is made to sterilize the child at age 4. Several years later medical science finds a way to overcome the child's retardation. The child becomes normal, but the sterilization cannot be reversed.

Finally, you'd make the improvements suggested by your evaluation, your effort to bridge the controversy, and your consideration of the common changes that occur in refining solutions. They are as follows:

Evaluation of your argument   You made no revision in your argument, so no improvement would be suggested.

Bridging the controversy   You identified two situations with negative effects. The first involved the possibility of an unscrupulous doctor giving in to parental pressure and certifying sterilization improperly. To overcome this situation you might decide to have a *board* of doctors, rather than a single doctor, responsible for certifying cases where sterilization is warranted. The second situation involves the possibility that medical science will find a way to overcome retardation after sterilization has occurred. Although it might not be possible to overcome this problem completely, its frequency could be reduced by requiring that no sterilization be permitted before the onset of puberty.

Consideration of common changes   Here you would decide such matters as how many members the board of certification should have and what specializations they should represent (all surgeons? one or more psychologists? a mental retardation expert?).

A final note about refining your solutions to issues. It requires real self-discipline to critically examine a solution you are enthusiastic about and feel strongly is the best one that can be devised. But that self-discipline is one of the qualities that sets outstanding thinkers apart from all others. Moreover, it is one of the principal reasons for their effectiveness in persuading others to endorse their views.

WARM-UP EXERCISES

13.1. Willy Joe and Joe Willy are having a conversation of sorts:

> WILLY JOE: There's no such thing as reality, man.
> JOE WILLY: No way . . . like I mean . . . it makes no sense that way . . . No, there's no way.
> WILLY JOE: OK, man, you say there's a reality. So describe it to me.
> JOE WILLY: Um . . . Ah . . . Uh . . .
> WILLY JOE: You can't describe it, so it can't exist. Case closed.

How would you answer Willy Joe? Explain your thinking carefully.

13.2. Three girls and three jealous boyfriends went to a distant movie theater on a motorcycle that would hold only two. How did they all get there without leaving any girl in the company of a boy other than her boyfriend unless her boyfriend was also present?[2]

13.3. A man is walking up on the down escalator, and it is moving down faster than he is moving up. Is he going upstairs or downstairs? Explain thoroughly.

APPLICATIONS

13.1. The concept of statutory rape is somewhat controversial. Essentially the concept means that below a certain age (18 in many states) a person, usually a girl, is not legally able to consent to sexual intercourse. Any adult who engages in sexual intercourse with a person below that age is technically guilty of rape and may be so charged. Some people believe the concept ridiculous, others that it is very sensible, and still others have no quarrel with the concept, but disagree over the age. Identify and resolve the issue, then refine your best solution as explained in the chapter.

13.2. Woodrow Collums stood at the foot of his brother's nursing home bed, raised his .38 caliber pistol, and pumped five bullets into his brother's chest and abdomen. The act was a mercy killing. Collums loved his brother and couldn't bear to see him lying helpless, unable to speak, his brain cells degenerating from Alzheimer's disease, slowly sliding toward death.[3] The case was widely publicized and excited anew the controversy over mercy killing. Identify the issue in mercy killing and resolve it, then refine your best solution as explained in the chapter.

13.3. In February 1981, Steven Michael White pleaded guilty to first degree manslaughter in the strangulation death of Mary Collins. (Both were patients at a psychiatric center when the slaying occurred.) In December 1981, the Appellate Division of the New York Supreme Court overturned White's conviction on the grounds that when he confessed to the crime, he had not understood his right to remain silent.[4] There is much disagreement over whether this right is a reasonable one and, if so, how much weight it should be given in cases involving serious crimes. Identify and resolve this issue, then refine your solution as explained in the chapter.

13.4. Environmentalists believe the government has an obligation to protect plants and animals threatened with extinction. Others believe that if individuals want to take up that cause, that is their right, but that it is not the government's business. Identify and resolve this issue, then refine your solution as explained in the chapter.

13.5. Some people believe that religious proselytizing (attempting to convert people to one's religion) is not only morally justifiable, but a moral obligation. Others believe it is morally wrong. Identify and resolve this issue, then refine your solution as explained in the chapter.

13.6. For years a controversy has raged over pornography. Some people believe it affronts human decency and should be outlawed. Others regard it as quite harmless. Still others claim it is beneficial, that it helps people overcome their inhibitions and provides a means to ventilate strong sexual urges. Identify and resolve this issue, then refine your solution as explained in the chapter.

13.7. Controversy extends even to such a basic question as the nature of mankind. Are human beings essentially good and noble creatures who are corrupted by society in the course of their development? Or are they inherently violent and savage, their darker tendencies kept in check only by the threat of punishment? (There have been intelligent and educated supporters of each view.) Identify and solve this issue, then refine your solution as explained in the chapter.

13.8. "Not guilty by reason of insanity." That decision would be heard no more if a majority of Americans had their way. A nationwide poll revealed that 87 percent of those surveyed believe too many people accused of murder are using the insanity plea to escape prison. Sixty-nine percent favor abolishing the insanity defense in murder cases.[5] Yet many knowledgeable people argue that the insanity defense is absolutely necessary. "How can a person be held guilty for an act he wasn't aware he was committing, an act he had no control over?" they ask. Identify and resolve this issue, then refine your solution as explained in the chapter.

13.9. The idea of sex education classes in the upper grades and high school is not as explosive an issue as it was 10 or 15 years ago. But feelings still run high on both sides, some believing that the teaching of sex belongs in the home and others believing that many parents simply cannot do the job properly because of ignorance or embarrassment. They believe the school has an obligation to help students understand this vital aspect of life. Identify and resolve this issue, then refine your solution as explained in the chapter.

13.10. In 1981, Albert Goldman published a biography of Elvis Presley entitled *Elvis*. Many people objected to Goldman's negative descriptions of Presley's looks near the time of his death, home, manner of dress, relationship with his mother, and sexual habits. They felt Goldman had grievously wronged a man's good name and that the offense was compounded by the fact that Presley could no longer defend himself. Yet the law is on Goldman's side. It is impossible under the law as it stands to libel a deceased person. Only the living are afforded that legal protection. Identify and resolve this issue, then refine your solution as explained in the chapter.

13.11. After years of educating the children of *illegal* aliens without charge, the state of Texas passed a law in 1977 cutting off the state's share of the cost of educating these children. Some localities announced that all children of illegal aliens would have to pay a tuition fee if they wished to enroll in the public schools. A group of parents asked the federal courts to intervene, and in June 1982 the U.S. Supreme Court decided, 5 to 4, that the Texas law was unconstitutional. In other words, the Court declared that Texas must provide free education for the children of people living there illegally.[6] Identify and resolve this issue, then refine your solution as explained in the chapter.

13.12. More than half a million young men have failed to register for the military draft, even though the law requires every youth to register after his eighteenth birthday. The law provides for a maximum penalty of five years in prison and a $10,000 fine, but only a handful of violators have been prosecuted. Many people feel the government is making a mistake in not applying the law more rigorously. Others feel that the law is ill-conceived, that no one should be made to register if he morally opposes the draft. Identify and resolve this issue, then refine your solution as explained in the chapter.

four

COMMUNICATE YOUR IDEAS

chapter *14*

Anticipate Negative Reactions

Boris Noodnik is just finishing his presentation to the Parent-Teachers' Association meeting. "To summarize my proposal, ladies and gentlemen, every teacher in our school system should make students write a composition of from one to three paragraphs every day of the school year and make helpful suggestions for improvement on each paper submitted. This is the only sensible way to have our students become proficient in their use of the written word." He pauses while the audience applauds his presentation, and then asks "Are there any questions?"

A woman in the back of the room raises her hand, Boris acknowledges her, and she stands to speak. "Mr. Noodnik," she begins, "I have done some rough calculating while you were making your presentation. Each teacher in our system has, on the average, 27 students in class. Figuring an average of 7 minutes to correct a composition, a conservative estimate, it will take each teacher an additional 15 hours a week to correct those papers. Teachers already do most of their planning for class in the evenings and on weekends. Just when do you expect them to get the time to correct all those papers?"

Boris' face reddens. "Uh-h-h, well, u-h-h-h, ma'am," he stammers, "ah, let me see . . . I'll have to check out those figures. I really don't know right this minute." Poor Boris. However viable his idea seemed to him, and perhaps to many in the audience, it is very likely dead now. And it's not really the woman in the audience who's responsible for its demise. Boris is. If he really wanted the audience to accept his proposal, he should have taken the trouble to anticipate any negative reactions and been prepared to answer them.

Although readers' reaction is less dramatic and less potentially embarrassing than the reaction of a live audience, it is no less real and no less critical. They may not be able to stand up and ask the hard questions in person, but they can still think them. Any audience, whether to the spoken or the written word, has a right to expect that those offering a solution to a problem or issue be prepared to answer objections that might be raised to it. If they prove to be unprepared, the audience quickly loses confidence in them.

"Forewarned is forearmed," as the saying goes. This chapter will teach you how to determine in advance the reactions your solutions are likely to receive, so you can plan a presentation incorporating your answers to those reactions.

HOW COMMON ARE NEGATIVE REACTIONS?

It is tempting to think that when you unveil your creative responses to problems and issues, people will shout "Bravo! Magnifique!" and schedule ticker-tape parades for you. Unfortunately that is not the case for anyone, even the geniuses later generations honor.

When Nicholas Copernicus presented his original idea that the sun, rather than the earth, is the center of the solar system, he was not applauded, but scoffed at. Martin Luther responded to the idea by saying "This fool wishes to reverse the entire scheme of astronomy." And John Calvin said mockingly, "Who will venture to place the authority of Copernicus above that of the Holy Spirit?" Thirty-one years later, Copernicus had the death-bed reward of seeing his ideas published—but even then they were not accepted.

When Galileo took up Copernicus' cause, he fared no better. He was thought to be a madman, and would have been executed as a heretic had not good friends in high places interceded for him. The price he had to pay for his life was public renunciation of the idea he knew to be true.

The history of ideas is filled with similar examples. When Charles Newbold invented the cast-iron plow, farmers rejected it because they believed it would pollute the soil. When Horace Wells first used gas as an anesthetic to pull teeth, his peers ridiculed him. Joseph Lister's pioneering of antiseptic surgery was dismissed as needless housekeeping. William Harvey's discovery of the blood's circulation was rejected for 20 years and earned him derision, abuse, and the loss of much of his medical practice. Secretary of State William H. Seward's purchase of Alaska from Russia for 2¢ an acre was considered a mistake and dubbed "Seward's Folly." Ignaz Semmelweiss was rewarded for his discovery of the cause of puerperal fever by being fired from two university medical centers and hounded into a lunatic asylum.

Even Ted Geisel, better known as Dr. Seuss, whose delightful books bring untold pleasure to adults and children alike, was not well received at first. In fact, his manuscript was rejected by so many publishers that he almost burned it in frustration. The lesson in all these cases, and thousands of others like them, is that negative reactions to creative ideas are not only common—they are predictable. Knowing that, wise thinkers do their best to anticipate negative responses and prepare to meet them before they occur.

WHY PEOPLE REACT NEGATIVELY

It is easier to deal successfully with negative reactions if we understand *why* people react that way. Sometimes it seems that meanness or resentment or simple jealousy is the reason. To be sure, one or another of these is often involved, at least to some extent. But these emotions do not explain the numerous cases where the rejected ideas are beneficial to the very people who spurn them. As we will see, the causes usually are less personal and petty than these.

One cause of negative reactions to solutions is *lack of understanding* about what the solutions are and how they will work. Most people don't listen or read attentively. One study showed that the average person listens with between 25 percent and 50 percent accuracy.[1] The level of reading attentiveness is often not much better. And even where readers do make a conscious effort to grasp the ideas presented, they may grow apprehensive and confused if the subject or treatment *seems* difficult.

A second cause is *bad thinking habits.* If you recall the habits hindering effective thinking that were discussed in Chapter 3, and consider the difficulty you had overcoming those that you acquired, you'll appreciate how seriously those habits can affect the thinking of people who don't realize they have them. Mine-is-better thinking, face saving, conformity, stereotyping, self-deception, and particularly resistance to change can effectively block acceptance of your new solutions. And the more insecurity, laziness, or blind acceptance of tradition that underlies their resistance, the greater the obstacle. *Thobbing* (<u>th</u>inking out the <u>o</u>pinion that pleases them and <u>b</u>elieving it) will pose a formidable threat to your solutions.

Still another cause of negative reactions is *ignorance of creativity.* It's important to remember that the creative process is not widely known. Few textbooks treat it at all; few colleges offer courses that introduce it, even to future teachers. Most people are more likely to be familiar with popular misconceptions about creativity than with the facts. They themselves probably approach problems and issues vaguely and without any conscious strategy, therefore producing only the most common and unimaginative responses. So the independence and originality of your thinking, and your confidence in it, may frighten them away. Your most creative ideas may seem bizarre to them, and you may appear to be a "radical."

All this is especially true of your solutions to issues. Many people are so used to seeing controversial matters in either/or, right/wrong fashion that they will not understand your efforts to bridge controversies. And because they find it extremely difficult to achieve a balanced perspective on issues, they will be suspicious of your perspective. On occasion you may find that your very effort to bridge a controversy not only fails to win the approval of both sides, but actually alienates both.

There is yet another cause of negative reactions to solutions. It is markedly different from the other three. They represent failures on the part of the audience. This final cause is *a real or apparent flaw in your solution.* It therefore represents, not the audience's failure, but yours. It is extremely difficult to anticipate negative reactions caused by flaws in your solution, but it is crucial that you do so. There is nothing quite so disheartening as to have a solution rejected by others because of legitimate negative reactions you could have anticipated and headed off. The time to make the effort, to scrutinize your work carefully, is at this stage, not later. Later is often too late.

COMMON NEGATIVE REACTIONS

Exactly what kinds of reactions can you expect your solutions to receive? It is impossible to predict all of them, because they can vary with the particulars of your solutions. Nevertheless, certain broad reactions tend to occur again and again. The following are the most common kinds of negative reactions.

- The solution is *impractical.*
- The solution is *too expensive.*
- The solution is *illegal.*
- The solution is *immoral.*
- The solution is *inefficient.*
- The solution is *unworkable.*
- The solution will be *disruptive of existing procedures.*
- The solution is *unaesthetic.* (That is, ugly or lacking in taste.)
- The solution is *too radical.*
- The solution will be *unappealing to others.* (For example, to the public.)
- The solution is *unfair.* (That is, it favors one side of the dispute at the expense of the other.)

ANTICIPATING SPECIFIC REACTIONS

Your aim in anticipating others' reactions is twofold. First, you want to identify any areas of valid criticism so you can strengthen your solution before presenting it to others. Secondly, you want to identify all negative reactions resulting from misunderstanding and confusion, bad thinking habits, and suspicion of new and creative ideas, so you can construct your presentation to avoid those reactions— or at least prepare responses to them.

There are two useful techniques for stimulating your speculation about negative reactions. They are the brainstorming technique and the imaginary dialogue technique. Let's examine each in turn.

The Brainstorming Technique

This technique is an adaptation of the third stage of the creative process, the production of ideas. The aim here is to think of as many possible objections to your solution as you can, however outlandish they seem. Here's how to use this technique. Look back at the common negative reactions above and use them as a checklist to guide your brainstorming. In other words, first ask if anyone might find your solution impractical, and then list as many possibilities as you can think of. Next ask in what ways people might find your solution too expensive, and list the possible ways. And so on, proceeding through all the common reactions.

Caution is in order here. Whenever you use the brainstorming technique, be sure to withhold all judgment so the flow of ideas isn't interrupted. Keep in mind that extended effort will always reward you—some of the most helpful reactions will not occur to you at first, but will wait until the more obvious ones are out of the way. When you've completed brainstorming all 11 common reactions, then you can decide which possibilities are most likely to occur.

The Imaginary Dialogue Technique

This technique, as the name implies, consists of imagining yourself in a discussion of your solution with someone who objects to it. For best results, think of a specific person, preferably someone you know quite well and are sure would disagree with you. Be sure to put aside any feelings of awkwardness or embarrassment while using this technique. If you find yourself thinking "What would people think of my talking to myself this way?" tell yourself that no one need know, and that you are not doing it out of compulsion, but as a deliberate strategy to aid your thinking.

Here is an example of how the imaginary dialogue technique works. You will recall that in Chapter 2 (p. 29) we discussed the case of Ralph, the father who befriended the coaches and used that friendship to gain a special advantage for his son Mark over the other players. We decided that Ralph behaved immorally—that though his actions achieved some good (the development of his son's skills), they caused more harm. They deprived other players of the opportunity to develop their basketball skills, probably caused those players to become bitter, and undoubtedly caused Mark to believe that it is acceptable to disregard other people's rights and needs in order to achieve his own goals.

If you were addressing the larger issue this case raises, the issue of at what point a father's helping his son or daughter athletically slips from morally acceptable into morally unacceptable behavior, and attempting to resolve the issue by offering guidelines for parents to follow, you would have to anticipate negative reactions. And if you wanted to use the imaginary dialogue technique to help stimulate your speculation, what better person would there be to talk with than Ralph himself. Surely *he* would not look upon your disposition of his case favorably.

Just how would you conduct the dialogue in your imagination? First you'd make an assertion expressing your view. Then you'd put yourself in his position, enter his frame of mind, and answer for him. Next you'd express a second view, construct the answer he'd likely give to it, proceed to a third view, and so on. The resulting dialogue might go like this:

> YOU: Your actions were immoral, Ralph.
> YOU-AS-RALPH: That's ridiculous. All I did was help my boy.
> YOU: But you developed those friendships with the coaches so that you could use them later. That's dishonest.
> YOU-AS-RALPH: You mean I have no right to choose my friends, that I have to avoid friendships with coaches if my boy is an athlete?

YOU: Not at all. There's a difference between developing a friendship because you like someone and developing it to use the person for your son's advantage.

YOU-AS-RALPH: It's a rough world out there. A boy needs an advantage to get ahead.

YOU: But you gained that advantage at other people's expense. Look at what you did to the other boys on the team.

YOU-AS-RALPH: I can't be concerned with them as much as I am concerned about my own son. That's unrealistic.

YOU: That's true enough. But we're not talking about your being concerned or not concerned. We're talking about specific actions you took, deliberately, that hurt them.

YOU-AS-RALPH: But they didn't have the interest or the talent my Mark had.

YOU: That was not for you to judge. It was the coaches' decision to make. Besides, if you were so sure of your son's talent, there would have been no need for you to gain an unfair advantage for him. His talent would have given him all the advantage he needed.

YOU-AS-RALPH: I did it because I love my son. Is it immoral to help your own flesh and blood?

YOU: Is it an act of love to teach your son that the rules of decency and fairness don't apply where his desires are involved, that he can do whatever he wants because he's special?

This dialogue shows the benefit of this approach to your thinking. Used properly, it not only reveals the negative reactions you are likely to get from others, but also helps you develop better responses to shallow or uninformed reactions. In actual practice, however, it is not necessary for you to detail your own responses while you are conducting the dialogue. It is sufficient to contribute just enough to move the dialogue along, to prod the "other person" to respond. The most important part of the dialogue, after all, is not your views, but the other person's thoughts and feelings about them. The more you are able to focus on the other person's reactions, the more you will gain the insights necessary to make an effective presentation.

There is no limit to the number of imaginary dialogues you can conduct. If your audience is complex, and you have reason to expect a variety of reactions, you should consider doing numerous dialogues.

One final point. After you become used to the imaginary dialogue technique and develop your confidence in using it, you will notice that a dialogue will often gather enough momentum to require little conscious direction from you. It will, in a sense, direct itself. When this happens, don't worry. It is a good sign, an indication that you have fully engaged your imagination and given yourself to the intellectual exchange with your imaginary opponent. Let the dialogue continue —what develops will usually be very useful. If it begins to turn away from the important concerns involved, just steer it back again.

WARM-UP EXERCISES

14.1. If I say "I'll see you tomorrow" three days in a row, am I saying the same thing each time? Explain your answer thoroughly.

14.2. Do you agree with the reasoning in the following passage? Explain your answer thoroughly.

No honest lawyer would agree to represent a person accused of a crime because if the person is innocent, he doesn't need defending, and if he is guilty, he doesn't deserve defending.

14.3. Suppose that you are looking at a star, say Sirius, on a dark night. Astronomers tell us that light waves started to travel from Sirius many years ago. After all that time they reach earth, strike your retinas, and cause you to say you are seeing Sirius. But the star about which they convey information to you, the star that existed at the time the rays began their journey, may no longer exist. To say that you see what may no longer exist is absurd. Therefore, whatever you see, it is not Sirius. Is this reasoning sound?[2] Explain your thinking thoroughly.

APPLICATIONS

14.1. Each of the cases indicated below was presented in an earlier chapter's applications. Turn back to the chapter in each case and reread the application. Then recall the position you took on it. (If you wish, you may rethink the problem now.) State your position on the matter and the reasons supporting your position. Then anticipate the negative reactions you would probably receive, proceeding as explained in this chapter.

a. The marijuana warehouse case, Application 3.4, page, 48.

b. The adoption case involving the homosexual minister, Application 3.7, page 48.

c. The case of the illiterate high school graduate, Application 3.8, page 48.

d. The case involving the Jewish dietary laws, Application 3.5, page 48.

e. The case of the owner's responsibility for the accident involving the car he loaned, Application 4.5i, page 60.

f. The case of the woman ordered not to become pregnant, Application 4.5c, page 61.

14.2. Overweight boys and girls are usually rejected for membership on high school cheerleading squads, drill teams, and similar performing groups. The committees responsible for selecting members would defend their decisions. But many people believe such rejection constitutes discrimination. Identify and resolve this issue, then refine your solution, giving special attention to your consideration of negative reactions.

14.3. The age of kiddie cosmetics has begun. A cosmetic company is now marketing a line of Tinkerbell products, including powders, perfumes, lip glosses, and nail polish, for girls aged 3 to 14. Other companies will undoubtedly follow suit. This marketing move has drawn the criticism of many individuals and groups who believe that kiddie cosmetics will make children mature too fast.[3] Identify and resolve this issue, then refine your solution, giving special attention to your consideration of negative reactions.

14.4. Should the death penalty be permitted in this country? The controversy continues. Advocates of the death penalty argue that some crimes—for example, the brutal beating of infants, sex crimes against small children, the murder of on-duty police officers, and particularly vicious rapes and murders—are so heinous that nothing short of the death penalty would achieve justice. Opponents believe that for society to take a criminal's life is a criminal act. Proceed as you did in previous applications.

14.5. Eileen Stevens received the call at 1:20 in the morning. The dean of students at the college informed her that her son Chuck had died of an alcohol overdose. She was puzzled—he was not a drinker. She took the first plane available to the college, visited the hospital morgue, talked with the pathologist, visited the campus, and talked to students and college officials. Bit by bit she pieced the story together. Her son had been the victim of fraternity hazing. On a cold winter night the fraternity brothers had ordered Chuck and two other boys into the trunk of a car, handed them a bottle of wine, a six-pack of beer, and a pint of Jack Daniels, ordering them to drink it all. Hours later Chuck was dead of acute alcohol poisoning. The months and years that followed left Eileen Stevens not only grieving, but angry. The college, she felt, had handled the matter insensitively, perhaps trying to cover up what had happened. The district attorney concluded that no one was criminally responsible for Chuck's death, and refused Mrs. Stevens access to his investigation. Moreover, Chuck's was not the only needless death from fraternity hazing. Mrs. Stevens knew that each year a number of pledges die in this country. She felt she should do something, but didn't know what.[4] Identify Mrs. Stevens's problem and address it as you did the issues in the previous applications.

14.6. Jack Anderson reported several years ago that employees at a secret weapons-testing site in California were using sophisticated government video equipment, designed to test navy weapons, to show hard-core pornographic films for their own entertainment during working hours.[5] Many citizens consider such activities a moral outrage. Others believe there is no reason to be concerned. Address this issue as you did the issues in previous applications.

14.7. Occasionally the media carry a story about corporal punishment, like the story from Titusville, Florida concerning the $45,000 lawsuit a couple brought against a Baptist grammar school. The principal of the school had paddled their 13-year-old son across the buttocks as punishment for not running in physical education class.[6] Informed people are divided on the issue of corporal punishment, some supporting its use in the schools (provided it is done in moderation and with restraint), others attacking it as barbaric. Proceed as you did in previous applications.

14.8. A great number of Americans find boxing not only distasteful but a throwback to mankind's more violent past. A crowd of fans at a boxing arena seem to them the twentieth-century counterparts of the Roman Coliseum patrons who found the murder of one gladiator by another (or the feasting of lions on Christians) entertaining. Most boxing fans, of course, regard such a view as ignorant nonsense. Identify the issue here and proceed as you did in previous applications.

14.9. Every year, it seems, one or more school boards around the country decide to ban certain books from school library shelves, and the issue of censorship burns bright again. The banned books vary from case to case, but some recent examples are Bernard Malamud's *The Fixer,* Kurt Vonnegut's *Slaughterhouse Five,* and Eldridge Cleaver's *Soul on Ice*. (These books were characterized by one school board as "anti-American, anti-Christian, anti-Semitic, and just plain filthy.")[7] The school boards believe they act in the interests of the students and the community. But many individuals and community groups around the country disagree. They oppose censorship in any form. Proceed as you did in previous applications.

14.10. The issue of whether religion belongs in the schools continues to divide Americans. Many people believe that learning about a particular religion and saying prayers are activities that belong in the church and in the home, but have no place in public schools. Others believe that these activities should be allowed in schools because the country was founded on religious principles and spiritual development makes better citizens and a more stable society. Proceed here as you did in previous applications.

14.11. Identify the issue in the following dialogue and address it as you did the issues in previous applications:

> TARA: The communist countries have the right idea about one thing—they don't allow people to have absolute rights to real property.
>
> ANDREA: What do you mean "real property"?
>
> TARA: I mean real estate, land and the buildings on it. They let people own cars and stereos and clothing because those things aren't part of the country, the nation. But land is, so people can't ever really own it.
>
> ANDREA: What about a house? That's not part of the country—it's built by someone. Can they own that?
>
> TARA: Yes, in a way they can. They can build it and live in it and no other person can take it from them arbitrarily. But they have no permanent right to it because it rests on the land and that belongs to the nation on behalf of all the people. Understand?
>
> ANDREA: Yeah, I understand. But what's the big deal about that system? I think ours is a lot better.
>
> TARA: Think about it for a minute. In our system everyone is free to own land in theory, but in practice the wealthy are the ones who own most of it, and the better parts of it. And if you trace it back far enough, most of the land they own was stolen from the Indians, or given to the man who beat everyone else to the claims office. The communist way is fairer.

14.12. Read the following dialogue carefully. Then identify and resolve the issue behind it, and refine your solution as explained in the chapter:

> BETTY: I can't understand how anyone with any intelligence can argue in favor of freedom of thought.
>
> GRACE: What do you mean?
>
> BETTY: I mean it's ridiculous to allow people to think anything they wish.
>
> GRACE: But thinking isn't the same as taking action.
>
> BETTY: Wrong. Thinking is a form of action, a mental action that precedes physical action. Most rotten deeds are first conceived in the mind.

Rape, burglary, shoplifting, treason, even the simple act of lying —all of them occur first as ideas. Then the person acts on the idea.

GRACE: Are you saying some thoughts are wrong and should be outlawed?

BETTY: Now you've got it. Even the Bible supports my view. It says "Everyone who looks at a woman with lust for her has already committed the sin in his own heart."

GRACE: How would you outlaw them?

BETTY: I'd revise the laws to stipulate that thinking of a crime is the same as committing that crime. It won't always be possible to determine when a person is thinking of a crime, I admit, but where it can be determined—where there is evidence—he should be arrested and brought to trial. That would nip lawbreaking in the bud.

GRACE: I don't know. It seems to me such a law would do more harm than good.

BETTY: You've got to be kidding. Now the police and the courts can react only *after* a crime occurs. That puts us all at the mercy of criminals. With my law they'd be able to *prevent* crime from happening. This country would be a lot safer place to live.

chapter 15

Build a Persuasive Case

Persuasion* involves changing people's minds, getting them to accept ideas they have not previously accepted, or at the very least influencing them to accept those ideas at some later time. Persuasion is a necessary part of all problem solving when other people's cooperation or approval is required for a solution to be implemented. It is therefore of special importance in resolving issues.

Persuasive writing often asks readers to set aside familiar ideas and ideas they are committed to, and accept in their place strange ideas they have never considered before or, worse, ideas they have considered and rejected. In many cases persuasion asks not just acceptance of new ideas, but active endorsement of them. In the case of solutions to workplace or societal problems, persuasion also asks the investment of time and money and the running of risks.

For all these reasons, success in persuasion does not come easily. Therefore, when you set out to persuade your readers, you must approach the job seriously and prepare for it effectively.

HOW PERSUASION IS ACHIEVED

The first crucial requirement in persuading others is to put yourself in their place and determine where they are likely to stand on the problem or issue—that is, what they know, what they don't know, and what they believe. Because your readers may take significantly different views of the matter, you must consider all possible views and focus on the most probable or dominant ones. In doing this

---

*Although this chapter focuses on persuasive *writing,* the principles and approaches discussed here also apply to persuasive *speaking.*

it is helpful to consider how the concerns discussed in this book apply to those views. The following questions may be used as a checklist for consideration:

Is your readers' intellectual foundation likely to be weak in any way? This question does not suggest your readers are stupid or uneducated. As we saw in Chapter 1, there is a great deal of confusion today about such matters as free will, truth, knowledge, opinion, and morality. Many intelligent and educated people have fallen victim to ideas and attitudes that cripple their creative and critical faculties. By recognizing that your readers are inclined to think "one idea is as good as another" in, for example, sexual ethics, you are preparing to deal with that problem and to remove the obstacle to understanding it poses.

Is your readers' perspective likely to be narrow? This question directs you to consider how your readers' tendencies to mine-is-better thinking, face saving, resistance to change, conformity, stereotyping, and self-deception may interfere with their comprehension of your views. A clue to the way those tendencies are likely to influence your readers on a particular problem or issue is the way they have influenced *you* in the past. (The more honest you are with yourself about your own occasional irrationality, the more sensitive you will be about its influence on your readers.)

Are your readers apt to be unobservant about important considerations? We noted in Chapter 4 that most people give up their curiosity at a rather early age, and never fully regain it. Chances are your own experience with the Chapter 4 applications and the later applications in this book have made you more aware of the difficulty of developing curiosity, even when you make a conscious and sustained effort to do so. If your readers have not made such an effort, their observation is likely to be careless, and they have probably missed many of the subtleties you have observed. By considering where the subtleties lie, you can determine what you need to explain more fully to your readers.

Is your readers' understanding of the problem or issue likely to be as clear as yours? We have seen how many people rush into a problem with only a vague notion of exactly what the problem is. You have learned the value of expressing the problem or issue in a number of ways and then selecting the best and most promising expression of it. Many of your readers may not have done so. And if they haven't, they won't realize that your view of it is the best one. It may help open them to persuasion if you discuss the various views of the problem, or at least explain what your view is and its advantage over other views.

Are your readers likely to be familiar with the facts you found in your investigation? It is easy to forget that once you have investigated a problem or issue, particularly a complex one, you have a tremendous advantage over those who have not investigated it. Their ignorance of the facts can be an obstacle to accepting your solution. By identifying what facts and interpretations they are probably unaware of, you are identifying matters that must be emphasized in your presentation if you are to be persuasive.

Do your readers appreciate the various solutions possible? Have they considered them critically? Again, your effort to produce as many solutions as possible to the problem or issue sets you apart from most of your readers. The best way for them to appreciate your solution's soundness is to realize that other solutions are inferior. As long as they remain convinced that some inferior solution will work, they are not likely to be impressed by your solution. But if you show them how the others *don't* work, that their imperfections and complications are too great to overcome easily, then you will have conditioned them to accept yours.

The more deeply you probe these matters, the more sensitive you will become to the demands of the particular situation. Beyond this sensitivity, you persuade in two ways—by using your evidence effectively and by presenting your ideas skillfully.

USING EVIDENCE EFFECTIVELY

In persuasive situations it is not enough to know the best solution. You must also *show* that solution to others. In other words, you must help them to understand how it works not only in general, but also in specific situations—particularly, if possible, in situations where your readers tend to believe it won't work. This means you must help them to visualize the solution and appreciate why it is superior to other solutions. Doing this effectively means providing as many details as you can, consistent with the length of your presentation. In all but the most restricted presentations, in which you are required to be brief, you should consider including all the significant results of your investigation.

To ensure that you use your evidence effectively, ask and answer the following questions. They are based on the approach detailed in Chapter 8:

- What experience and observations of your own did you find relevant to this issue? (Be sure to include in your answer any experiences or observations you originally classified under a different heading, but then decided were connected with this problem or issue.)
- What experiences and observations of friends did you find relevant to this problem or issue?
- What information did you obtain from interviews with authorities?
- What information did you obtain from the library?

Your answers to these questions will provide you with a substantive presentation. To be sure you squeeze your data for all its potential, don't settle for summary answers. Remember: You not only want your readers to understand your data, but also to appreciate its significance. Experiences and observations demand that you make them see as you (or others) saw, feel what you felt. If they have never had similar experiences, this will be difficult. So, aim for vividness wherever possible and try to convey a sense of immediacy and the drama of the original event. In addition, make your interpretation clear and reasonable.

Use the same kind of thoroughness with the data you obtain from interviews and library research. Your readers will likely be unaware of the authorities' views unless you make them aware. And if you cover this data in too brief and undeveloped a fashion, and without the necessary emphasis, you will have failed to make your data serve your persuasive intent.

PRESENTING IDEAS SKILLFULLY

Presenting your ideas skillfully means, first, meeting the basic requirements of all good composition. These are discussed at some length in Appendix A. Secondly, it means applying these four guidelines:

- Respect your audience
- Begin with the familiar
- Select the most appropriate tone
- Answer all significant objections

Respect Your Audience

Whenever there is strong disagreement over ideas, as there is with controversial issues, there is also, sadly, heightened potential for ill will. It is easy to believe, once we feel strongly about a point of view, that those who disagree with us are stupid or villainous or both. That kind of attitude not only poisons debate—it also makes persuasion difficult or impossible.

Since people are not likely to be persuaded by someone who shows disrespect for them, respecting your readers is not merely a matter of courtesy or good sportsmanship. It is a psychological imperative. You may be inclined to believe that you don't have to really respect your readers, but can get by with *pretending*. But that is a mistake. Your own experience surely demonstrates that respect and disrespect are difficult to hide. Your manner or expression usually betrays strong feelings no matter how you try to hide them. Attitudes tend to show through what you say and the way you say it.

What can you do to make yourself feel respect for people whose views you disagree with? First, you can remember to distinguish between the idea and the person. It is possible for a decent, admirable person to have a foolish idea, or a disreputable person to have a sound one. Secondly, in the case of a controversial issue, you can remind yourself that disagreement is more likely to reflect the complexity of the issue than any shortcoming in your opponent.

Begin with the Familiar

First impressions may not be very reliable, but they are usually quite strong. They are therefore difficult to overcome. If you begin your presentation on a point your readers are unfamiliar with (or in disagreement with), they will be wary (or disagree) throughout your presentation. At best it will be difficult to change their reaction. That is why it makes sense to begin on a point they are familiar with, if possible a point on which they agree with you. This approach puts the psychology of first impressions to work for you instead of against you.

Beginning on a familiar point does not, however, mean that you should be dishonest and hide your disagreement. You are merely preparing them for the point of disagreement, helping them to see your solution more objectively than they otherwise would—not avoiding disagreement. There is nothing deceitful about this approach. Nor does it mean you should manufacture a point of agreement. If you look, you will usually be able to find at least several significant points of agreement, even in situations of sharp disagreement. As a last resort, if you can't find anything else that you and your readers are likely to agree on, you can begin by stating the significance of the issue and pointing out that it, like all controversial issues, tends to fan emotions more than is helpful for debate.

Select the Most Appropriate Tone

The concept of tone is a subtle one. It may be defined as the mood or attitude suggested by a presentation. It is therefore closely related to the idea of respecting your audience. Certain tones are always inappropriate in persuasive writing. The now-hear-this tone, for example, goes beyond being authoritative to being *authoritarian,* and suggests that the writer is forcing his views on his readers. Another inappropriate tone is the only-an-idiot-would-think-as-you-do tone, characterized by mocking and sarcastic remarks. Still another inappropriate tone is the you've-got-to-agree-right-now—there's-no-time-left tone. This tone is too excited to be effective. Even the most momentous problems and issues demand careful consideration. It is irresponsible to make any important decision impulsively. To demand an instant decision from your readers can only make them suspicious of your motives. "If the writer really has a solid case," they reason, "why doesn't he want to give me time to examine it carefully and ponder it?"

The safest and most appropriate tone in persuasive writing is the calm, objective, courteous tone. That will reflect quiet competency and a sense of balance toward the issue, as well as a proper view of your readers.

Answer All Significant Objections

You may think that if you identify any *valid* objections to your solution and modify your solution to eliminate them, you have done enough. That view is incorrect. Even *invalid* objections may act as obstacles. Therefore, you must deal with all objections, directly and thoroughly. This can be done very subtly and smoothly, without reminding your readers that it is their objection, and without interrupting the flow of your presentation.

Say, for example, you are presenting a solution bridging the extreme positions on the abortion issue. You wish to answer, among other probable objections, the pro-choice objection that your solution would deny women the right of free choice. Here are several possible approaches you might take, with comments on the appropriateness of each:

You may object that this solution would deny many women the right of free choice in deciding whether they wish to terminate a pregnancy. It does indeed	*Comment:* This is an awkward and ineffective way to answer the objection. The personal reference to the audience (*You*) is best avoided, if at all possible, in persuasive communication.

deny them absolute freedom
of choice. Nevertheless,
it preserves their freedom
in a number of circumstances,
and . . .

It focuses on the person
instead of the idea, a dangerous
focus if disagreement exists.
In addition, the word *object* is
an unnecessary reminder of a
reaction you want to lead your
readers *away from.*

Some readers will object
that this solution would
deny many women the right
of free choice in . . .

Comment: This approach avoids
the personal reference contained
in the first passage, but still
contains an unnecessary reminder
of a negative reaction in the word
object.

This solution may seem to
deny many women the right
of free choice in deciding
whether they wish to terminate
a pregnancy. It does indeed
deny them absolute freedom
of choice. Nevertheless,
it preserves their freedom
in a number of circumstances,
and . . .

Comment: This approach is
subtler, smoother, and more
effective than either of the
other two.

THE IMPORTANCE OF TIMING

There is one additional element in building a persuasive case. It is not, properly speaking, a guideline for preparing your presentation. Nevertheless, it does have a major bearing on your presentation's effectiveness. It is your *timing* in presenting your case. Many a creative idea was defeated by simply being presented at the wrong time. People's attention, interest, and openness to ideas are not constant. At some times they are greater than others. It is not always possible to appraise an audience's state of mind, particularly when the audience is large and complex. Still, wise thinkers make an effort to do so, as much as they can. There are three favorable conditions they look for in selecting their timing:

1. The audience should recognize that the problem or issue exists and be aware of its importance. A controversial issue should be currently in the news or at least have been there recently.
2. The audience should be relatively free to address your idea. That is, they should have no other pressing concerns commanding their attention.
3. The audience should have no commitment to a competing solution. It is not likely they will be interested in considering your solution to a problem or issue if they have endorsed another, competing solution. In such cases, your wisest course of action is to withhold presentation until the competing idea proves unworkable.

A SAMPLE SITUATION

You are sitting in the cafeteria one day and happen to overhear the following conversation at the table next to yours:

FIRST
PERSON: The matter is simple. Vince Lombardi summed up the intelligent perspective on winning when he said "Winning isn't everything—it's the *only* thing."

SECOND
PERSON: That's nonsense. Lombardi was a good football coach, but a lousy philosopher. The traditional view is the right view—"It's not whether you win or lose, but how you play the game."

FIRST
PERSON: With an attitude like that how can you ever be a winner.

SECOND
PERSON: Everyone who plays hard in sports can't help but be a winner.

FIRST
PERSON: Wow! If only my Little League coach could hear that. He used to tell us "If you lose, you're not the best, and if you're not the best, you're nothing." You know what he'd say to you? He'd say "Man, you're a big nothing."

At that point the two get up and leave. But the conversation doesn't leave your mind, and you know why. It's because you were on a varsity team in a high school where winning was stressed above all else. Your coach taught the Lombardi philosophy, your teammates accepted it as gospel, and so did the fans. Even then you were not completely comfortable with it. You felt that it was wrong somehow, but you weren't quite sure how.

Now your curiosity is aroused. You begin to examine the issue the dialogue recalled. That issue, you decide, is as follows:*What is the purpose of interscholastic and intercollegiate athletics, and how important is winning to its realization?* You begin talking to friends about it, then to several teachers, including your physical education instructor. Then you decide to do a little library research on the subject, purely for your own interest. Before long, you decide that there are a lot of people with the view of the first person in that cafeteria conversation, that our entire society seems to have an unhealthy view of winning. More importantly, you begin to want to persuade others that there is a better, more reasonable attitude. And so you decide to write an opinion piece for the campus newspaper.

After identifying the issue, completing your investigation, producing a range of solutions, refining your best solution, and anticipating negative reactions, you face the challenge of building a persuasive case for your solution. Let's see how you would use the approaches explained in the chapter to do this effectively.

Your readers will undoubtedly have mixed reactions to your presentation. Some will agree with you, but if your assessment of the extent of our society's emphasis on winning is correct, most will disagree—many strongly. Those are the ones you must consider carefully. Here are the questions suggested earlier in the chapter, with some of the most significant answers:

Is your readers' intellectual foundation likely to be weak in any way? One problem area that may exist for many readers concerns a moral question—is an action right and proper just because it proves successful? There is a tendency today to answer yes to this question. If you intend to argue that overemphasis on winning has the effect of promoting dishonesty on the court or playing field, or a lack of respect for one's opponent, then you should be prepared to have some readers think "So what? If such actions help the person win, then they're ok."

Is your readers' perspective likely to be narrow? A number of problems are likely to arise here. If many of your readers grew up thinking, and being taught, that the "winning philosophy" is the right philosophy, then they will certainly tend to identify with that view. Undoubtedly, a good number of them apply it in their own athletic activities. Hence your suggestion that it is wrong and harmful will trigger their mine-is-better, face saving, and resistance to change responses. In addition, they are likely to view you stereotypically, as a loser or someone who doesn't participate in or understand sports.

Are your readers likely to be unobservant about important considerations? Chances are that a number of your readers will never have wondered about the prevailing attitude toward competition. They will merely have accepted what they were told or shown by others' example. Moreover, because they lacked your curiosity, they may not have noticed the negative effects this philosophy produces at various levels of competition—from Little League to the professional levels of sport—and to fans as well as athletes. You'll need to show them.

Is your readers' understanding of the issue likely to be as clear as yours? Chances are most of them don't even see the matter as an issue. It hasn't nagged at them the way it has at you; they haven't felt the need to define it. They assume winning is the purpose of sports. The central question you have crystallized will seem new and strange, perhaps even pointless, to many of your readers. Therefore, you must present it with care, and deepen their understanding of it gradually. Without helping them to understand that there is a real issue involved, you have no hope of gaining their acceptance.

Are your readers likely to be familiar with the facts you found in your investigation? There is little chance they will be familiar with views against winning, because this issue—unlike issues such as abortion and capital punishment—is not highly publicized. No widespread public debate has yet developed over it. For this reason, any important facts you find should be presented as if the readers are likely to be unaware of them, and be suspicious of them.

Do your readers appreciate the various kinds of possible solutions? Have they considered them critically? The answer to both questions is probably not. Most of them undoubtedly think that the only alternative to winning at all costs is *not caring about winning at all.* Thus, they tend to see any argument against the prevailing athletic philosophy as an argument against athletics. One of your greatest challenges will be to make them see that the enjoyment and satisfaction athletic competition offers exist independently of the "winning philosophy."

After answering these questions and deciding how to approach your readers most effectively, you would prepare the piece for the campus newspaper. Here is how that piece might read:

ONLY WINNERS

Only a fool would deny that winning is more pleasurable than losing. Anyone who has ever stood on the football field or the basketball court as those final seconds ticked away and victory was complete, or who watched the ball explode off his racquet and land out of his opponent's reach to end the tennis match knows the emotions that accompany the experience. The joy, the excitement, the feeling of mastery are incomparable.

Those personal experiences are reason enough for preferring winning. But when you add to them the media effects created in the past 10 or 20 years —the on-field cameras capturing every emotion in the faces of the athletes, sweeping shots of cheering crowds, pregame buildup and postgame analysis —it's not surprising that winning has come to dominate the American view of sports. With phrases like "the thrill of victory and the agony of defeat" indelibly impressed on our minds, the traditional idea "It's not whether you win or lose, but how you play the game" seems rather anemic.

But perhaps we've gone too far with the philosophy of winning. Vince Lombardi's famous expression "Winning isn't everything—it's the only thing" was only the start. Lombardi said it in the context of coaching a professional team. But then many college coaches, high school coaches, and even Little League coaches adopted it as a philosophy. Some have gone far beyond it in their emphasis on winning.

A student at this college told me his high school soccer coach told his team before every game "Defeat is worse than death because you have to live with defeat." Another student said his Little League coach told his young players "If you lose, you're not the best, and if you're not the best, you're nothing." I believe that is a terrible idea to plant in the minds of children. Terrible, and false! After all, Fran Tarkenton, the great Minnesota Viking quarterback, never was on a championship team. And basketball star Wilt Chamberlain won a coveted championship ring very late in his phenomenal career. Those athletes were certainly not losers.

There are worse effects than slogans, too. In high school I played on a football team that won the state championship. We were winners, yes, and we were honored with a parade through town, a big dinner, and speeches by a lot of dignitaries. But one of the main reasons we won all those games was our coach's win-at-all-costs philosophy. He showed us films about how to hurt our opponents. He taught us to clip and to hold, and how to pile on an opposing player in ways that would injure him. Whenever we played a team with an outstanding player, the coach would urge us to disable him. I can still remember him saying "I want to see some stretchers out there today." More than once he got his wish. In one case, the opposing player, a boy with outstanding college prospects, suffered a permanent injury to his spine.

At the time we won the championship and were hailed as winners, I was as happy as the next guy on the team. But today I see it differently. According to the win-at-all-costs philosophy, the fact that we won should be the only important thing—how we won shouldn't matter. Yet somehow it does matter to me. I've taken my trophy off the shelf and put it in the attic.

Bill Russell is certainly no loser. He played basketball on one of the winningest basketball teams in history, the Boston Celtics. And he is regarded by many authorities as one of the best players ever to set foot on a court. Yet he has some interesting things to say about winning in his book *Second Wind.*

To be sure, he doesn't advocate losing, and he expresses pride in the qualities that made the Celtics a winning team. But his view of winning is not the common view. He writes, for example, "If you fix your mind on the goal of winning and stay honest with yourself, you'll come to realize that winning isn't about right and wrong, or the good guys and the bad guys, or the pathway to good life and character, or statistics. Winning is about who has the best team, that's all."

Russell is remarkably balanced in his view of the importance of winning. He tells about something that was more important to him than winning—the feeling that the particular contest being played might be lifted to an unusual level of excellence on the part of both teams. At times like that he wasn't just rooting for his own team—he was rooting for his opponents too. He wanted everyone to excel, to make the game something special. When that happened, he explains, he lost his feeling of competitiveness for a time, even while he was competing with every ounce of his strength. More importantly, when such a contest was over, he really didn't care who had won. The joy of participating in such a game was so fulfilling that winning was no longer important.

I believe amateur athletics would be much better if we returned to the traditional philosophy of "how you play the game." I'm not advocating trying to lose, nor even taking away the intense competitiveness that sports tend to generate. After all, competitiveness can be a positive force. The spirit that makes an athlete press himself forward in sports is the same spirit that makes men and women accept the challenge of invention, and discovery, and to triumph over such formidable problems as poverty and disease and ignorance.

What I am advocating is a shifting of the emphasis from winning to excellence. With this emphasis, coaches can continue to teach boys and girls to practice self-discipline, to extend their limits, and to perfect their talents. But they can also teach them to cope with failure, to accept losing gracefully and with honor, to deepen their understanding of life, and to gain self-knowledge and self-mastery. When the participants in athletics learn these things, whatever the final score of the game may be, everyone wins.

WARM-UP EXERCISES

15.1. In Strangeville it was decided that the local barber should shave all those, and only those, who did not shave themselves. Did the barber shave himself? Explain your thinking thoroughly.

15.2. Decide whether you accept or reject the logic in the following passage. Then explain your reasoning carefully.

It is wrong to blame people for being born with a disease. Criminality is a disease some people are born with. Therefore it is wrong to blame people for committing crimes.

15.3. A logician died and left this will: "I leave $1000 to be divided among my four daughters. Some of the money is to go to Annabel or Beatrice. I know that Beatrice and Clarissa are under Deirdre's thumb, so if any of the money goes to either of them, she is to have none. I want Beatrice and Clarissa treated alike—in fact, all four, or as many as possible, are to receive equal treatment. Who was the logician's favorite daughter, and what was the size of her legacy?[1] Explain your reasoning fully.

APPLICATIONS

15.1. Application 14.1 directed you to anticipate the negative reactions you would probably receive to your view on each of six specific cases. Take *one* of those cases, review your findings on it, and write a persuasive paper on it, following the approach explained in this chapter.

15.2. One of the most difficult considerations in divorce cases is who should be awarded custody of the children. Traditionally, the courts have favored the mother. Today, however, different judges decide differently. Given all the complex factors involved, there is no easy solution to the question of child custody. What guidelines would you follow if you were a family court judge? Apply all the approaches you have learned in this book and then write a persuasive paper in answer to this question.

15.3. Centuries ago, when there was little or no distinction between children and adults in daily life, children who committed crimes were treated exactly as adult offenders were treated. More recently, they have been treated quite differently—they are given special consideration for first offenses, lighter sentences for second and subsequent offenses, and are placed in special reform schools and rehabilitation centers rather than in prison. But in the past few years, many people have begun to question the wisdom of that special consideration. They reason that the crime in question, and not the criminal's age, should dictate the punishment. That thinking has begun to have an impact on legislative and judicial decisions. Vermont, for example, lowered the adult criminality age from 18 to 10 in 1981. In 1982 an Alabama court sentenced a 15-year-old boy to life imprisonment. In the same year, the Supreme Court refused to ban the death penalty for teenagers, and in Gainesville, Florida a 6-year-old girl was scheduled to be tried as an adult for hitting another child in the nose with a stick. (The 6-year-old's case was later dismissed.) What is your position on the issue of whether children should be treated as adults for their crimes? Apply all the approaches you have learned in this book and then write a persuasive paper in answer to this question.

15.4. There has been a growing feeling in this country and abroad that the continued production of nuclear weapons must be halted soon or civilization itself will be imperiled. Some military experts disagree, arguing that the existence of sophisticated nuclear weapons is a deterrent to nuclear war, even urging that the United States be ready to use nuclear weapons *first,* if necessary. Decide your position on this issue and follow the directions in Applications 15.2 and 15.3 above.

15.5. Most people in the United States today regard higher education as a necessity for a secure future. Yet some critics of education believe that the college degree should be abolished. They argue that it has little relation to the world of work, even in the professions. Many jobs that today carry a B.A. or M.A. education requirement, they claim, could be performed satisfactorily by a fairly bright high school graduate. And where further training is required, they believe, it could easily be given on the job. Decide your position on this issue and follow the directions given in previous applications.

15.6. Is it reasonable to believe that unidentified flying objects (UFOs) exist and that they are manned by intelligent beings from outer space? Decide your position on this issue and follow the directions given in previous applications.

15.7. Every morally sensitive person would agree that rape is a terrible crime and should carry a severe penalty. Everyone would agree, too, that for justice to be swift and meaningful, there should be no unnecessary obstacles to prosecuting rapists, and the victims should be spared further humiliation. But exactly how this is to be achieved is a matter of some controversy. Some propose accepting the victim's word that she (or, less commonly, he) was raped and not requiring corroboration. Others disagree, arguing that this would provide no protection against false charges. False charges do sometimes occur. Two such cases were reported in the news in January 1982. In one, a man who had served 2 years of a 12-year rape sentence was granted a new hearing when the victim admitted she had lied. In the other, a grade school teacher was acquitted of statutory rape charges when the two boys who had accused her were found to have lied. Where do you stand on the issue of whether to require corroboration in rape cases? Follow the directions given in previous applications.

15.8. The American public seems divided on the question of whether homosexuality disqualifies a person from legal protection against discrimination. The Council of the City of New York defeated five different versions of a gay rights bill more than 10 times in the 1970s and early 1980s.[2] Yet other political leaders take a very different view of homosexual rights. Former governor Brown of California, for example, appointed two homosexuals and a lesbian to judgeships. Do you believe homosexuals should be protected against discrimination of all kinds, including job discrimination in government and education? Follow the directions given in previous applications.

15.9. One of the hottest controversies in 1981 was over the teaching of creationism in the schools. It began when the state of Arkansas passed into law a bill requiring the public schools to give equal weight to "creation science" and the theory of evolution in public classrooms. The law was then challenged in the courts, and the debate raged for months in the media as well as in the courtroom. Then in January 1982, a federal judge ruled that "creation science" was not really science but religion, and that the Arkansas law had the effect of advancing religion, which is prohibited by the Constitution.[3] The debate, however, is not closed. Should creationism be taught in the schools? Follow the directions given in previous applications.

15.10. Birth control clinics believe they should be allowed to consult with minors about birth control, and even to prescribe such devices as the birth control pill or a diaphragm without having to notify the patient's parents. Many parents disagree. Decide your position on the issue and follow the directions given in previous applications.

15.11. Most of the assignments given in this book stop short of setting up the problem completely for you, in order to give you practice in defining problems yourself. Nevertheless, in the great majority of cases some minor help was given—at very least the presentation *suggested* some possible directions for you to take. These last problems in the book will be different. They will give not even the slightest suggestion of the nature of the problem or issue, or of the direction you should take. They merely present some interesting facts. What you do with them is entirely up to you. If you have learned your lessons well, each item will suggest a number of ideas.

a. Bill Tomaszewski, a Selkirk, New York farmer, drenched a grain field surrounding his corn field with a pesticide the conservation department had restricted to use as an insect repellent. Tomaszewski stated that his intention in using the pesticide was to protect his crop from birds. More than 2000 birds were killed by the pesticide.[4]

b. A report prepared for the Equal Employment Opportunity Commission revealed that for every dollar paid to men in the workforce, women received less than 60¢.[5]

c. The National Coalition on Television Violence, a television monitoring coalition, reported that network television shows portray an average of six violent acts an hour.[6]

d. In 1958, the rate of divorce was 2.1 for every 1000 people in the population. In 1981 the rate was 5.3.[7]

e. In New York City there were 993,372 reported felonies and misdemeanors, 168,861 arrests, and 95,115 convictions in 1980. As a result, 47,647 people went to jail, and 12,639 remained imprisoned for six months or more.[8]

f. Each of the following products was banned from television advertising in 1952: feminine hygiene products, hemorrhoid remedies, tampons and sanitary napkins, body lice cures, enemas, pregnancy test kits, jock-itch remedies, and incontinence products. The ban was lifted for every one of these products during the past 30 years.[9]

g. For several decades the National Education Association has surveyed the status of public school teachers at regular intervals. The most recent survey finds a growing discontentment among the nation's teachers. In 1961, 77 percent said they would "certainly" or "probably" choose the same career if they were starting over. In 1981 only 47 percent gave that response.[10]

h. A nationwide Gallup poll, described as "the most comprehensive survey on beliefs about . . . the afterlife that has ever been undertaken," revealed that 67 percent of the American people believe in some kind of afterlife. In addition, according to the accompanying analysis of the survey, "college-educated Americans are more likely to hold such a belief than those with a high school education or less" and "eighteen-year-olds are just as likely to believe in life after death as people over fifty."[11]

i. The Amateur Athletic Union has developed a physical fitness test for teenagers, based on 39 years of testing. When the test was used in 1980–1981, it was found that only 43 percent of American teenagers were able to meet physical fitness standards that should have been attainable by the average healthy teenager. Moreover, in some categories the average older teenager could not perform as well as he or she did at an earlier age.[12]

j. A survey published in the May 18, 1982 issue of *Redbook* magazine revealed that more and more younger women in various walks of life are becoming alcoholics. "The responses confirmed," the study said, "that almost two out of three women now being treated for alcoholism are under the age of 35."

k. A 5-year UCLA research study that followed a group of Los Angeles-area teenagers from junior high school through high school concluded that a certain type of teenager is more likely than others to go from drinking alcohol to using marijuana and hard drugs. That type of teenager is extroverted and rebellious, and tends to be sloppy.[13]

l. In New York City in 1981 a team of doctors aborted one of twin fetuses, but left the other undisturbed. (The latter was born naturally seven months later.) The abortion occurred because the terminated fetus had been diagnosed as having Down's syndrome. The doctors explained that the parents "desperately wanted a normal child but found themselves personally unable to cope with a lifelong responsibility for a retarded child and . . . were unwilling to shift the burden to society at large."[14]

APPENDIXES

Doing the Warm-Up Exercises

The warm-up exercises at the end of each chapter are intended to limber up your mind for the thinking demanded by the applications. Try not to see them as a chore but as an enjoyable activity, an opportunity to develop the playful attitude toward problem solving that creative people have. Some of the problems will, of course, resist solution. Even more frustrating, some will be relatively simple to figure out but very difficult to explain clearly to your readers. However, none of these difficulties will be insurmountable if you apply the right strategy.

SEVEN HELPFUL STRATEGIES

1. If the exercise consists of a single statement to be analyzed, read it again carefully. Be sure you understand what it says. Ask yourself "Does this make sense?" If you find yourself answering with a firm *yes* or *no,* decide precisely what makes you respond that way. Often that will be what you should explain to your readers.

2. If words fail you at the outset, try using a diagram to get you out of your rut. This will not work with all problems, but some lend themselves to the approach very nicely. If, for example, the passage were "All dogs are animals. Fido is a dog. Therefore Fido is an animal," you might diagram it this way:

The diagram would suggest the way to explain your analysis:

It is correct to classify dogs under the general heading *animals.* Moreover, this applies not just to some dogs, but to *all* dogs. There is no other category under which to classify dogs. Fido is correctly classified as a dog, so he must be an animal.

3. When the statement presents as fact something that is not fact, identify the error and explain how it invalidates the statement.

4. When the statement confuses two terms or ideas, identify the confusion and show its effect on the statement as a whole.

5. When the statement presents a conclusion as the only possible conclusion, and other conclusions are also possible, present the other conclusions and demonstrate that they too are reasonable (perhaps more reasonable).

6. When the statement, or some part of it, is open to interpretation, use the if-then approach to analysis. Consider, for example, the statement "Everyone must die." Here's how the if-then approach works:

The statement as it stands is ambiguous. If it is taken to mean "At present there is no known way for human beings to avoid death," then it is a statement of fact. But if it is taken to mean "There will never be a way for human beings to avoid death," then it is presumptuous. For, however unlikely such a development may seem, we cannot say for certain it will never occur.

The if-then approach is also useful when you are uncertain of the facts. In other words, you might say, "I am uncertain of the facts in this matter, but if they are as stated, then the conclusion is sound because. . . . If, however, they are not as stated, then the conclusion is not sound because. . . ."

7. If the exercise consists of a dialogue, read it several times, each for a different purpose. First, read it to understand the discussion in its entirety. Then read each person's comments individually, noting the progression of his thoughts and their degree of logical consistency. Finally, read for implications and assumptions. These are ideas that are not stated directly, but are nevertheless identifiable by what *is* stated directly. (The dialogue in Exercise 2 below contains an unstated idea.)

SAMPLE EXERCISES AND RESPONSES

Each exercise you do will have its own particular details and will therefore demand a special response. For that reason, no one formula can be given for responding to exercises. The following sample exercises and responses, though fairly typical, are illustrations of what can be done, but not models to be slavishly imitated.

Exercise 1

The Assignment   Analyze the following statement, deciding whether it is reasonable and, if so, to what degree. Explain your thinking thoroughly.

The results of a recent national examination reveal that 75 percent of America's high school students are below average in reading ability.

The Response

I don't know if the statement is a factual one. But I can say that it may have different meanings, depending on how the word *average* is interpreted. And the various meanings affect the reasonableness of the statement.

Below average may mean "below a score which half the high school seniors have achieved in previous years." Or it may mean "below a score now regarded as an acceptable minimum." In either of these cases, the statement is a reasonable one and could very well be factual.

But there is a more technical definition of below average. It may mean "below the arithmetic mean (the score derived from dividing the total scores of all high school students by the total number of high school students)." I am not sure whether it is even mathematically possible that 75 percent could fall below the mean. But I do know that it is highly unlikely. So if this is what the statement is saying, it is not very reasonable.

Exercise 2

The Assignment Read the following dialogue carefully. Then decide whether what is stated (or implied) makes sense. Explain your reasoning thoroughly.

> John: Do you think the masses really have any power in the United States today?
> Bill: That depends on what groups you include in "the masses." Would you include professional people—doctors, lawyers, teachers . . . ?
> John: *Teachers?* They don't make that much money.

The Response

John's last comment reveals the assumption that money is the basis for determining professional status. That assumption is unwarranted. If money were the measure, then a lawyer with a small practice would not be considered a professional, but a plumber with a good business would be. If an apprentice clerk in a store inherited a large sum of money from his aunt, he would be a nonprofessional one day and a professional the next. No, a professional person is one engaged in one of the *professions*—those fields requiring a liberal arts or science education and some form of subsequent specialization. The amount of money a person earns is beside the point.

appendix *B*

The Fundamentals of Composition

Writing is a diverse art. Although millions of pieces of writing have been produced each day for thousands of years, no two pieces have been exactly alike. Yet for all this remarkable diversity, every effective piece of writing reflects the same basic principles. By using them to guide your efforts, you can elevate the level of your written expression.

THE MAJOR PRINCIPLES

The major principles of composition are unity, coherence, emphasis, and development:

Unity

Every piece of writing must have a central idea around which all other ideas are arranged.

This principle is essential for writing to be understandable. Without a central idea, you have no basis for determining what arrangement of your thought is most effective. A central idea provides control over what to include in the composition and what to exclude, where to begin and where to end, and what arrangement of thoughts is best. In order to provide this guidance, the central idea should be clear to you *before you begin writing*. It saves no time to rush headlong into a composition expecting to find an idea somewhere along the way, and then, half an hour later, after much head scratching and eyebrow furrowing, to decide that you are hopelessly lost or at a dead end. Never assume you know what you want to say. Put it down in a clear sentence or two, change it several times, if necessary, to be sure it is what you want to say, and refer back to it for direction while you are writing.

Coherence

Every piece of writing must provide sufficient direction for the readers to achieve understanding with reasonable effort.

Immature writers have the idea that the world is waiting breathlessly to hear from them. Their attitude is "If the readers have trouble figuring out my meaning, let them struggle to do so—my thoughts are worth their effort." That attitude is naive. Readers of your writing will react to incoherence just as you do when you encounter it in others. In other words, they'll think to themselves "This person is confused—if he couldn't make clear what he wanted to say, I'm not going to waste my valuable time trying to figure it out." Then they'll throw it aside.

To avoid such a reaction and make your writing coherent, you must be sure that the order of your ideas is sensible. You must also finish one idea before moving on to the next whenever possible (so that your readers don't have to jump back and forth between ideas unnecessarily), and provide helpful connecting words or phrases to signal significant shifts from one idea to another.

Emphasis

Every piece of writing must give each idea it contains the attention it deserves.

There may be occasions when every idea in a composition has exactly the same degree of importance as every other. But those occasions are extremely rare. Much more often, the ideas differ significantly in their importance. To determine the relative importance of the ideas in a piece of writing, consider their exact relationship to your central idea. The larger the role they play in communicating that idea, the more important they are. Use these approaches to give greater emphasis to more important ideas.

1. Assign an important idea more space—that is, provide more information about it, develop it further than other ideas.
2. Give important ideas, whenever possible, the positions of greatest emphasis. The end is the most emphatic position, and the beginning the next most emphatic. Thus, if you had four points or arguments in the body of your composition, you'd put your most important point last, your next most important point first, and the others in the middle.
3. Repeat key words occasionally, or use echo words. The latter are words that do not repeat the key words, but whose sense is similar enough to call them to mind. In a composition about love, words like *respect, devotion,* and *affection* would be echo words. One caution, though—both repetition and echo words must be used judiciously or they will make your composition seem inflated.

Development

Every piece of writing must include sufficient elaboration of important ideas to achieve the writer's purpose.

This principle does not mean that every detail of every idea must be provided. To do that would violate the principle of emphasis. It means, rather, that you must be sensitive to the development necessary to elicit the response you want from the reader, and then must provide that development—for example, by using cases in point, descriptions, definitions, explanations, and so on. When your purpose is to *persuade* your readers, many of your ideas may require considerable development.

THE STAGES OF COMPOSING

The composition process consists of three separate stages—planning, writing, and editing. Beginning writers often think they can save time by eliminating the first and third stages. The result is usually unfortunate. Either they produce a shabby, ineffective piece of work violating one or more of the principles of composition, or they make so many false starts that in the end they spend more time than if they had used all three stages. All three stages deserve careful attention.

Planning

In this stage you design the composition, creating a blueprint to follow in the writing stage. It is easier to experiment with different formats when ideas are in rough, abbreviated form than when they are fully developed in sentences and paragraphs. This is no small concern in situations (such as in the applications of this book) where you are dealing with a large number of complex ideas and a number of different perspectives. The steps you should follow in planning your compositions follow.

1. List all the ideas you will include in the body of your paper. There's no need for complete sentences here and no need to worry about spelling, mechanical errors, and neatness. The list is for you alone.

2. Decide on the clearest and most effective arrangement of those ideas, following the principles of coherence and emphasis.

3. Number the ideas in the order you wish to present them.

4. Decide whether you will need a special introduction and conclusion, or whether two of the ideas already listed could be effective in these positions. If you need a special introduction and conclusion, try to make the introduction capture the readers' attention and arouse their curiosity, and make the conclusion reinforce your central idea. (Restatement is one way of reinforcing, but it is usually not the best one, particularly in a brief composition.)

5. Note where you will need connecting words to show the relationships between your ideas and establish coherence for the readers. Provide the connecting words.

6. Note in the margins of your list which ideas need development, and the kind and amount of development each requires. Consider the following kinds of development:

- Presenting factual details
- Describing someone or something
- Presenting brief or extended examples
- Defining a term
- Detailing a process
- Using analogy
- Making a comparison
- Classifying things
- Identifying causes or effects
- Evaluating an idea or line of reasoning
- Tracing the development of something
- Summarizing another viewpoint
- Quoting or paraphrasing an authority
- Explaining further a subject in your presentation that the readers might be confused about

Writing

In this stage, you carry out your composition plan and produce a rough draft. Complete the entire draft at a single sitting, with as few interruptions as possible. Choose your words as carefully as you can, write complete sentences, and break your writing into paragraphs.

But do *not* let yourself get bogged down in doing these things. If the right word doesn't come to mind at once, write down one that does. If you aren't sure whether a paragraph break is appropriate, make a tentative decision. *Never* pause during the writing stage to look up the meaning or spelling of a word, or to check some rule of usage or grammar. These are important tasks, but the time for them is later. The more carefully you follow this advice, the better the flow of your writing is likely to be.

Editing

Your purpose in this stage is to polish your rough draft and make it presentable. This is the time to check your word choice, paragraphing, grammar, usage, spelling, and punctuation. More importantly, it is the time to be sure you have observed the principles of effective composition. The most efficient way to edit your writing is to read your paper through several times, looking for something different each time. It is best to read it *aloud,* because then you will have two senses working for you instead of one. Here's what to look for in the various readings.

First Reading Look for any lapses in observing the major composition principles— unity, coherence, emphasis, and development.

Second Reading Look for problems in paragraphing. Though paragraph length may vary from a few lines to perhaps 15 or more, it is a good idea to keep the length of your paragraphs moderate, say from 8 to 10 lines long. Remember that a series of short paragraphs is distracting to the reader, and a series of long ones seems formidable. Break paragraphs at any of the following junctures—between techniques of development, within a technique when there is a change of time or place or focus, and between speakers in dialogue.

Third Reading Look for specific errors that tend to recur in your writing. After you have corrected the weaknesses and errors your editing has revealed, rewrite your composition in polished form.

DEVELOPING A READABLE STYLE

As a literate person, a college student, you have done considerable reading. You have encountered a variety of prose styles, some of them so awkward and difficult to follow that you have almost wished you'd never learned to read, and others that have delighted you and made you sorry to come to the end of the piece. Perhaps you've concluded that writing style must be a matter of genetic endowment. There's probably some truth to the idea— after all, some people do seem to have a special talent for verbal expression, just as some have a mechanical aptitude. But writing is essentially a learned activity, so habit is more significant than heredity. If the habits you acquired through trial and error or imitation are bad habits, you will be a poor writer. If they are good habits, you will be a good writer. Observing the following guidelines can help you build better habits.

1. **Make your writing sound good.** Many people who write poorly speak fairly well. In fact, some are very lively and interesting conversationalists. If you are such a person, you can improve your writing by making it reflect your speech. This doesn't mean, of course, all the little flaws of speaking— the um-ing, ah-ing, pausing and repeating yourself. It means the rhythm of your speaking voice. To accomplish this, read your rough draft

aloud and note passages that don't sound natural. Revise them so that you feel comfortable saying them aloud.

2. **Strive for brevity.** The idea of brevity may seem inconsistent with writing longer papers and developing your ideas. But it is not inconsistent at all. A paper may be long because it has a lot of unnecessary words in it, or because it is filled with ideas. You can develop your thoughts fully and still have your writing be a model of brevity. Simply express each idea in as few words as you can, consistent with conveying the meaning and creating the understanding you intend.

3. **Express your ideas in simple language.** This doesn't mean to avoid all big words, just the ones that are *unnecessarily* big. George Orwell said it best, "Never use a long word where a short word will do."

4. **Put some variety into your sentences.** What is the most boring quality in a speaker? Most people would say speaking in a monotone. A monotone is the use of a single, unvaried tone of voice. The word derives from the same Greek word that gives us *monotonous.* Monotones are monotonous. The equivalent of monotone in writing is sentences that begin the same way, have the same structure, and are the same length. They are perfectly predictable—that's why they put readers to sleep. To get the monotony out of your writing, begin some of your sentences differently, vary their structure, and include an occasional short sentence among a series of longer ones (or vice versa).

5. **Paraphrase more often than you quote.** Quotations are valuable. But used too often, they shift the focus from your style to someone else's. Whenever it is possible to paraphrase (to express the other writer's idea in *your* words) without making the idea suffer in the process, do so. You must, of course, give the same credit for paraphrased ideas as you do for quoted ideas—that is, by mentioning the person informally in your sentence, or by including a formal footnote.

6. **Be lively.** Purge your writing of bland, mechanical expression. Try to express your ideas colorfully and imaginatively. Your writing will take on a new vitality when you do. Here are two brief examples of lively, imaginative expression:

> As you turn the pages of that American history book, the story gets more and more polluted. The pilgrim lands in the New World and discovers a land that is already occupied. How do you find something that somebody else has and claim you discovered it? And we talk about crime in the streets!
>
> That is like my wife and I walking down the street and seeing you and your wife sitting in your brand-new automobile. Suppose my wife says to me, "Gee, I'd like to have a car like that." And I answer, "Let's discover it." So I walk over to you and your wife and say, "Get out of that damned car. My wife and I just discovered it." The shock and surprise you would naturally feel gives you some idea of how the Indians must have felt.[1]

> Only a very soft-headed, sentimental, and rather servile generation of men could possibly be affected by advertisements at all. People who are a little more hard-headed, humorous, and intellectually independent, see the rather simple joke and are not impressed by this or any other form of self-praise. If you had said to a man in the Stone Age, "Ugg says Ugg makes the best stone hatchets," he would have perceived a lack of detachment and disinterestedness in the testimonial. If you had said to a medieval peasant, "Robert the Bowyer proclaims, with three blasts of a horn, that he makes good bows," the peasant would have said, "Well, of course he does," and thought about something more important. It is only among people whose minds have been weakened by a sort

of mesmerism that so transparent a trick as that of advertisement could ever have been tried at all.[2]

A SAMPLE ANALYTICAL PAPER

The following analytical paper illustrates how your responses to the end-of-chapter applications can be presented in traditional composition form, observing the principles of writing explained in this appendix. The composition below is a response to the issue of violence in contemporary films. Specifically, it answers the question "What is the most reasonable reaction to the recent trend toward the graphic portrayal of violent scenes in films?"

FILM VIOLENCE SHOULD MAKE US SICK

I walked out of the movie after half an hour. It was either leave or throw up. The movie was *An American Werewolf in London*. In an early scene a wolf attacks two young men, killing one and badly slashing the other. Then, while recovering in the hospital, the survivor dreams he is running nude through the forest, spies a deer, pounces on it wolflike, and devours it.

Two more nightmares quickly follow. In one, the survivor's family is brutally assaulted and killed by monsters with hideous faces. In the other his nurse is similarly attacked. Soon the young man's dead friend visits him in the hospital to warn that he will become a werewolf. The camera lingers on the dead man's disgustingly mutilated face.

In each of these scenes, no gory detail is left to the imagination. Yet somehow many people around me in the theater found the visual assault enjoyable. They laughed and laughed. I left.

Like that audience, some critics have taken the film lightheartedly. The *Newsweek* critic, for example, titled his review "Cool Ghoul," and termed the film "a nearly perfect specimen of the wise-guy movie" in which the hero turns into a werewolf and "masticates half of Piccadilly before the bloody climax." That kind of critical reaction reflects a casual attitude toward film violence that has become very fashionable in recent years. That attitude rests on four widely accepted ideas, each of them flawed.

The first idea is that any time an audience is made to laugh, the effect is wholesome. This is nonsense. There's a big difference between laughing at someone making a fool of himself or at an ironic development, and laughing at someone being raped or torn to shreds. Some things—mental retardation, physical handicaps, and terminal illness, for example—just aren't funny.

The second idea is that films don't affect our attitudes and values. This view ignores the most obvious findings of psychology. Psychologists tell us that most people aren't born sensitive or insensitive, kind or cruel. Rather, they are shaped one way or the other by their experiences, including their vicarious experiences on the larger-than-life movie screen.

Chicago film critic Roger Ebert reports that in viewing another film on two separate occasions, he observed both audiences laughing in scenes showing a woman beaten, raped, and cut up. One respectable-looking man next to him kept murmuring, "That'll teach her. Give it to her." Ebert found that reaction frightening. So should we all. But we shouldn't be surprised by it. Like any powerful emotional experience, film viewing has the capacity to brutalize us, make us feel enjoyment where our humanity demands we feel revulsion.

The third popular notion is that films don't affect people's behavior. This idea is questionable at best. Consider the case of the 24-year-old Brockton, Massachusetts man who, believing himself to be a vampire, killed his grandmother and drank her blood. Or the case of the Cincinnati publisher who marketed the 1982 Cat Hater's Calendar, featuring color photos of cats being hanged and wrapped in foil on a grill. No particular film may be responsible for inciting such actions, but surely the climate of violence generated by horror films contributed to them, at least by stimulating the person's imagination.

Finally, it is widely believed that the idea of democracy forbids any restriction on artistic expression, including that of filmmakers. To approve of even the most general guidelines is considered an attack on the U.S. Constitution. This belief is too extreme to be reasonable. Individual rights should not be allowed to take precedence over public rights. No one, for example, should be permitted to poison the air the rest of us breathe. And neither should a filmmaker have the right to poison the social climate.

This is not to say that the movie industry should be forbidden to explore the unpleasant side of reality. On the contrary, no subject should be forbidden to filmmakers because no subject is good or bad in itself. It is the *treatment* that makes the difference. In the hands of a genuine artist, even the most unspeakable violence can be handled inoffensively. Alfred Hitchcock's *Psycho* generated incomparable suspense without the knife once touching the victim on camera.

Not only is there no good reason to approve the kind and amount of film violence we have been subjected to in recent years—there is compelling reason to reject it. Across this country, from small communities to great cities, crime and violence are a daily threat to millions of people. If we are ever to conquer that threat, we must retain our capacity to be outraged by it. But it is precisely that capacity that is diminished every time we suppress revulsion and watch a succession of violent acts on the movie screen.

The Fundamentals of Logic

Logic is the study of the principles of reasoning. Its main concerns are the structure of arguments and the process by which conclusions are derived from premises. Thus its focus is not on statements as such, but on the *relationships* between them. In other words, in logic the question "Are the statements in this argument true or false?" is less important than the question "Is the conclusion in this argument validly drawn?"

THREE BASIC PRINCIPLES

There are three principles that underlie the subject of logic:

- The principle of identity—if a statement is true, then it is true.
- The principle of excluded middle—a statement is either true or false.
- The principle of contradiction—no statement can be both true and false.

Each of these principles has been challenged from time to time, but properly understood, each is true and does not admit exceptions. At first consideration we might, for example, think that some realities change and so the principle of identity isn't correct. The statement "Infant Charles Jackson weighs 8 pounds, 2 ounces" is true at birth but false for the rest of Charles Jackson's existence. Yet on closer inspection, we see that the statement is an assertion about his weight at a particular moment of time. His later weight change has no bearing on that truth.

Similarly, it might seem that the principle of excluded middle is challenged by a statement that is partly true and partly false, like "Ronald Reagan, the thirty-fifth president of the United States, was at one time governor of California." But closer examination reveals that the statement is really *two* separate statements fused into one—the false statement that Reagan is thirty-fifth in the line of presidents, and the true one about his prior office.

Finally, it may be possible to think of a statement that seems to be both true and false, but only if it is given two different interpretations. The sentence "Leonardo is Italian" cannot be both true and false at the same time in the same way. It may be, of course, that Leonardo is Italian by birth, but American by naturalization. Yet to understand the sentence in that way is to read "is Italian" in two different senses. Such an example does not challenge the principle of contradiction.

FORMAL ARGUMENT

The traditional way of expressing a logical argument is in a syllogism. A syllogism is a kind of verbal mathematics: a + b = c (or 1 + 2 = 3). It is composed of three statements: the *major premise,* the *minor premise,* and the *conclusion.* Here is a famous example of a syllogism:

> All men are mortal.
>
> Socrates is a man.
>
> Therefore Socrates is mortal.

The major premise is the first statement. It is called major because it contains the *major term* of the syllogism (in this case *mortal*). The major term always appears as the predicate of the conclusion; the *minor term* (in this case *Socrates*) always appears as the subject of the conclusion. The *middle term (men/man)* does not appear in the conclusion, but is the common element, the connector, between the premises.

For analytic ease, and to help themselves focus on structure instead of content, logicians often substitute symbols for the terms in a syllogism. The symbols most often used are P, Q, and R. The above syllogism would be expressed symbolically as follows:

> All P are Q.
>
> R is P.
>
> Therefore R is Q.

COMMON ERRORS IN SYLLOGISMS

Before we turn to specific errors, it is necessary to clarify the concept of *distribution.* Distribution means making an assertion about *every* member of a class. Thus, in the statement "All colleges offer degrees," the subject is distributed. However, in the sentence "Some colleges offer degrees" the subject is undistributed.

There are four errors that frequently occur in syllogisms and two related errors that, though technically not syllogistic, are similar in form. These errors are:

- Undistributed middle
- Illicit process
- Affirming the consequent
- Denying the antecedent
- Converting a conditional
- Negating antecedent and consequent

Undistributed Middle

Each middle term in a syllogism must be distributed at least once. If it is not distributed in either of the premises it is intended to connect, then the error of undistributed middle exists and the reasoning is invalid. The symbolic expression of an undistributed middle syllogism is as follows:

> All P are Q.
>
> All R are Q.
>
> Therefore all P are R.

Since the middle term (Q) is undistributed, it is possible that P and R fall into different parts of Q and are therefore not related as the conclusion asserts. (To see this more clearly, substitute *hamsters* for P, *elephants* for R, and *mammals* for Q.)

Illicit Process

Any term in a syllogism that is distributed in the conclusion must also be distributed in the premise in which it occurs. If either the major or the minor term is distributed in the conclusion but not in the premise in which it occurs, the error of illicit process exists. The symbolic expressions of this error are as follows:

ILLICIT MAJOR	ILLICIT MINOR
All P are Q.	All P are Q.
No R are P.	Some R are P.
Therefore no R are Q.	Therefore all R are Q.

The four remaining errors occur in hypothetical (if-then) reasoning. They are all corruptions of the following *legitimate* form of hypothetical reasoning:

> *If P, then Q. P. Therefore Q.*

The corrupted forms are:

Affirming the Consequent

> If P, then Q.
>
> Q.
>
> Therefore P.

Denying the Antecedent

> If P, then Q.
>
> Not P.
>
> Therefore not Q.

Converting a Conditional

> If P, then Q.
>
> Therefore if Q, then P.

Negating Antecedent and Consequent

> If P, then Q.
>
> Therefore if not P, then not Q.

These, then, are some of the most commonly encountered errors in syllogisms. Be alert to them in your reasoning.

appendix **D**

Solutions to Sample Problems

THE THREE GLASSES PROBLEM

The key to solving this problem is to use one or more of the glasses as a measuring device. Here's how to proceed:

1. Fill the 3 ounce glass and empty it into the 5 ounce glass. Fill it a second time and empty as much as will fit into the 5 ounce glass. Now the 3 ounce glass will contain 1 ounce of liquid, the 5 ounce glass 5 ounces, and the 8 ounce glass 2 ounces.
2. Empty the 5 ounce glass into the 8 ounce glass. Then empty the 3 ounce glass into the 5 ounce glass. Now the 3 ounce glass will be empty, the 5 ounce glass will contain 1 ounce of liquid, and the 8 ounce glass 7 ounces.
3. Fill the 5 ounce glass from the 8 ounce glass. Each will then contain 4 ounces.

THE YOUNG GIRL/OLD HAG PROBLEM

If you have trouble seeing the young girl: She is looking away from you. You can only see the side of her face.

Her nose and eyelash

Her left jawbone

A velvet choker

If you have trouble seeing the old hag: She is looking down, her chin touching the top of her chest.

A wart on her nose

Her eye

Her mouth

THE VASE AND FACES PROBLEM

To see the vase, focus on the white object against a background of shadow. To see two faces, imagine a bright light shining through a window and two people standing nose to nose, in silhouette.

Notes

CHAPTER 1

1. Arthur Koestler, *The Act of Creation* (New York: Macmillan, 1964), p. 173.
2. James Mursell, *Using Your Mind Effectively* (New York: McGraw-Hill, 1951), pp. vi–vii.
3. For a more detailed discussion, see D. Galin, "Two Modes of Consciousness and the Two Halves of the Brain," in *Symposium on Consciousness,* eds. P. Lee et al. (New York: Viking, 1976).
4. See, for example, Sidney Parnes, *Creative Behavior Guidebook* (New York: Scribner's, 1967), p. 32.
5. E. Paul Torrance, *Guiding Creative Talent* (Englewood Cliffs, N.J.: Prentice-Hall, 1962), p. 5.
6. Brewster Ghiselin, *The Creative Process: A Symposium* (Berkeley: University of California Press, 1954), p. 115.
7. See, for example, J. Dewey, *Art as Experience* (New York: Milton Balch, 1934), p. 73.
8. Quoted in W.I.B. Beveridge, *The Art of Scientific Investigation* (New York: Norton, 1951), p. 56.
9. Koestler, p. 146.
10. This definition is Henry Hazlitt's, quoted in Koestler, pp. 72–73.
11. Benjamin Bloom and Lois J. Broder, *Problem-Solving Processes of College Students* (Chicago: University of Chicago, 1950), pp. 25–30.
12. Ernest Dimnet, *The Art of Thinking* (New York: Simon and Schuster, 1928), pp. 103–104.
13. Virginia Adams and Tom Ferrell, "Inside the Crater a Stone-Age People," *New York Times,* 21 May 1978, p. 7.

CHAPTER 2

1. According to CBS newsprogram "60 Minutes," September 17, 1978, the most popular street names are, first, Park (avenue or street), and second, Washington. Main is thirty-second on the list, and Broadway is not in the top 50.

2. John Phin, *The Seven Follies of Science,* 3rd ed. (New York: Van Nostrand, 1912), p. 202.

3. Phin, p. 208.

4. Robert P. Crawford, *Think for Yourself* (New York: Fraser, 1937), p. 118.

5. Harold A. Larrabee, *Reliable Knowledge,* rev. ed. (Boston: Houghton-Mifflin, 1964), p. 22.

6. *New York Times,* 6 December 1981, p. 27.

7. "Computer Points to Single Author for Genesis," *New York Times,* 8 November 1981, p. 7.

8. The correct answers are as follows: a) An English playwright. Although history books have traditionally credited Nathan Hale with the statement, Hale actually said "It is the duty of every good officer to obey any orders given him by his commander-in-chief." His biographer borrowed the playwright's words. b) The signal that was used is not known. The poet Henry Wadsworth Longfellow invented the well-known "one if by land and two if by sea" signal. (Both this and the answer to a are found in Michael T. Kaufman, "Myths of '76 Revolution Deflated at Yale Parley," *New York Times,* 4 May 1975, p. 1f. c) Fur. The idea of a glass slipper occurred because the French word for fur was incorrectly translated. d) Siberian squirrel fur. (Both this and the answer to c are found in Phin, p. 208.)

9. *New York Times Magazine,* 1 December 1974, p. 31.

10. "The Great Change in Children," *Horizon,* Winter 1974, p. 4.

11. Walter Lippmann, *Public Opinion* (New York: Harcourt, Brace, 1922), p. 90.

12. George Seldes, *Freedom of the Press* (Indianapolis: Bobbs-Merrill, 1935).

13. *Oneonta Star* (New York), 6 February 1982, p. 3.

14. Edwin L. Clarke, *The Art of Straight Thinking* (New York: Appleton, 1929), p. 269.

15. Frederick C. Bartlett, *Remembering : A Study in Experimental and Social Psychology,* (New York: Cambridge University Press, 1932, pp. 205–207).

16. Columbia Associates in Philosophy, *An Introduction to Reflective Thinking* (Boston: Houghton-Mifflin, 1923), p. 189.

17. Larrabee, p. 203.

18. Martin Gardner, *Fads and Fallacies in the Name of Science* (New York: Dover, 1957), p. 123.

19. See, for example, John Altrocchi, Abnormal Behavior (New York: Harcourt, Brace, Jovanovich, 1980), p. 17f.

20. Gardner, pp. 155–157.

21. The story of Raoul Wallenberg is detailed in John Bierman, *Righteous Gentile* (New York: Viking, 1982).

22. "Starving Children Saved by NYC Police," *Oneonta Star,* 13 October 1981, p. 13.

23. Joseph Jastrow, *Effective Thinking* (New York: Simon and Schuster, 1931), p. 121.

24. Warren Hoge, "Machismo 'Absolved' in Notorious Brazilian Trial," *New York Times,* 28 October 1979, p. 24.

25. Gordon W. Allport and Leo Postman, *The Psychology of Rumor* (New York: Henry Holt, 1947), pp. 214–215.

26. Quoted in E. L. McKitrick, ed., *Slavery Defended: The Views of the Old South* (Englewood Cliffs, N.J.: Prentice-Hall, 1963), p. 53.

27. "Doctor Convicted of Rape Accused of Raping Others," *Oneonta Star,* 19 September 1981, p. 2.

28. "Respirator Plug Pulled, Girl Dies," *Oneonta Star,* 11 August 1977, p. 1.

29. "U.S. Ensign Admits Selling Secrets," *Oneonta Star,* 20 January 1982, p. 2.

30. "Family Steadfast Despite Girl's Death," *Oneonta Star,* 17 November 1981, p. 2.

31. "Iran Charged with Bleeding the Condemned," *Oneonta Star,* 11 November 1981, p. 2.
32. Richard Haitch, "Defense Coup," *New York Times,* 20 September 1981, p. 49.
33. "Father Dogs Daughter's Murderer," *Oneonta Star,* 29 December 1981, p. 1.
34. Diane Henry, "Parents of Three Retarded Girls, . . ." *New York Times,* 2 October 1977, p. 1f.

CHAPTER 3

1. John Godfrey Saxe, quoted in Don Fabun, *Communication: the Transfer of Meaning* (Encino, Ca.: Glencoe, 1968), p. 13.
2. D. Wallechinsky and I. Wallace, *The People's Almanac* vol. 1 (New York: Doubleday, 1975), p. 1089.
3. Wallechinsky, p. 1089.
4. D. S. Hiroto, "Locus of Control and Learned Helplessness," *Journal of Experimental Psychology* 102 (1974): 187–193. (See also C. Diener and C. Dweck, "An Analysis of Learned Helplessness," *Journal of Personality and Social Psychology* 39 (1980): 5.)
5. Maxwell Maltz, *Psycho-Cybernetics* (New York: Pocket Books, 1969), p. 49f.
6. Gordon W. Allport, *Becoming* (New Haven, Ct.: Yale University Press, 1955), pp. 27–28.
7. Nancy Larrick, "Children of TV," *Teacher,* September 1975, p. 75f.
8. Erich Fromm, "The Creative Attitude," in *Creativity and Its Cultivation,* ed. Harold H. Anderson (New York: Harper and Brothers, 1959), p. 48.
9. Rowland W. Jepson, *Clear Thinking* (New York: Longmans, Green and Company, 1967), p. 79.
10. Koestler, p. 75.
11. See, for example, May and Abraham Edel, *Anthropology and Ethics* (Springfield, Ill.: Charles C. Thomas, 1959), p. 88f.
12. Jepson, p. 81.
13. Edwin A. Burtt, *Right Thinking,* 3rd ed. (New York: Harper and Brothers, 1946), p. 63.
14. Jepson, p. 81.
15. James A. Emery, *An Examination of the Proposed 20th Amendment to the Constitution of the U.S.* (New York: National Association of Manufacturers, 1924), pp. 20–23.
16. Sam Walter Foss, reprinted in Parnes, p. 19.
17. Wallechinsky, p. 1091.
18. Abraham Maslow, *Toward a Psychology of Being,* 2nd ed. (Princeton, N.J.: D. Van Nostrand Company, 1968), p. 34.
19. Lippmann, pp. 119–120.
20. William J. Reilly, *The Twelve Rules for Straight Thinking* (New York: Harper and Brothers, 1947), p. 15.
21. Quoted in Ghiselin, p. 207.
22. Clarke, p. 242.
23. Claudia Wallis, "Going Gentle into That Good Night," *Time,* 8 February 1982, p. 79.
24. Jastrow, pp. 130–131.
25. "Police Sell Marijuana, Then Make Arrests," *New York Times,* 10 December 1979, p. 28.
26. "Mother to Lose Child Over Kosher Food," *Oneonta Star,* 4 February 1982, p. 21.
27. "Nazis 'Right to March' Upheld," *Oneonta Star,* 24 February 1978, p. 2.
28. "Gay's Adoption of Youth Approved," *Oneonta Star,* 21 June 1979, p. 2.

29. "Graduate Sues for One Million, . . ." *New York Times,* 26 November 1972, p. 41.
30. "Belief in Astrology Widespread," *Binghamton Press* (New York), 19 October 1975, p. 18a.
31. "Accord Reached in Suit, . . ." *New York Times,* 1 November 1981, p. 30.
32. "Minister Charged in Rooster Rite," *Oneonta Star,* 25 February 1982, p. 2.

CHAPTER 4

1. F. Lorimer, *The Growth of Reason* (London: K. Paul, 1929). Quoted in Koestler, pp. 616–618. Reprinted with permission.
2. Parnes, p. 29.
3. Alex Osborn, *Applied Imagination* (New York: Scribner's, 1957), p. 130.
4. Osborn, p. 172.
5. Beveridge, p. 92.
6. Beveridge, p. 28.
7. "Man Kills Wife in Spat Over Penny," *Oneonta Star,* 16 February 1982, p. 10.
8. Jane E. Brody, "Kinsey Study Shows Deep Predisposition," *New York Times,* 23 August 1981, p. 1f.
9. "Shyness Traced to Genetic Base," *Oneonta Star,* 5 January 1982, p. 1.
10. "Tests Said to Predict Criminal Traits," *Oneonta Star,* 8 January 1982, p. 7.
11. "Court Rules Inmate May Starve Himself," *Oneonta Star,* 2 February 1982, p. 2.
12. "Fickle Universe," *Time,* 25 January 1982, p. 61.
13. Associated Press wirephoto, *Oneonta Star,* 23 July 1981, p. 1.
14. "Working Youth' Report Stresses Appearance," *New York Times,* 14 February 1982, p. 56.
15. *Oneonta Star,* 5 February 1982, p. 1.
16. *New York Times,* 27 March 1964.
17. "Split Decisions," *Time,* 8 February 1982, p. 67
18. "Upstate Case Seen Expanding Definition, . . ." *New York Times,* 6 December 1981, p. 82.
19. "No Children, Judge Orders," *Oneonta Star,* 25 April 1979, 1.
20. "Unwed Mothers Avoid Marriage," *Oneonta Star,* 27 November 1981, p. 10.
21. "Free Speech for Religion," *New York Times,* 13 December 1981, p. 14.
22. "Motorist Returns License," *Oneonta Star,* 22 January 1982, p. 3.
23. *New York Times,* 28 January 1982, p. 14.
24. "Actors Send Aid to Salvador Rebels," *Oneonta Star,* 16 February 1982, p. 1.
25. Supreme Court of Washington, 119 Washington 547, 206, 6 (1922).

CHAPTER 5

1. Mursell, p. 217.
2. James Harvey Robinson, *The Mind in the Making* (New York: Harper and Brothers, 1921), p. 46.
3. "Family Life No Longer That Vital to America," *Oneonta Star,* 1 September 1981, p. 3.
4. "Photo of Dinosaur Needs Some Help," *Oneonta Star,* 29 December 1981, p. 2.
5. *Time,* 25 January 1982, p. 31.
6. *New York Times,* 7 November 1971, p. 30. © 1971 by the New York Times Company. Reprinted by permission.

CHAPTER 6

1. Paul Smith, ed., *Creativity: An Examination of the Creative Process* (New York: Hastings House, 1959), p. 17.
2. The best source of current works (as well as important older works) is the *Journal of Creative Behavior.*
3. George F. Kneller, *The Art and Science of Creativity* (New York: Holt, 1965), p. 2.
4. Quoted in Parnes, p. 7.
5. J. W. Getzels and P. W. Jackson, *Creativity and Intelligence* (New York: Wiley, 1962), p. 21f. Also Torrance, *Guiding,* pp. 5 and 63.
6. Ghiselin, p. 9.
7. Eliot Dole Hutchinson, *How to Think Creatively* (Nashville: Abingdon-Cokesbury Press, 1949), p. 79.
8. Harold H. Anderson, "Creativity in Perspective," in Anderson, p. 258.
9. Good sources of studies include Getzels, Torrance, and Parnes.
10. Quoted in C. P. Curtis and F. Greenslet, ed., *The Practical Cogitator* (Boston: Houghton-Mifflin, 1945), p. 231.
11. Quoted in William J. J. Gordon, *Synectics: The Development of Creative Capacity* (New York: Harper and Brothers, 1961), p. 116.
12. Quoted in Getzels, p. 53.
13. Joseph Rossman, *The Psychology of the Inventor* (Washington, D.C.: Inventors' Publishing Company, 1931), p. 82f.
14. Osborn, p. 130.
15. Getzels, p. 53.
16. "Couple Learns Golden Rule, . . ." *Oneonta Star,* 29 August 1981, p. 1.
17. "In Divorce, Kids Get the House," *Oneonta Star,* 20 January 1982, p. 1.
18. "Grafitti Gobbler Gets Attention," *Oneonta Star,* 30 November 1981, p. 2.
19. "Crippled Inventor Is Standing Proud," *Oneonta Star,* 6 February 1982, p. 1.
20. "Trouble Sleeping? Call Up the Sandman," *Oneonta Star,* 7 July 1982, p. 1.
21. "Waterbabies," *Time,* 10 May 1982, p. 87.
22. Hutchinson, for example (p. 38), lists four stages, but one of them is "verification," which involves the process of solution refinement classified in this text as critical thinking.
23. "New Jersey Town Decides How to Bury Frozen Elephant," *Oneonta Star,* 22 January 1982, p. 10.

CHAPTER 7

1. George Iles, *Inventors at Work* (New York: Doubleday, Page, 1906), p. 370.
2. Dan Kaercher, "School Closings: What Can Parents Do?" *Better Homes and Gardens,* August 1982, p. 17.
3. "Two Doctors Tell of Treatments, . . ." *New York Times,* 29 November 1981, p. 38.
4. Interview of "Good Morning America," 29 August 1980.
5. "Recluse Leaves $57,000 to Jesus," *Oneonta Star,* 11 December 1981, p. 7.
6. Ann Landers, *Oneonta Star,* 3 March 1982, p. 8.
7. From "If Japan Can . . . Why Can't We?" on NBC television 24 June 1981.

CHAPTER 8

1. A. E. Mander, *Logic for the Millions* (New York: Philosophical Library, 1947), p. 55.
2. Parnes, p. 40.

3. Koestler, p. 123.
4. "Dolphins May Help Train Retarded Tots," *Binghamton Press,* 28 February 1982, p. 5a.
5. "Bank Robber, 10, Back in Trouble," *Oneonta Star,* 13 February 1982, p. 1.
6. "Tot's Testimony Crucial in Murder Trial," *Binghamton Press,* 26 October 1975, p. 2.
7. "A Man Called Jamison," *New York Times,* 26 January 1975, section 4, p. 9.
8. "Expert Warns on Testimony, . . ." *New York Times,* 10 January 1982, p. 44.
9. "Kids' Dishonesty Sinks a Company," *Oneonta Star,* 26 January 1982, p. 4.
10. "Falsifying of College Records, . . ." *New York Times,* 29 November 1981, p. 1f.
11. "Birth Defects and Behavior, . . ." *New York Times,* 21 January 1979, section 4, p. 9.
12. "Fetus Born Alive After, . . ." *Binghamton Press,* 15 November 1981, p. 1a.

CHAPTER 9

1. This analogy was first made by Zbigniew Pietraskinski, *The Psychology of Efficient Thinking,* trans. B. Jankowski (New York: Pergamon Press, 1969), p. 134.
2. Parnes, p. 57.
3. Osborn, p. 149.
4. Osborn, p. 149.
5. Parnes, pp. 57–58.
6. Beveridge, p. 143.
7. Clarence D. Tuska, *Inventors and Inventions* (New York: McGraw-Hill, 1957), p. 88.
8. Parnes, pp. 55–56.
9. Graham Wallas, *The Art of Thought* (New York: Harcourt, Brace, 1926), p. 139.
10. Parnes, p. 57.
11. Max Wertheimer, *Productive Thinking* (New York: Harper and Brothers, 1945), pp. 169–173.
12. Koestler, p. 118.
13. See, for example, Hutchinson, pp. 35–40.

CHAPTER 10

1. "Functional Illiterates," *Parade,* 8 August 1982, p. 7.

CHAPTER 11

1. Hutchinson, pp. 182–183.
2. D. Wallechinsky and I. Wallace, *The People's Almanac,* vol. 2 (New York: Bantam Books, 1978), p. 817.
3. Wallechinsky, vol. 1, pp. 914–915.
4. Wallechinsky, vol. 2, p. 821.
5. Jepson, p. 194.
6. "30% of Cancer Deaths, . . ." *Oneonta Star,* 23 February 1982, p. 1.
7. "Off the Street and Out of the Cold," *Time,* 8 February 1982, p. 66.
8. John Leo, "Single Parent, Double Trouble," *Time,* 4 January 1982, p. 81.

9. "Moneyball," *New York Times*, 28 March 1982, section 4, p. 22.
10. "Restoring Values in Education," *American Educator*, Winter 1981, p. 20.

CHAPTER 12

1. "Frozen Embryo Plan Stirs Uproar," *Oneonta Star*, 29 January 1982, p. 8.
2. "Compulsory Alcoholism Treatment Gaining," *New York Times*, 9 May 1982, p. 10.
3. "College Forbids Pac-Man Admission," *Oneonta Star*, 6 June 1982, p. 9.

CHAPTER 13

1. "Some Schools Sideline Pudgy . . . Majorettes," *Binghamton Press*, 3 October 1982, p. 4a.
2. Roger W. Holmes, *The Rhyme of Reason* (New York: Appleton-Century, 1939), p. 458.
3. "Texas Indictment . . . Mercy Killers," *New York Times*, 10 December 1981, p. 1.
4. "Slaying Confession Barred by Court," *New York Times*, 11 December 1981, p. 32.
5. "Poll Finds Insanity Plea Opposed," *Oneonta Star*, 21 October 1981, p. 2.
6. "No Tuition for Illegal Aliens," *Oneonta Star*, 28 June 1982, p. 3.

CHAPTER 14

1. Rudolph Verderber et al., "An Analysis of Student Communication Habits," unpublished study, University of Cincinnati, 1976.
2. Max Black, *Critical Thinking* (Englewood Cliffs, N.J.: Prentice-Hall, 1952), pp. 156–157.
3. "Selling Make-Believe Makeup," *Time*, 24 August 1981, p. 58.
4. James Stolz, "Death of a Fraternity Boy," *New York Daily News Magazine*, 24 January 1982, p. 14f.
5. Jack Anderson, "Naval Base Runs Secret Porn Theater," *Oneonta Star*, 27 November 1981, p. 4.
6. "Student Awarded $10,000 for Spanking," *Oneonta Star*, 2 January 1982, p. 2.
7. Woodley B. Osborne, "High Court to Rule, . . ." *On Campus*, December 1981/January 1982, p. 20.

CHAPTER 15

1. Black, p. 157.
2. "Bill on Homosexuals Defeated Again," *New York Times*, 10 May 1982, p. 87.
3. "Darwin Wins," *Time*, 18 January 1982, p. 63.
4. "Poisoned Cornfield Kills 2000 Birds," *Oneonta Star*, 2 January 1982, p. 1.
5. "Women Come a Long Way But, . . ." *Oneonta Star*, 2 September 1981, p. 17.
6. "Monitors Say TV Averaging, . . ." *Oneonta Star*, 18 March 1982, p. 1.
7. "More Marriages, More Divorces," *Oneonta Star*, 29 March 1982, p. 6.
8. "Why Does Crime Pay?" *New York Daily News*, 28 February 1982, p. 3.
9. "Contraceptive Ads Found Unacceptable," *Oneonta Star*, 18 January 1982, p. 15.
10. "Teacher Discontent on the Rise," *Oneonta Star*, 18 May 1982, p. 2.
11. "Two-Thirds in Poll Believe, . . ." *Oneonta Star*, 18 May 1982. p. 7.
12. "Study Finds Teens in Poor Shape," *Oneonta Star*, 29 April 1982, p. 1.

13. "Study Finds Teens Drink First, . . ." *Oneonta Star,* 18 May 1982, p. 6.
14. "Physicians Deplore the Aborting of One Twin," *New York Times,* 12 November 1981, p. 13a.

APPENDIXES

1. Dick Gregory, *Write Me In!* (New York: Bantam, 1968), p. 13.
2. Gilbert Keith Chesterton, "A Meditation in Broadway," *The Man Who Was Chesterton,* ed. Raymond T. Bond (Garden City, N.Y.: Doubleday, 1960), p. 150.

Index

84 85 86 7 6 5 4 3 2 1